ATHEISM & FREEDOM

ATHEISM & FREEDOM

AN INTRODUCTION TO FREE THOUGHT

7TH EDITION
ENGLISH TRANSLATION

ANDRÉ CANCIAN

Author's edition
2023

When my eyes run through the tears that roll down these pages, I wonder if, in lullabies, my song was the Hail Mary and my poetry, our daily bread, I could hide from you — who knows, for a lifetime — a nothingness so immense and bitter that, the emptier it is, the heavier it becomes. My nothingness, old and customary, is a very light burden when faced with the pain of seeing you bleed, but with the pride of this being the fulfillment of the fruit of my womb, tearing himself up in a cruel revelation.

SUMMARY

PRESENTATION

One aspect that caused me a profound impression from the beginning of my contact with the Author's work was the intellectual precocity and the depth of his reflections, a rare characteristic for such a young person.

It is unusual to encounter unique personalities like this in such a troubled world, where the outside is highly valued, and there is no space for those precious moments of critical reflection and for the search for answers to perennial questions that cross the centuries.

Unfortunately, for the most part, humans are grouped into docile and obedient herds. They have always sought to give their minds to the first being willing to lead them along the path of illusion, of unreality, of easy answers, delegating to others the wonderful gift of freedom of thought.

They seek to calm their consciences by placing someone else in control of their lives. After all, those who cannot command themselves can only obey. And, as Nietzsche said: "How much truth can a spirit endure, how much truth can it dare?"

Unable to walk on their own legs, of focusing the responsibility of their lives on themselves and of enduring the anguish that this life causes us, they comfortably opt for easy solutions, repeating "ad infinitum" stories and bedtime songs which could be accepted more calmly in the past, when science was still taking its first timid steps, and there was fertile ground for ignorance and superstition.

Today, however, scientific discoveries have ended up burying, one by one, the follies that prevailed during the last millennia. It is unbelievable, therefore, that despite all the advances made by humanity, the vast majority of our race remains submerged in the murky waters of mediocrity.

Within our contemporary framework, religions persist, absurdly, offering their dogmatism and their doctrine, which do not allow any form of contestation. Quite the contrary, philosophy is born when we try to understand the world objectively, not through the acceptance of authority, but through reason and experimentation, remaining open to questioning and criticism, without closing the question on any subject.

Thus, the fact that the origin of life is a mystery does not mean that we have to create supernatural agents to explain what current science is still unable to fully explain. Our profound ignorance about why we exist and about all the grandiosity and mystery of the Universe should not open the doors to superstition, but rather to the continuation of research efforts that will lead us to acceptable, plausible, coherent explanations that are based on what's real.

It is within this context that this young thinker emerges, already centered on himself, occupied with essential human issues, issues that commonly do not belong to individuals of his age group.

The book with which he presents us is didactic, technical, and highly enlightening, providing the most different types of readers — skeptics or spiritualists — with substantial information about the possibility of the existence of a supernatural creator of the Universe.

Starting with the foundations of atheism, it encompasses all possible reflections involving the belief in a personal god, trying to demonstrate why there is no reason to believe in such an entity. He then continues his work by explaining the fundamental consequences of the non-existence of God in the personal life of each individual, but also for humanity as a whole.

The entire text is punctuated by the author's fine irony, who points out the puerile contradictions existing in the belief in personal gods, and all the fragility of the explanations about the origin and meaning of life that institutionalized religions have to offer.

Throughout the reading, there is a feeling of being harshly stripped of the veils and illusions, of the chimeras that have been transmitted to us through the ages. In this way, we must be, in a certain way, prepared to endure such a degree of lucidity and intellectual honesty that come to us through the author's reflections. Perhaps not everyone can digest so much information without feeling a certain sense of strangeness, as if they had taken a hard blow without knowing exactly where it came from. It is necessary, at some points in the reading, to take a deeper breath, as an attempt to bear the truths that show themselves to those who are able to see them.

At the end of the book, readers will receive, as a reward, the inevitable end of all their vain convictions, and the lesson that the best thing a man can do is to "cultivate his garden", as said Voltaire, an Enlightenment thinker, for whom the important thing was to reach heaven on Earth, without worrying about any form of survival, believing in the possibility of human perfection, but only through reason.

I believe that a thought that defines well the way I see the Author in his worldview would be an aphorism by the German philosopher Friedrich Nietzsche, which says: "I followed the vestiges of the origins. Then I became a stranger to all venerations. Everything became strange around me, everything became solitude".

The strangeness before oneself and the feeling of loneliness are the price paid by those who yearn for the answers to the eternal questions, which hover above all centuries.

The author, at such a young age, follows in the footsteps of those who have left behind the wide and easy road of the commonplace, of simplistic solutions, in order to tread unknown paths. He thus comes to enjoy an unexpectedly widened vision, which is the strange blessing of understanding the total impossibility of understanding anything. As the speaker for many other voices, he now carries the torch that, at the end of the road, another will carry.

Sílvia Gabas

PREFACE

This seventh edition, fully revised, has several improvements, remodelings, and additions, which aimed to deepen some points, fill in some explanation gaps, and clarify certain passages that seemed a little unclear to me.

I decided that this will be the definitive edition of my work, not because it exhausts the subject or because it is error-free, but because it is impossible to keep it eternally updated to a dynamic reality in which the truth of today is an error tomorrow. Some ideas will remain, while others will be discarded — and this is as inevitable as it is healthy and necessary.

I hope this book will be instructive in the various subjects it proposes to address. I have tried to make it as didactic, clear, and organized as possible. Therefore, I wrote the chapters in an interconnected way, presenting the ideas gradually, in order to facilitate their general understanding. The argument of each chapter is based on the conclusions of the previous one, with an increasing degree of intertwining between them.

I therefore suggest reading them in the order in which they are presented, as I have tried to simulate the real way in which such thoughts were formed in me, with the aim of presenting a significant part of my worldview in the most crystalline, intuitive, and natural way possible.

I wrote exactly the way I like to read. For this reason, whenever I could, I dispensed with the linguistic flourishes that I deemed unnecessary, which could certainly compromise the full understanding of the ideas presented. But, at the same time, I tried not to sacrifice elegance, precision, or deviate from language standards. I did my best to make this reading an invitation to reflection, raising questions for a debate in which this book is only my word.

I know that the subject is difficult and delicate, and that there are many authors who could, no doubt, do this job much more fully and profoundly than I can. I wanted, with the present work, just to sow some seeds of free thought, encouraging individuals to take a deeper and more impartial look at themselves and at the reality in which they live, hoping, with this, that some of the seeds will end up germinating in some minds that will know how to cultivate them and, I hope, transform them into a tree capable of bearing fruit.

However, it should be well understood that it was not my objective to destroy anyone's beliefs, or to impose points of view, because what I defend, before and above all, is intellectual freedom. Nor was it my desire to make everyone blindly believe everything I say. I just thought that, at the end of several years of study, I had something to say that was important. I have tried to synthesize in this modest intellectual work the most relevant aspects of what I have learned.

So, what I want is just to share the conclusions I have reached, and the only thing I hope is that the ideas presented are useful to those who are also trying to solve the great puzzle of our existence, and thus represent a small intellectual victory in the eternal war we wage on error — a drop of lucidity in the sea of ignorance in which we live.

However, if that drop is not of lucidity, but of error, I apologize, for I am not perfect: I am human, limited, and I also make mistakes. However, I say this being fully certain that every line in this book was written in all honesty, and at no time have I spoken contrarily to what I think is true.

André Cancian
2002

PART I

What is wanted is not the will to believe, but the will to find out, which is the exact opposite.

— Bertrand Russell

GENERAL INTRODUCTION

I think we ought to read only the kind of books that wound and stab us. If the book we're reading doesn't wake us up with a blow on the head, what are we reading it for? So that it will make us happy, as you write? Good Lord, we would be happy precisely if we had no books, and the kind of books that make us happy are the kind we could write ourselves if we had to. But we need the books that affect us like a disaster, that grieve us deeply, like the death of someone we loved more than ourselves, like being banished into forests far from everyone, like a suicide. A book must be the axe for the frozen sea inside us.

— Franz Kafka

The problem that we will analyze throughout this work is by no means recent. We could say that it is one of the issues that have been most debated and investigated in the entire history of humanity. It is the problem of human beings questioning the most fundamental realities, seeking in this their identity, their origin, their roots.

What is man, and what is his place in the world? What is this world? Where did it come from? Is there a reason? Is there any purpose in everything we're experiencing? After all, what am I doing here? Why do I exist? Some of the best intellects that ever lived have tried their answers, and given their blood to demonstrate that there is a hidden reason behind our existence. However, regrettably, everything leads us to think that their efforts were in vain, at least in the sense of finding a positive answer.

Some think that we will never find answers to such inquiries. But isn't that because we're asking the wrong questions? Before we ask what is the meaning of life, wouldn't it be wise to ask if life has any meaning at all? Before we ask who created the world, wouldn't it be wise to ask if the world was actually created? In conclusion, couldn't this reluctance, this desire to remain in the unknown, be seen as a symptom of a great fear, the fear that we really are what we seem to be? So we prefer to remain in doubt — because we can't bear the answer?

As Francis Bacon pointed out some time ago:

The human understanding is no dry light, but receives infusion from the will and affections; whence proceeds sciences which may be called "sciences as one would". For what a man had rather were true he more readily believes. Therefore, he rejects difficult things from impatience of research; sober things, because they narrow hope; the deeper things of nature, from superstition; the light of experience, from arrogance and pride; things not commonly believed, out of deference to the opinion of the vulgar. Numberless in short are the ways, and sometimes imperceptible, in which the affections color and infect the understanding.

However, a new reality began to unfold before our eyes with the emergence of modern science. The scientific method provided us with the means of investigating reality in an impartial manner, outlining the boundary that distinguishes objective knowledge from opinion and belief, separating individual reality from universal reality, the subjective from the objective. From then on, we began to realize that the universe in which we live is governed by natural and impersonal laws. This allowed us to dispense with gods and mysticism to explain it satisfactorily.

Thus, after the word "natural" began to be used to dethrone God, every naturalistic explanation was forcibly seen as something cold, reductionist, profane. Science has dethroned man from his divine pedestal, taking away his sense of importance and his hope of an eternal existence, and perhaps that is why its materialism is the target of so much hatred and contempt. Is the scope of science limited? Yes, without a doubt: limited to dealing with what exists, not with what we wish existed.

So far, all findings made by science point to an answer that few would want or even bear to hear. After all, what is left of us, if we are really empty biological machines, living in a meaningless world? Without such illusions, what can we say about morality, values, love, progress, beauty, happiness? Everything annihilated and reduced to an existential tragicomedy that we're afraid to laugh at?

These are some of the subjects that we will handle with due care, in order to show the errors and distortions that led man to create so many fictions and chimeras, and also to nurture so many great hopes that are now so painfully uprooted by modern discoveries.

This intellectual discipline that led man to the accumulation of knowledge has slowly matured his consciousness, and with it humanity has begun to overcome its intellectual childhood. We are opening our eyes to a life and a reality that are very different from what we thought we knew.

Taking responsibility for a life without gods is something for which civilization as whole has not yet reached sufficient maturity. But, without a doubt, there is no other perspective, because, evidently, there comes the point where the individual who walks towards enlightenment can no longer close his eyes to himself and to the reality in which he lives without, in so doing, denying his own condition as a rational being.

Well then, this book is intended for readers who are mature enough for this new vision of the world. It is aimed at those who have decided to place themselves in an impartial position and, as critical observers, seek the real meaning of what we are experiencing, without making any concessions to the intangible ghosts created by our fear and fed by our hope.

Therefore, anyone looking for consolation, soft words, delicate poetry, euphemistic truths, and peace of mind should not continue this reading. The following pages are a desert, and few men can survive in them. Few have enough courage and strength to withstand the enormous aridity that hides behind our illusions.

To those who wish to proceed, looking the challenge in the eye, we must always ask this question: why do we want to bear the full weight of reality? Indeed! Why should we live amidst suffocating and torrid deserts, why should we rise, climbing the mountains of thought, to almost suffocate with the rarefied atmosphere of glacial mountain peaks — if, on the surface, we have shade, comfort, and fresh water? We have no reason to explain it: what drives us to do so is a passion.

What is this dominant passion that leads us into the wilderness, makes us deny comfort, and puts us at its service? It is the passion for knowledge, the yearning for truth, guided by reason. When genuine, this passion leads us to many dangerous adventures in the labyrinths of thought, confronts us with crossroads of unsolvable problems, poses terrible and ambiguous questions, gives birth to internal conflicts, and turns our spirit into a battlefield.

However, in this war, all soldiers are volunteers. They are soldiers who fight out of passion and who, from the depth of their souls, believe in the cause for which they are fighting. Our sword is called discernment, and our virtue, intellectual integrity.

Possessing intellectual integrity means being totally honest with oneself; it means pledging allegiance to the truth, even in matters that are crucial to our happiness. This requires the ability to face painful questions head-on; the ability to admit ignorance, even when that ignorance corrodes us, even when there is a burning desire for answers; and also the ability to admit the facts, even when there is dirt in such facts, and we have to accept them almost reluctantly, being unable to quench our thirst.

Impartiality is also necessary, and only men who are fully free, courageous, and uncompromised possess this valuable prerogative. To be intellectually free, it is necessary to be able to look with suspicion even at what is most dear to us. It is necessary to become indifferent to the fact that the truth may be useful or harmful, making this intellectual search a selfless adventure, without fixed objectives — he who has eyes only for what he seeks becomes partial and blind to everything else. In short, being a freethinker means being able to say: it doesn't matter how I would like reality to be — what I want above all is to know the truth.

At this point, an impasse could arise: after all, what is the truth? What is certain is that, not rarely, a great deal of fuss is made to define it. This fuss, more often than not, is just a cynical attempt to bend the truth to our will, interests, and prejudices. For this reason, we are always displeased with hearing the following lies: "each one has their own truth", "the truth is relative", "this is my truth", "this is what I believe and, therefore, for me, this is the truth". Well, we are not interested in that kind of truth. After all, what respect could we possibly have for a kind of truth that prostitutes itself to the whims of the individual? A small grain of integrity makes us admit that such things should be called something else: opinions or convictions or preferences or points of view, but never truth. Yet, let it be said, how easily our ego is persuaded — by our vanity, perhaps? — that our convictions are the Alpha and the Omega of all reality!

Again, what is the truth? Truth is reality, just reality, and nothing else. What is true? True is every judgment that conforms to the real; every proposition that finds correspondence in reality is true. This notion had its origins in Greek thought, according to which truth — *aletheia* or *alethé* — corresponds to reality itself. This will be our criterion of truth.

This, however, leads us to another question, certainly no less problematic: what is reality? Isn't every notion of reality inescapably relative, even arbitrary? Indeed. But we will not presuppose non-existent agreements, we will not try to turn a blind eye to the philosophical battles that crossed the centuries regarding this subject. However, we have to start from something. This insecurity in the face of dispersion is inherent to every incursion into the unknown. Each step in the dark must be taken with caution and circumspection. For it is certain that if we seek enlightenment, this demands of us some audacity: not in the position of one who understands, but in the position of one who wants to understand and, to do so, launches himself, soberly, to the core of the absurdity of our existence. Whatever results from this journey will indicate the value of these presuppositions, on which we walk, uncertainly.

Our premise, therefore, will be that reality corresponds to being, to effectiveness, to existence. Real is that which is independent of us, that exists by itself, and that would continue to exist even if all life were wiped out of the Universe. It is something completely disconnected from our will, from our senses, from our opinions, from our objectives, from our ideals: in short, disconnected from what we are. Naturally, we are referring to objective reality, in relation to which our subjectivity is reduced to an ephemeral shadow of poetry.

And, although there is only one objective reality, let us close our ears to that siren song that so easily hypnotizes those who seek the truth: the certainties, the absolute truths. Those famous eternal and superior truths, those sublime edifices of dogmatism! How much mendacity dwells in all certainties, and how much indolence! Let us not listen to the pompous chatter of those who claim to possess it: truth has never been found by wandering the paths of the absolute. Only tiredness and insecurity would have us believe in the truth of such absolute lies.

The search for truth must never be confused with the search for certainties. What is proposed here is something else, something entirely different. What is proposed here is not the search for certainties, but the search for the most probable. For this, as said, we must be warriors, and as warriors we will be in our endless battle against our immortal enemy: the error. Yes, in its essence, the search for truth is the war against error — an indestructible enemy to which we owe the highest respect, which stalks us in every reasoning, and against which we must never let our guard down.

Therefore, to be merciless to all that is chimerical, to strike death blows to all that is false, to be ourselves the embodiment of hostility to error — this is precisely our kind of humanity. To restore what is truly human in man.

The following pages are some of the trenches in this battle. To those who are on our side, we wish victory, even a small victory, in this fight against error, for discovery. And let us always keep in mind that the reward for all this will only be given in coins of knowledge and enlightenment, and they do not glitter like gold.

I

THE FOUNDATIONS OF ATHEISM

By simple common sense, I don't believe in God; in none.

— Charles Chaplin

Etymologically, the word *atheist* is formed by the prefix *a* — which denotes absence — and the Greek radical *theós* — which means *God, divinity, or theism*. Thus, the word *atheist* can mean *without God* or *without theism*. Since the vagueness of this first meaning makes it inadequate to represent the notion of atheistic disbelief, the second meaning, *without theism*, is used as a basis, theism being the *belief in the existence of some type of god or gods of a personal nature*. We thereby arrive at a coherent and clear definition of an atheist individual: one who does not believe in the existence of any god or gods. Thus, when we want a word that represents such a perspective, we use the term *atheist* linked to the suffix *ism*, which *is used to refer to a set of ideas or system of beliefs or behavior*. In this way, we arrived at a very clear definition of what atheism is: a state of lack of belief in the existence of any god or gods.

It is important to point out that most atheists, when referring to their position, simply state that they don't believe in gods/gods. This is not incorrect, but by this the individual means that he does not believe in the *existence* of gods/gods. Simply stating "I don't believe in God" may give rise to the erroneous interpretation that the person in question believes in God's existence, but is against God, against his commandments, or that he does not give him any credit, that he discredits him, defames him, a fact that often gives rise to various prejudices towards the atheistic position. Having clarified this point, let's see what types of atheism exist.

There are several types of atheism, which differ fundamentally in terms of the individual's attitude toward the idea of a deity. It is worth remembering that such classifications are merely didactic, made only to outline the most common circumstances in which atheism can be found. The two core modalities are: 1.0) *implicit atheism*; 2.0) *explicit atheism*. The first, philosophically, is not very relevant, and is subdivided into: 1.1) *natural atheism*; 1.2) *practical atheism*. The second is divided into two other varieties that are commonly referred to as: 2.1) *negative atheism* or *skeptical atheism*; 2.2) *positive atheism* or *critical atheism*.

1.0) *Implicit atheism*, as its name indicates, is the variety of atheism that exists tacitly. In this case, atheism is not based on the conscious and deliberate rejection of the idea of God, based on philosophical and/or scientific concepts, but simply exists as a way of living that does not take into account the hypothesis of the existence of a god to be used as a guide. As stated, *implicit atheism* can be divided into *natural atheism* and *practical atheism*.

1.1) *Natural atheism* is the state of lack of belief due to ignorance or the inability to position oneself before the notion of divine existence. This category includes all individuals who have never had contact with the idea of a god. For example, some tribe, group, or people that are isolated from civilization and that are unaware of the idea of a god. Also included in this category are individuals who are unable to conceive the idea of a god, either because of intellectual immaturity or because of mental disabilities. For example, we could mention young children; people who suffer from some disabling mental illness also belong to this category.

1.2) *Practical atheism* includes those who have had contact with the idea of God, that is, who know the theories about deities, but who do not take any action to deny, reject, or affirm it, thus remaining neutral on the subject. The members of this category are commonly classified as agnostics, that is, those who think it is impossible to know with certainty whether there is a deity.

From this perspective, because of this impossibility, they affirm that any intellectual effort to prove or refute the existence of a god would be useless. Anyone who is aware of the existence of religions and their theories, but lives without worrying about whether or not there is a god, or considers it impossible to know it with certainty, without rejecting or explicitly asserting the idea of God, is classified as belonging to *practical atheism*.

2.0) *Explicit atheism* is the conscious rejection of the idea of God. The cause of this rejection is normally the result of philosophical deliberation. However, it is not possible to make any kind of generalization as to the specific cause of the disbelief, as each person individually judges which reasons are valid or invalid to corroborate or refute the idea of the existence of a god. *Explicit atheism* can be divided into these two categories.

2.1) *Negative* or *skeptical atheism* is the disbelief in the existence of God(s) due to the lack of evidence in its favor. This variety can also be found under the designation of *standard skeptical position*, since it reflects one of the most fundamental axioms of skeptical thinking, which is: we should not accept a proposition as true if we have no reason to do so — or, in its laconic version: no evidence, no belief. Atheists in this category merely find reasons to justify their rejection of the idea of God, sometimes striving to demonstrate why the supposed proofs of divine existence are invalid, but without worrying about denying the possibility of the existence of a god.

2.2) *Positive or critical atheism* is the most difficult variety to defend, since it is a disbelief that involves the denial of the possibility of the existence of a god. Atheists in this category typically call themselves rationalists and follow the principle that attack is the best defense; that is, they literally attack the idea of God, highlighting the contradictions and incongruences present in this concept, striving to demonstrate, through rational arguments, why the existence of a god — as defined by religions — is logically impossible.

At first glance, it might seem that such definitions are too simple to be able to encompass all possibilities, but they are not. That is because the atheistic position, in itself, is not positive — it does not have any content, as it does not represent something, but the mere *absence* of something (including the case of *positive atheism*). Even in its more elaborate forms, atheism is an absence linked to a rejection or denial of something widely accepted — which, in this case, is theism, in its various forms.

Thus, the definition of atheism does not imply any kind of practical description of the individual. In this classification, what atheists do with their lives is not taken into consideration at all. Unlike other "isms" — such as Catholicism, Judaism, Hinduism, Islamism —, atheism is not a lifestyle or a doctrine endowed with a body of knowledge or principles, but only a classification about the position or intellectual state of the individual in relation to the idea of God. This means that atheism has no analogous nature to religions.

Since atheism is just a classification — and not a doctrine or a worldview — it logically does not incorporate any values, moral principles, or notions of ethics. It is precisely because of this fact that many individuals inadvertently classify atheists as immoral. It should be clear, however, that the absence of a set of moral values refers only to atheism itself, so that, in practice, this does not entail any incompatibility between the two.

Like theists, atheists do have moral values that guide their actions. There is no empirical evidence whatsoever to support the accusation of immorality so often thrown against unbelievers. It is clear that atheists, as a whole, do not share a single moral code; they do not have a morality based on the authority of "atheistic principles", which would be "absolute" or "superior", similarly to the values linked to theism. In reality, atheists choose individually — considering their objectives, their needs — which are the values that will best serve them to guide their lives according to the meaning they have chosen for them. So, what does not exist is an atheistic morality in the sense in which we speak of Christian morality. However, there are, of course, moral atheists, who rely on human nature factors to rationally substantiate their values — for it is clear that, without a god, such factors could never be absolute or transcendental.

The great frequency with which people try to corroborate or refute atheism through moral judgments only demonstrates a sad superficiality (e.g.: "atheists also do charities" or "many atheists are criminals"). Of course, if they wish, some atheists can be kind, compassionate, sympathetic, and so on. Perhaps, due to the fact that most religious people identify themselves with this type of morality, their typical dislike of the word "atheist" can even be softened a little.

However, claiming that goodness has, in itself, some truth value, that it offers any credibility to the position, is, to say the least, an absurdity. The most "dogmatic" of atheisms is still nothing more than a mere denial — "God does not exist", affirmatively —, so that assuming an atheistic position takes us to a much more fundamental plane of discussion, much broader than the mere question of right and wrong. In other words, in addition to being independent of morality, atheism also precedes it in philosophical depth. Thus it will only be possible to deduce, individually, values from atheism, but never atheism from personal values. Hence the impossibility of goodness, for example, supporting it, and the same goes for objections to atheism based on crimes committed by atheists.

There is also a strong tendency to link the responsibility for one's actions to one's worldview, and this tendency is linked to the idea that every worldview is always loaded with values and duties — in this case, also linked to the misconception that atheism is a positive belief. For example, if a Christian does charity work in the name of God and uses the Bible to justify this, then one can say that Christianity is to some degree responsible for his action. This is because every religion has its dogmas, its truths, its higher principles, in short, its "thou shalt". Therefore, it defines what is good and what is evil, what is right and what is wrong, and so on. Atheism, on the other hand, is alien to this whole conglomerate of values that humans cultivate. If an atheist does something good or bad, it is not because of atheism itself, as atheism says nothing about what we should or should not do. Atheism does not say what is good or bad, much less what is right or wrong. It does not carry with it any kind of value, which is why no kind of practical responsibility can be attributed to it. Since everything rests solely on the shoulders of the individual will, it is not possible to generalize the cause of his actions to include atheism.

Therefore, every atheist who defends specific moral values — even if they are of benevolence and charity — without making it clear that this has nothing to do with his disbelief, will be, without realizing it, doing a disservice to atheists. Perhaps the intention is good, that is, he thinks that, in doing so, he is reversing the negative stereotype that is typically held of atheists — according to which they are all perverted, frustrated, immoral, insensitive, criminals. The problem, of course, is that this counterattack presupposes the false idea that atheism must defend itself against moral accusations — and that only creates more confusion. The personality of atheists has no direct relation to atheism. All these social stereotypes about what atheists are like are nothing but prejudice, fantasy, because, as we have seen, atheism is not able to justify any of that.

Whether an atheist is selfless or selfish, kind or mean, compassionate or cruel is only a reflection of his temperament and the values adopted by the individual. Failure to make this distinction between atheism and morality leads people with little insight into the subject to become accustomed to viewing the behavioral patterns of unbelievers as a direct consequence of their atheism — thus, just as charitable atheists will give atheism a good image, criminal atheists will tarnish and disgrace its image. Not only does this give rise to several undesirable stereotypes, but these still obscure the true face of atheism: neutrality.

So atheists don't necessarily share any similarities — other than disbelief, of course. Atheists can be good or bad, saints or perverts, altruistic or selfish, individualists or collectivists; they can be democrats, socialists, anarchists, or monarchists; they can be philosophers, doctors, psychologists, teachers, garbage collectors, merchants, writers, actors, or anything else. Atheism, in itself, is strictly neutral, and therefore free of any moral or philosophical implications. Atheism is just the name given to the state of absence of theism, i.e., just the absence of belief in the existence of any gods. So, if atheists can be said to have something in common, that something is exactly having-nothing-in-common — at least not necessarily, as a general rule.

All animals are atheists, and all people were once atheists — without exception. All babies are born without sufficient discernment to understand the notion of God. As we saw, this state is framed as a category of atheism. Of course, it's not a deliberate disbelief, but it shows how absurd it is to try to derive any direct consequence from the fact that someone is an atheist. Certainly, the most fervent religious people will frown upon this idea, saying that it is "unfair" to label anyone unable to form their judgment on the matter as an atheist. However, let's see: why unfair? Is there anything wrong with being an atheist? Is it a sign of perversion, of insanity? No, and there's no reason for us to think that way.

In this situation, the word *atheist* is describing perfectly well the individual's perspective regarding the idea of the existence of divinities. For example, surely no one would object to classifying a baby as an apolitical individual because it is incapable of understanding what politics is and of taking a stand on it — nor to the idea that they are all illiterate. Richard Dawkins also pointed this out, asking *How can you possibly describe a child of four as a Muslim or a Christian or a Hindu or a Jew? Would you talk about a four-year-old economic monetarist? Would you talk about a four-year-old neo-isolationist or a four-year-old liberal Republican?* The problem lies in the incoherence of attributing positive positions to those who cannot answer for them — who cannot even understand such notions. However, in our society, the word atheist has become so loaded with prejudice, so stigmatized, that to call a person an atheist, far from being a mere classification, actually seems to be a kind of insult.

Objectively, we see that there is nothing reasonable, impersonal, or disinterested about this hostility to the definition of *natural atheism*. The problem is certainly not with the definition, but with the prejudices that are held against the atheistic position. The degree to which a religious person is uncomfortable with the idea that an uninformed child is an atheist can be used as a measure of his level of prejudice and intolerance in relation to atheism. Whatever they say, atheism is not a perversion, nor a stubbornness, nor an insensitivity, nor anything else but a lack of belief in the existence of God.

Even so, if we analyze this issue from a religious perspective, it becomes understandable that such prejudices exist. The fact that someone rejects the "obvious truth" that there is a creator, declaring himself openly as an atheist, can only mean that he is an insensitive, cynical, resentful person, frustrated with life and disgusted with God. But, logically, such reasoning is wholly one-sided. The problem is not with atheists, but with the fact that total conviction makes people prisoners of their own perspectives. Anyone who pledges absolute loyalty to a particular doctrine or point of view inevitably turns a blind eye to everything else, and thus impartiality becomes impossible. People who are committed to one point of view lose their freedom of thought; they become incapable of seeing reality except through a partial and personal lens, and so everything becomes divided into two groups: those who, like them, know the truth, and the others, who are all wrong and lost. This is undoubtedly an unfortunate attitude, since any reasonably enlightened person knows that using conviction — or faith — as the sole criterion of truth can only lead to blind partiality.

Regarding the origin of such prejudices, it is impossible to know exactly what occurs in the religious mind, but we can use an analogy that seems quite reasonable to explain it. Let's say that, from a religious perspective, an individual declaring himself an atheist is perhaps as shocking as a beloved and well-cared child who claims not to love his parents. Something like saying: "What does it matter if they love me? What does it matter if they raised me, fed me, and educated me? They did it because they wanted to. I didn't force anyone to do this, so I don't owe them any gratitude!"

For most people, such a statement certainly sounds shocking. The immediate impression that comes to our minds is that such a person is cynical and insensitive, and it is difficult to imagine that he is happy and mentally healthy. However, we must admit that this person's words make sense, and are strictly rational. The fact is that we all have prejudices — and thinking that everyone should blindly love their parents just because they were kind and took good care of us is just another one of them. This is probably rooted in instincts — but even so, on an objective level, it remains a prejudice. This is a good example to demonstrate that beliefs held by emotional reasons seem to have a curious immunity to rational criticism. Therefore, assuming that religious beliefs are based on emotional factors, this would explain why stating that "we do not love our creator" may sound very strong to religious people, fatally resulting in prejudices of all kinds.

Realizing that they cannot stereotype atheists morally or philosophically, the critics of atheism move on to another tactic. They focus on the field of practice and affirm that disbelief is pure negativism; that it destroys, but does not rebuild; that it leaves a void in people's lives; that it is useless. But this argument is clearly biased, as it attempts to belittle the atheistic position by comparing it with theism in a distorted way. If atheism is not a set of values, if it is not an explanation or a guide for people's lives, why should it be useful in such aspects? There is no point in making such a comparison. Atheism is not an alternative to theism, and was never intended to be. However, naturally, without dogmas to be followed, the task of choosing and judging values inevitably falls on our own shoulders, that is, to position ourselves individually in the face of the world in which we live. But this task must be understood in terms of freedom of choice, not of existential emptiness. Atheism, contrary to what some make it out to be, is not the curse of a meaningless life, but the "curse" of having meaning in our hands. Anyhow, it's hard to imagine what could be bad and negative in the fact that everyone is free to create their own rules and pursue their own goals, instead of being forced to follow someone else's rules and goals.

Another common misconception of those who oppose atheism is to treat such a position as analogous to theism, as a "religion of disbelief". In other words, they claim that atheists, similarly to theists, hold some kind of dogmatic belief in the non-existence of God(s). Based on this premise, they conclude that atheism would be no more valid than any religious belief — just as theists believe in God and are unable to prove his existence, atheists would be disbelievers equally unable to prove his inexistence.

From what we saw above, such an objection is a tremendous misunderstanding of what atheism is. Firstly, because atheism is not a dogmatic belief in the non-existence of God, but only the absence of belief in that type of supernatural entity. Secondly, because there is a very simple logical rule — and conveniently ignored by theists — which goes as follows: it is not reasonable to believe in something without having reasons to do so. Any sane individual must agree that the attitude of *not believing* in something — because there is no convincing evidence in its favor — is not a belief, nor does it need to be supported by evidence.

Furthermore, proving universal negatives, for logical reasons, is extremely difficult, and certain theists gladly use this idea to assert that no one is capable of proving the non-existence of God. At first sight, that seems reasonable, and should be sufficient to even the scores. However, with a little critical thinking, one soon realizes the incoherence: we cannot prove the non-existence of almost anything. To make the idea clear, we just need some free time to let our imagination run wild. For example, let's formulate some bizarre hypotheses:

1) Our universe is a space aquarium made by aliens who are growing humans;

2) There are immaterial mushrooms that live in a parallel dimension, which are constantly watching us, even though we cannot detect them;

3) The true deity, who created the world and mankind, is Zeus, with the help of Apollo and Dionysus; they and countless other gods are all on the Olympus watching us;

4) The planet on which we live is an electron; the Sun is a collection of protons and neutrons; our planetary system as a whole is a gigantic fluorine atom; modern physicists disagree with this statement, but that is because mankind does not yet have sufficient technology to analyze reality accurately;

5) The universe just seems mechanical and impersonal; in reality, the world in which we live is self-aware;

6) There is a peaceful civilization that inhabits the core of the Sun, which protects itself from the heat through a hyper-technological system that is inconceivable to us; it is home to millions of unicorns, centaurs, and minotaurs at a much higher level of development than ours;

7) There is a large fire-breathing red-winged dragon in my room; however, every time someone tries to observe or confirm its existence, it mysteriously disappears.

Such ideas are sufficient. Now let's ask: how would anyone be able to refute such propositions? We have no reason to consider them true, but even so, we have no way to prove that they are definitely false. That's the problem with universal negatives.

For example, in the case of the sixth hypothesis, the only way to prove that such beings don't exist would be to go to the Sun's core and see if they're there or not — but that's not really a good idea, since going to places that are at millions of degrees Celsius is relatively dangerous. So, basically, this means that we can't prove the non-existence of this supposed helionuclear civilization. However, does it make any sense to claim that this impossibility serves as *evidence* of its existence? Definitely not. Furthermore, the fact that someone firmly believes in such a hypothesis is irrelevant to its veracity.

The same, of course, applies to the idea of God: it is just an unsubstantiated hypothesis — pure speculation, really. We just need to replace the statement "there are living beings at the center of the Sun" with "God created the world" or "God exists". It's the same situation, and there's no reason to think that the divine hypothesis should escape the rule. For the same reason that most people think it is foolish to believe that we are being watched by immaterial mushrooms, atheists think it is foolish to believe that we are being watched by immaterial gods.

We should note, however, that this in no way implies the impossibility of the existence of immaterial mushrooms or gods. In fact, none of the propositions presented above are totally impossible. We simply don't believe them because we have no reason to think that they are true. If we had reasons, we would — but we don't. As we can see, there is no trace of extremism in such reasoning, as it might seem at first.

This counter-argument of theists — "prove to me that God doesn't exist" — , which is usually accepted as valid by the unsuspecting, is an argumentative fallacy called *inversion of the burden of proof*, in which those who affirm the veracity of a proposition place the duty of proving its falsehood on the skeptics — and, if they are unable to do so, the veracity of the proposition would immediately be stablished. The mistake, as we can see, is obvious: how could we do this — prove the non-existence of such a god — if there is not a single proof of its existence to refute?

In reality, the duty to prove the truth lies with the part who affirms something. Thus, if an individual says "God exists", it is up to him to prove the truth of such proposition, that is, to prove the existence of God. If he fails to prove it, we'll have no reason to accept his idea — and so the disbelief will be automatically justified.

We see, therefore, that atheists have no duty to prove anything, because, in the act of disbelieving, they are not stating anything. In general, what they say is simply the following: "I don't believe in God because I have no reason to. If I had a reason, I would believe in it. But I don't have any." In the absence of evidence, being an atheist is simply a matter of intellectual honesty. This notion was very well summarized by Bertrand Russell in this passage:

Many orthodox people speak as though it were the business of sceptics to disprove received dogmas rather than of dogmatists to prove them. This is, of course, a mistake. If I were to suggest that between the Earth and Mars there is a china teapot revolving about the sun in an elliptical orbit, nobody would be able to disprove my assertion provided I were careful to add that the teapot is too small to be revealed even by our most powerful telescopes. But if I were to go on to say that, since my assertion cannot be disproved, it is intolerable presumption on the part of human reason to doubt it, I should rightly be thought to be talking nonsense. If, however, the existence of such a teapot were affirmed in ancient books, taught as the sacred truth every Sunday, and instilled into the minds of children at school, hesitation to believe in its existence would become a mark of eccentricity.

We've already made a good case for atheism, but that's not enough to close the issue. There is a phrase — which, in fact, is quite famous among atheists — that serves as a warning for us to always keep our minds open: absence of evidence is not evidence of absence. The mere lack of evidence is not sufficient to justify the belief in the non-existence of God — and most atheists really don't believe in a definitive way in the non-existence of God.

However, we cannot ignore the fact that there are certain atheists who believe in the non-existence of God(s). As we have seen, they are the ones that belong to the category of *critical atheism*. To justify such a position, the absence of evidence is not sufficient. In this case, it becomes necessary to demonstrate the impossibility of divine existence. Thus, perhaps one could say that this position is dogmatic, since it is impossible to prove definitively the non-existence of any god. However, the small detail that makes all the difference lies in the fact that they do not try to prove the impossibility of each and every god, but of specific ones, as defined by this or that religion.

In this case, the critical atheist uses the belief of the theistic individual to substantiate his own arguments. So, if someone says "I believe in God", the critical atheist asks things like "what is God?", "what is the nature of this god?", "which are its attributes?". For example, studying the definitions of the biblical god, the critical atheist could look for contradictions in the attributes of that divinity and, using the logical rule of non-contradiction — everything that contradicts itself is necessarily false —, uses that information to argue against the existence of such a being. Thus, just as the rule of non-contradiction justifies the belief in the absence of entities whose attributes are mutually exclusive — such as spherical cubes or hexagonal circles —, it also justifies the belief in the non-existence of a god whose attributes are contradictory. In this situation, the belief is rationally justified, and it is therefore not possible to accuse it of dogmatism.

In "theism *versus* atheism" type discussions, it is easy to see that most people don't understand what atheism is. This is why most of the arguments used against it are remarkable for their absolute irrelevance. For example, when some atheist openly takes up his position, he is soon attacked with verbose arguments and all kinds of nonsense. Some examples: "do you want to go to hell?"; "are you another one of those who believe that everything came from nothing?"; "then explain the origin of life and the Universe"; "it's a shame that you're so unhappy".

The first and the last examples don't even deserve a serious answer. However, we must bear in mind that the fact that someone is an atheist says nothing, absolutely nothing about what they think regarding such subjects. This is because atheism has a negative character, and denials are extremely weak in providing data. For example, if someone were to say "my name is not Joe", what could we infer from that, other than the fact that his name is another, other than Joe? It would be absurd to think that such information provides any significant clue as to his real name. For the same reason, there is no way to deduce from the fact that someone is an atheist what are his philosophical, moral, or scientific views on any subject.

Of course, religious people often ask this type of question because most atheists adopt a scientific approach, which is based on experimentation and rationality, but not necessarily. The atheist individual may have his own theories or, without any problem, may refrain from answering these questions, claiming that, in the absence of corroborative data to elaborate any plausible theory, any statement would be nothing more than a guess.

In the latter case, the typical answer to questions of this nature is simply this: *I don't know.*

How did the Universe come about? I don't know.

Why do we exist? I don't know.

Does God exist? I don't know. I only affirm that I was born into this world and that I am ignorant of all these facts. Our existence seems like a great mystery. So it's pointless to say "it was God" if, in reality, I have no reason to believe that. I prefer to accept my ignorance rather than embrace an unfounded hypothesis — trying foolishly to mask my ignorance in the face of this great question mark that is the world in which we live.

Intellectual integrity prevents question marks from being used as arguments in favor of comforting hypotheses, such as that of divine existence. The fact that we don't know where we came from, how life came about, etc., does not at all mean that "it was God". Not knowing where it all came from just means that we don't know where it all came from — and that's it; it doesn't even mean that it came from something. Ignorance is definitely not an argument, and the frequent attempt to use it as an argument only reveals a deplorable partiality, most likely born from the need to believe.

This god who only inhabits the recesses of our ignorance is typically nicknamed "god of the gaps", since he only survives in the shadows of the unknown. It is because of this explanatory subterfuge that, in the past, due to ignorance, natural phenomena — such as thunderstorms — were interpreted as manifestations of a god dissatisfied with humans. Of course, at that time, that seemed as plausible and respectable an explanation for natural phenomena as it is today to say that the Universe was created by a god, since both things were equally unknown. But today, science has shed light — the greatest enemy of the God of the Gaps — on the processes responsible for thunderstorms, turning ridiculous the claim that they are due to the manifestation of an angry god. Hippocrates, born around 460 BC, considered one of the fathers of medicine, in his time already understood the human tendency to mystify the unknown, and said: *Men think that epilepsy is divine merely because they don't understand it. If they called anything they don't understand divine, there would be no end to divine things.*

Let's be honest about ourselves: we're complex beings, capable of remarkable undertakings, but also limited, and we don't have all the answers at our fingertips, at least not currently. Therefore, those who do not want to be deceived by explanatory and comforting fables must learn to live with such limitations, since the attitude of answering a question with a mystery does not explain anything.

This, of course, does not mean completely closing ourselves off to other points of view. In our knowledge, there is — and must be — room for doubt, for uncertainty, because in this way our knowledge will not be crystallized in the form of beliefs impervious to the new evidence that may arise. If we don't accept that our worldview is provisional, that it will always be subject to revision, it will quickly become obsolete. So, if the idea is to keep our minds open, should we grant the hypothesis of the existence of a god any plausibility? Certainly: the same plausibility of a very unlikely speculation that, for thousands of years, has been waiting for evidence to prove it.

Here, it is worth making a brief comment on the position called *agnosticism*. Wrongly, it is often thought that agnosticism lies on the threshold of doubt between theism and atheism. In fact, agnosticism is independent of the issue of belief/disbelief in a god. This view relates only to the impossibility of the human mind conceiving, understanding, or judging some types of issues, stating that such issues are beyond the scope of our rationality and, therefore, it would be impossible to formulate any reliable judgment regarding them.

Thus, it is wrong to think of agnosticism as a "middle ground" between the two perspectives — a perspective that neither affirms nor denies the existence of a higher entity, supposedly representing a position of wise questioning rather than mere atheistic extremism. Agnosticism is certainly not a third choice between theism and atheism, and it's easy to see why: does agnosticism involve belief in a god? No. Does it involve disbelief in a god? No. So what necessary relation does it have with this issue? None. As George H. Smith explained, *the term "agnostic", in itself, does not indicate whether someone believes in a god (...) agnosticism is not an independent position or a middle ground between theism and atheism, since it classifies according to a different criterion.*

Strictly speaking, the word *agnostic* means just *without knowledge*, that is, it is a generic term that concerns only the impossibility of obtaining knowledge about something or some subject. So it would be more correct to say something like: this individual — atheist or theist — is agnostic in relation to the question of the existence of God, or to any "question x" — e.g., the famous unknowability of the "thing-in-itself".

There is, therefore, no middle ground between believing and not believing, that is, between theism and atheism — and stating "I think it is impossible to know for sure" is not a solution, but an evasion. What comports a middle ground is the gap between the denial and the affirmation of the existence of God, and such a gap corresponds to *skeptical atheism*, not to agnosticism. This notion of "agnostic-middle-ground" is an erroneous position commonly adopted by those who are not theists, but who don't consider the existence of God an absurdly unlikely hypothesis, like some more fervent atheists. But, without a doubt, agnostics of this type are, technically, atheists. Many probably call themselves agnostics because they are afraid of the social stigma linked to atheism, which is very strong. Then they transfer the meaning of their positions to milder-sounding terms, such as "agnostic". In this sense, it is clear that this type of agnosticism was born only as a social maneuver to avoid prejudice, not as an argument worthy of respect.

To understand more clearly how misleading this position is, it will be enough to think about the reason why so many are agnostic in relation to God, but no one is agnostic in relation to the Boogeyman. That being could very well exist in a parallel dimension. So, if there's that possibility, why aren't we agnostic about the Boogeyman? Simply because, when our emotions are not involved, we can admit that, in the face of the lack of evidence, the most sensible position is disbelief, not doubt.

So, under normal circumstances, if someone asks us if Santa Claus exists, and we say *no*, that's not an intolerable presumption of human rationality, it's simply common sense. This is because, if the question were to admit our limitations, we would have to admit that the question of the existence of Santa Claus is also something ultimately impossible to decide, in relation to which we would have to declare ourselves agnostics.

Of course, when it comes to the question of the existence of God, we are not absolutely certain, but the fact is that we can't be absolutely certain about anything, not just about God. In these terms, there seems to be no justification for the agnostic position to limit itself to the question of God alone. So, if we're not absolutely certain about anything, we should be agnostic about everything — including Santa Claus —, but we're not, because that line of thinking borders on ridicule.

To conclude, let us use the following parallel: just as Christians don't need faith to disbelieve Thor, atheists don't need faith to disbelieve Christianity. Likewise, just as agnostics don't need perfect knowledge to disbelieve Thor, atheists don't need perfect knowledge to disbelieve God. Thus, agnosticism, which presents itself as a compromise between believing and disbelieving, is sufficiently refuted, and can only be legitimately resurrected if we can satisfactorily answer the following question: *why be agnostic in relation to God, but not in relation to Thor?*

Returning to the main subject, it is always common to see, due to all the myths that exist surrounding atheism, individuals wondering what atheists are like. Maybe they think atheists are very rare exotic creatures that live in a hidden underworld, dress in black, and advocate for the destruction of all religions — but that is nothing more than fantasy. For the most part, atheists are really ordinary people, who simply construct their opinions about reality based on logic and evidence. The fact is that probably everyone has encountered at least a few atheists by chance, without realizing it — which is why they think atheism is so rare. In fact, if we don't ask individuals directly, it's nearly impossible to find out if they're atheists. There are few who shout from the rooftops that they don't believe in any god.

Of course, there are also some exacerbated atheists, typically referred to as militant atheists, some of whom maintain a hostile stance toward religion. Some believe that it is a major obstacle to the progress of humanity, especially those who have some knowledge of History. But this, as we have seen, cannot be viewed as a direct consequence of atheism, since there is no atheistic Holy Scripture that says "you will vilify religion and mock the belief of your neighbor". If an atheist acts in such a way, it is merely an individual position, and to link the cause of their aggressive behavior to atheism is a dishonest attitude.

Many also think that atheists are irreducible in their disbelief, that they are chronic nonbelievers, unable to change their points of view. If we can say that atheists are irreducible, they are only so in the attitude of not believing in unsubstantiated ideas. Certainly, if any theist were to come up with a truly valid proof for the existence of God, even the most stubborn atheist would reconsider his view, and there's no reason to think otherwise. After all, why would anyone oppose the existence of a creator? Who wouldn't want to be the crown of creation? Who would choose to be an ephemeral animal, a thinking speck of dust, if they could be the immortal essence of the Universe? To quote Peter Atkins:

> *[It would indeed be fascinating if the Universe had a purpose; it would probably be pleasant to have life after death. However, there is not a single shred of evidence in favor of either of the two speculations. Since it is easy to understand why people yearn for a cosmic purpose and eternal life, and there is no evidence for both, it seems to me an inescapable conclusion that neither exists.]*

It really would be great if we all were as special as we would like to be, but the fact is, we have no reason to believe that we are. Again, it is intellectual integrity that prevents us from believing something unfounded just because it is comforting.

From the above, we can see that atheism, contrary to the image that is painted of it, is not represented by a cult of fanatical, immoral, unbalanced iconoclasts who want to destroy religion at all costs. Undoubtedly, atheism presents itself as a perfectly reasonable, lucid, and sensible position when viewed from an objective perspective — that is, without taking into account subjective factors, such as "the way we would like reality to be", "what we need to believe in order to live", etc. And, as was pointed out at the beginning of this work, what freethinkers seek are not absolute certainties: they seek what is most likely to be true.

The purpose of this chapter was to undo some of the main myths, prejudices, and defamations that revolve around atheism, so that we can understand this position clearly. It is obvious how much effort made on the part of theists to misrepresent the true meaning of this disbelief. Instead of confronting the real issues, they create scarecrows of what atheism would be and, destroying them, they brag about having refuted it, when in reality such refutation is nothing more than a misunderstanding.

However, let us not think that they are all so naive and innocent: they slander because they cannot face it; they evade because they cannot answer. The fact is that theism always ended up as the loser every time it tried to confront facts and rationality, and it would simply fall apart if it tried, honestly, to confront all the questions that atheism presents.

Thus, if there is one question that truly incorporates the full weight of the challenge that atheism throws against religions, it is this: *what reasons do we have to believe in the existence of a god?*

II

ARGUMENTS FOR THE EXISTENCE OF GOD

Theologians say: these are unfathomable mysteries. To which we reply: these are absurdities imagined by yourselves. You begin by inventing the absurd, then make the imposition of it on us as a divine mystery, unfathomable and all the more profound the more absurd.

— Mikhail Bakunin

Having established the basic concepts of the logic underlying atheism and posed the central question — what reasons do we have to believe in the existence of a god? —, we must now confront the arguments that claim to prove God's existence — and certainly there has been no lack of effort in this direction, for, as Le Bon emphasized, *Believers, however convinced they may be, have always felt the need, at least in order to convert unbelievers, to find justifying reasons in their faith. The numerous elucubrations of theologians prove with what perseverance this task is employed.*

In the following pages we will analyze the main arguments proposed, and then we will present the reasons why they do not serve as justification for belief in God. We will first look at some simple arguments, which can be refuted without much difficulty, since they are based on very distorted notions of what a "proof" would actually be. Later, we will deal with more elaborated arguments, which will be analyzed more extensively. However, before we embark on such a task, it is worth making some remarks.

The notion of God discussed here will vary depending on the belief that the argument proposed was trying to prove. Sometimes it will be a personal god, sometimes simply a "higher intelligence", or else a "force responsible for the harmony of the Universe". In this way, we will attempt to refute the arguments that were proposed only regarding the deity whose existence they intended to prove.

Since, throughout this chapter, we will be dealing with logical arguments and syllogisms — formal deductions —, it is also worth remembering that pure logic is not the criterion of truth. Logic is a human creation, consisting of a series of systematized concepts that attempt to represent the way in which reality works. Thus, it is a very useful tool to guide our investigations, but not to determine them completely. The fact that an argument that seeks to prove the existence of something is based on impeccable logic, strictly speaking, means nothing if the conclusions reached with it are not subject to proof and verification. This is because it is possible to conceive several explanations based on an equally massive logical rigor to defend opposing causes, and it is impossible, of course, that both could correspond to reality simultaneously. Therefore, the only way to know which of them is true is to confront them with reality, and then see which of them survives. If theories cannot be falsified — if they cannot be refuted or confirmed — they should not be seen as proof.

Furthermore, all allegations of unintelligibility must be viewed with great suspicion, since in most cases they are just evasive maneuvers. Such statements are incoherent because, analyzing them, we realize that they are contradictory. For example, assuming that an "abstraction x" is unintelligible, how could we possibly know that, if it is unintelligible? The paradox is that, in order to know that something is impossible to understand, we would first need to understand it, so that we could be aware of what we are ignoring, that is, to know exactly what we are referring to when we claim that impossibility — otherwise it would be an empty and useless statement.

Since the limitation of reason is an assumption of rationality itself, we are forced to conclude that it is impossible to know whether the unintelligible even exists — it is only a conjecture impossible to be proved. That is why the individual who claims unintelligibility usually simply postulates the unintelligible as a given, without further explanation: in other words, it is just an irrational belief covered by a thin film of logic.

The arguments presented below serve as an example of the kind of reasoning that is typically used to substantiate *skeptical atheism*, that is, the modality that is limited to refuting the arguments by which supposedly the belief in a god would be justified, without worrying about denying the possibility of the existence of such a deity, which is a characteristic of *critical atheism*.

PART I

Being alive is proof that God exists.

Those who have participated in debates about the existence of God have most likely heard this classic argument. This is a very naive statement, and it would really be useless to look for a better example of the logical fallacy that bears the name *circulus in demonstrando* — commonly known as a circular argument —, which consists of admitting as a premise the very conclusion that one should be proving. Thus, starting from the completely unjustified assumption that the only possible cause for the existence of life is God, then life itself is used as proof for the existence of God. The misconception becomes even more clear with this example: if we had been taught as children that elves are the true cause of earthquakes, every time an earthquake happened we would say: "this is the proof that elves exist!" Blatant nonsense, of course. Such a statement is nothing more than a belief disguised as an argument.

God must exist because, without him, life would have no meaning.

Regarding this issue, we simply limit ourselves to asking one question: why does life have to have any meaning? Just because it makes things more organized in our minds, making us feel important? Without a doubt, it is a mistake to imagine how we would like reality to be and then to declare that the requirements that satisfy us must necessarily exist. It would be like saying that God must exist because, otherwise, we would have nothing to do on Sunday mornings. The same can be said about statements like this: "God must exist because, without him, there would be no guarantee of justice in the world". Again, we only need to ask: from where can one infer the idea that some kind of "universal justice" must necessarily exist? From nowhere, except our desire that things were such.

When, in prayer, I ask God for things, my prayers are answered.

Asking God for something and interpreting a favorable coincidence as a "heavenly gift" could demonstrate the existence of as many gods as we wanted: I prayed to God and, in the supermarket, I found my favorite soft drink, which is almost always in short supply. That's what that argument tells us. Sifting through positive accidents and calling perfectly normal things "miracles" only shows that our minds are located in a magical and anthropomorphic world where everything surrounds us in image and likeness. So, although many people claim this type of "divine intervention", it's easy to see where, most of the time, the misunderstanding lies. When we "ask" something from God, we begin to pay attention to all the facts that happen around us, and we weigh them according to their relevance, that is, we classify them as positive, negative, or irrelevant to the objective we are pursuing. In this context, if something positive happens, we immediately interpret that something as caused by God, because in this situation we are looking for connections between our request and our objective. However, the causal connection, of course, is only psychological. This association seems valid and logical to us because our brain is "programmed" to scan situations in search of cause-and-effect patterns — often finding them where there are none. This is also called "magical thinking", which, as James Alcock explains, *is the interpretation of two close events as being cause and effect, without any concern with the causal link.* For example, if you believe that crossing your fingers brings good luck, you associate the fact of crossing your fingers with a subsequent favorable event and establish a causal link between them. In this way, we realize that "divine help" is just a personal interpretation of the facts, not an objective description of what we actually saw happening. If, for example, when we asked God for something, that something was supernaturally fulfilled, then we would have reason to think that we are facing a divine intervention. However, to claim that natural facts are "miraculous" just because they are sometimes confluent with our objectives is unfounded, and does not prove anything other than that we are calling God what really is blind chance. The fallacy that consists of assuming that something is the cause of a fact simply because it preceded it is called *post hoc ergo propter hoc*.

The proof of God's existence are the miracles he performs daily.

If, for example, a cure proves the existence of God, then the fact that he gave us a disease, what does it prove? If it does not demonstrate its non-existence, it places God in a very problematic situation. Be that as it may, testimonies of "miracles" that God supposedly works in people's lives are common. Mysterious illnesses are cured, for which medicine had no answers; drug-dependent individuals who "find the light" and overcome addiction; alcoholics regenerate through faith, and so on. However, if we adopt a consistent definition of the term "miracle", we see that the value of such testimonies falls apart. In addressing the issue, the philosopher David Hume states that:

> *Nothing is considered a miracle if it occurs in the normal course of nature. It is no miracle that a man, apparently in good health, dies suddenly, because it turns out that such a kind of death, although more unusual than any other, occurs frequently. But it's a miracle that a dead person can be resurrected, because this has never been observed in any time and in any country. Therefore, there must be a uniform experience against every miraculous event, otherwise the event would not deserve this denomination. And since a uniform experience is equivalent to a test, there is here direct and complete proof, taken from factual nature against the existence of a miracle; such proof cannot be destroyed nor can the miracle be made credible except by means of an opposite proof that is superior to it. (...) The plain consequence is — and it is a general maxim worthy of our attention — that no testimony is sufficient to establish a miracle, unless the testimony be of such a kind that its falsehood would be more miracu-*

lous than the fact which it endeavors to establish.

Therefore, the more unlikely an event is to occur, the more convincing the evidence must be in its favor. Is it more likely that the theist was mistaken in his testimony or that a supernatural intervention took place? Both hypotheses are possible. However, if there is no conclusive evidence, all we can say is that there is a question mark hanging over the fact — and that invoking the improbability of a miracle to explain it is not the most probable answer. A possible natural explanation for such "miraculous healing" phenomena is what's called the placebo effect. In humans, the power of suggestion is very powerful, capable of carrying out profound changes, including biological cures. For example, if an individual with a headache firmly believes that he is taking aspirin but mistakenly takes a multivitamin complex, it is very common that the simple belief that his pain will stop due to the supposed aspirin will be sufficient to cure it. Similarly, when a theist projects, with solid conviction, his expectations into an entity that he imagines to be infinite and perfect, and that would be helping him overcome his addiction or illness, that is something very strong, and such trust can generate a motivation powerful enough for the individual to really achieve such things. However, in this case, as we can see, it is not God who brings about such changes, but the belief in God, that is, the individual's conviction, the faith-placebo complex — something much more likely than the occurrence of a miracle.

The happiness and peace that come from faith prove its truthfulness.

When we're arguing about the veracity of something, happiness shouldn't be presented as an argument. If believing in something makes us happier, it just means that, for some reason, that belief is pleasant or comfortable, but not necessarily true. In this sense, if we only used happiness, in isolation, as the criterion of truth, would we even know anything? If we were sufficiently capable in the art of self-deception, we could believe that we are immortal, that we are millionaires, that misery and inequality do not exist, that there are no diseases, that we are more intelligent than Einstein, that the holocaust never happened, and that all our dreams will come true tomorrow morning. If such beliefs made us happier, would that mean that they are true? No. Suppose that a close friend had suffered a serious accident and was admitted to intensive care. To have a chance of surviving, he would need to undergo a high-risk operation. The operation is performed, but our friend doesn't resist. Then we call the hospital to know about the result of the operation, and the doctor in charge says: "the operation was an incredible success, he's already out of danger. Come visit him, he's waiting for you!" So we feel very happy and relieved, but is such happiness based on anything real? No, it's based on being mistaken. As Bernard Shaw's brilliant quote says: *The fact that a believer is happier than a skeptic is no more to the point than the fact that a drunken man is happier than a sober one.*

Nobody can live without God. Everyone needs to believe in some higher force.

To declare the non-existence of atheists, who are concrete beings, to defend the existence of an incorporeal entity does not seem like a very logical posture. Be that as it may, we know that nonbelievers live very well without God. To say that "deep down" all atheists believe in the Creator is nothing more than egocentrism disguised as an argument. It's simply not impossible to live without believing in God — or "higher force" — and all the atheists in the world are living proof of that. This need to believe, in the end, only shows that some are psychologically dependent on imaginary consolations — and it is truly regrettable that so many people are unable to live without placing themselves under the yoke of a "divine constitution". Is freedom such a terrifying thing? Maybe. But the thing is, if a theist is unable to live without believing in something "superior", that doesn't mean that every human being is also incapable. This is an absurdly generalized personal belief. It would be something like a smoker saying: "I learned to smoke from an early age; I am unable to live without tobacco; therefore, the entire humanity smokes; glory to nicotine!"

Bertrand Russell, using another approach, also highlights the contradictory nature of this argument, which suggests that only in the case of the belief in God would it be valid to ignore the evidence:

People will tell us that without the consolations of religion they would be intol-

erably unhappy. So far as this is true, it is a coward's argument. Nobody but a coward would consciously choose to live in a fool's paradise. When a man suspects his wife of infidelity, he is not thought the better of for shutting his eyes to the evidence. And I cannot see why ignoring evidence should be contemptible in one case and admirable in the other.

It is certain that God exists because no one, until today, has been able to prove his non-existence.

Here we are clearly faced with the old logical fallacy called the *reversed burden of proof*. It's virtually impossible to confirm a universal negative. Therefore, the task of providing the evidence falls on the defenders of a proposition, and not on the skeptics who "afford" to demand evidence to substantiate their opinions about reality. Theists themselves follow this logical rule most of the time — but conveniently ignore it when it goes against their personal beliefs. It is true that theists follow it because they do not believe in Greek gods — such as Zeus, Apollo, Dionysus — nor in unicorns, winged horses, dragons, elves, cyclops, and so on, although they cannot prove that such beings do not exist in some remote region of our universe. Therefore, in these cases, the most reasonable thing is to admit that those who affirm the veracity of a proposition are automatically responsible for providing evidence that supports it — and, if they fail to do so, there will be no reason for us to accept their statement as true, thus justifying the disbelief. Carl Sagan draws an interesting analogy between "special entities" and an invisible dragon, making it clear how erroneous it is to believe that something is true just because it cannot be refuted:

Now, what's the difference between an invisible, incorporeal, floating dragon who spits heatless fire and no dragon at all? If there's no way to disprove my contention, no conceivable experiment that would count against it, what does it mean to say that my dragon exists? Your inability to invalidate my hypothesis is not at all the same thing as proving it true. Claims that cannot be tested, assertions immune to disproof are veridically worthless, whatever value they may have in inspiring us or in exciting our sense of wonder.

Science cannot answer the "big questions" of existence. The answer can only be God.

It is often said that man is wildly ignorant about the world in which he lives, that science cannot answer the "big questions". This reluctance that many present to accept that we know something probably has its origin in the terrifying possibility that we really are what we seem to be, and that there is nothing very spectacular about the fact that we exist. As far as we can see, they deny that we have or may have found any answer because they already have another kind of preformed answer in mind, and they are looking for evidence that supports just that idea, turning a blind eye to the evidence that points in any other direction. We have countless reasons to think that we are just biological complexes that emerged through organic evolution and no reasonable motive to think otherwise — other than, perhaps, the desire for it to be so. This approach of denying that scientific knowledge of objective reality can answer subjective questions seems to be the way some find to flirt with comforting — but unlikely — hopes. Basically, this is a rather naive attempt to reduce man to complete ignorance in order to level all hypotheses to the same degree of probability — and thus give the impression that all points of view are equally plausible. However, regarding the relativity of wrong and the imprecision of our knowledge, Isaac Asimov reminds us that:

> *When people thought the Earth was flat, they were wrong. When people thought the Earth was spherical, they were wrong. But if you think that thinking the Earth is spherical is just as wrong as thinking the Earth is flat, then your view is wronger than both of them put together.*

Since ancient times, people have believed in God. If it didn't exist, surely such a belief would have already been discarded.

The fact that a belief is old does not imply its veracity. Truth isn't like wine; it doesn't get better by getting older. This only demonstrates our constant need to look "beyond" for answers to questions that have nothing to do with reality. We know that many false beliefs have been cultivated for thousands of years. For example, until Copernicus appeared, the Earth was considered the center of the Universe, and the Sun revolved around it. That mistake was believed for a long time. We also have astrology, which is ancient. It is estimated to have originated around 3500 years ago. This doctrine, which is based on the supposed influence that heavenly bodies exert on human behavior, despite having been widely refuted by modern science, has not ceased to be popular and have many followers to this day. And the same applies to God: the fact that this belief is old only means that it is old, and nothing more.

Belief in God is universal in humanity. It's impossible for the entire world to be mistaken.

This argument also seems to ignore history. Apart from the fact that a considerable part of the world's population does not believe in God, the popularity of a proposition contributes nothing to its veracity. Even if the entire world believed in the existence of God, that wouldn't mean anything, because in the past the whole world believed the Earth was flat and full of witches. What counts for or against a theory is *evidence*, not how many individuals consider it true. Whether we like it or not, reality doesn't bend itself to our beliefs. As Anatole France said: *If fifty million people say a foolish thing, it is still a foolish thing.* Technically, this fallacy is called *argumentum ad populum*.

The idea of God proves his existence / Talking about God is a tacit admission of his existence.

If that were true, then what could we say about characters from fictional books? What about all the countless gods of all religions? Does discussing Greek mythology mean admitting the existence of Zeus? Ideas are one thing, real beings are another. For example, RPG players discuss the attributes of many bizarre fictional creatures — goblins, orcs, minotaurs, centaurs, harpies, winged dragons —, but that certainly doesn't mean that such beings exist objectively. Imagination, by itself, can conceive things that have no correspondence with objective reality. Therefore, the idea of God, in isolation, does not serve as evidence in favor of its existence. If we insist otherwise, then it must be time to plan a vacation and take advantage of those ten million that we have in an offshore account, which has just materialized because we touched on the subject.

God exists, but it is incomprehensible to the human mind.

How can someone believe something they can't even understand? What exactly would the individual be believing when they say they believe in God? George H. Smith shows us very clearly the incoherence of this position:

When an atheist is told that God is unknowable, he can interpret that claim in two ways. He may suppose, first, that the theist has obtained knowledge about a being that, as he himself admits, cannot be known; or, on the other hand, he can assume that the theist simply does not know what he is talking about.

This type of allegation is not an argument, but an evasive maneuver, a way of trying to take the issue beyond the scope of rationality — thus ending any possibility of further discussing the matter. It would be like saying: "spherical cubes exist in unconceived dimensions, but it is impossible to prove it rationally because, due to the 'imperfection' of the human mind, we are unable to understand objects whose attributes are contradictory". Furthermore, this argument looks even more shaky when we see that it limits itself to *admitting* the existence of such a being, and then using the tactic of alleging the "unintelligibility of the divine nature" to manage to evade rationality, making the task of logically justifying such belief unnecessary. This is a typical tactic of the anemic arguments of religion, which are unable to keep themselves standing up when under the force of gravity that exists in the actual world — and so they flee to the beyond, to the metaphysical, to the inscrutable, to the nothingness.

Reason is limited; God is a transcendent being; believing in his existence is a matter of faith, not logic.

This argument is based on the dubious assumption that, if the existence of God could be proven logically or experimentally, then that God would not really be a transcendent being, but simply something mundane, that is, it would not be God. Therefore, a "leap of faith" would be necessary to substantiate the belief in God. From this perspective, faith seems to be just a tool to justify irrationality, to validate the adoption of an unfounded belief. Thus, again, we see that this is an evasion, not an argument, because a "leap of faith", in addition to not proving the existence of a god, would also justify any kind of absurdity imaginable: study religions, choose your favorite mythological character or deity, and then just take a "leap of faith" to justify it. Furthermore, as Nietzsche pointed out, *the characteristics that were given to the "True Being" of things are characteristics of Non-Being, of Nothingness. The "true world" was built based on the contradiction with the actual world.* In this way, jumping from the effective world to the transcendental unintelligible world would mean jumping from everything that is material to that which is only immaterial, from everything that is effective to what is purely non-effective, that is, to the non-being, to the irrationality of absolute nothingness. The difference is that, in such case, the abstraction of nothingness is renamed "God" and the incoherence is hidden by the pompous name of "divine transcendence". To deal with such metaphysical oddities that seem to have arisen from a mental seizure — reason is really limited.

God exists, but humanity has not yet evolved enough to have the capacity to prove it.

In that case, there's not much to be said. We are eagerly awaiting such "proof". It has been said that there are gods for thousands of years, and no one has been able to obtain evidence of this for thousands of years. If someone finds such evidence, atheism will end. That's it. But believing in advance is nothing more than naivety. Why should we believe, without reason, in a certain "entity", and then justify such belief by our current vast degree of ignorance? We could invent dozens, hundreds, or thousands of exotic theories and then claim that they're all true, but humanity hasn't yet "evolved enough" to prove them. Now, this is an unpolished and puerile argument — something that certainly comes as no surprise when it comes to the typical argument used to defend the belief in supernatural entities.

Part II

The cosmological argument (first cause)

Proposition: *Every effect has a cause. If the Universe exists, then it had a cause, because there is no effect without a cause, and it could not have created itself out of nothing, because in that case it would be cause and effect at the same time, which is impossible. If we go back in the chain of causes, we will have an infinite series, which must be interrupted, otherwise there would never have been a first effect and, therefore, we would not exist. This First Cause is God; an uncaused, immovable, eternal, sustaining and creator of the Universe in which we live.*

This is a classic argument, it's easy to understand, and apparently convincing — but obviously invalid, otherwise we would accept it. In principle, this argument distorts the meaning of the word "cause". At first, it is used in the scientific sense of "cause and effect" in the interaction between bodies — this is for us to accept the premise as valid. But later, it is used in a distorted way, meaning "to come into existence" — and this change in meaning is something quite typical of dishonest arguments. There's certainly a huge difference between creating and building. A man who is the cause of a book does not create it, but writes it using paper and ink. Likewise, no one creates a car from nothing, but builds it from pre-existing materials.

The second error in this argument consists in the fact that God himself escapes the premise used to arrive at him, that is, the argument is contradictory. The statement "every effect has a cause" is in direct conflict with the statement "God is uncaused" — so it is impossible for both to be true at the same time. Claiming that God can exist without a cause gives occasion to the same claim in relation to the Universe. If God can be uncaused, why can't the Universe? Just because the theist would like it to be so? It doesn't seem reasonable to accept that God should escape the very logic being used to prove its existence.

Furthermore, even if the argument were not flawed in such aspects, it also does not demonstrate at all that God created the Universe. All that such an argument demonstrates is simply the fact that we can go back in the chain of causal events until we reach a question mark — and not knowing proves nothing, other than that we are ignorant about something.

Thus, as we can see, there is a large gulf between the point at which the argument arrives and the statement that "this first cause is God". In addition to saying "it was God" being just a way of explaining the unknown by the most unknown, we could also ask: why is this cause God? How do you know that? Let's face it, it's obvious that nobody knows: we can never know anything about imaginary fictions, but only believe.

In this regard, Nietzsche aptly stated that *by searching out origins, one becomes a crab. The historian looks backward; eventually he also believes backward.* This is a very peculiar characteristic of humans, who are always looking for answers to satisfy their need for explanations for everything that exists — and even when they visibly cannot reach them, they are satisfied with merely believing that they have achieved them.

From what we saw above, it is clear that the idea that everything must be created is nothing more than a false analogy between the nature of the world and the nature of human creations, the confusion between "creating" and "building" — ultimately nothing more than a reflection of our anthropocentrism. Maybe the Universe didn't even have a beginning, maybe matter is eternal. Nobody really knows.

Since there are so many variants of this argument, it's not worth spending time refuting each of them. Basically, they all go back to question marks, make some distorted analogies, and then claim that only God can be the answer. That's why they're all equally invalid.

THE ONTOLOGICAL ARGUMENT

Proposition: *I have the idea of a being, of a perfect being. Now, since there is necessarily more reason in cause than in effect, the idea of perfection can only proceed from perfection itself. This perfect entity must exist because, if it did not exist, it would lack the perfection of existence, and in that way it would not be perfect.*

That argument was created by Saint Anselm. In his opinion, the very unsurpassed perfection of the idea of God proves its truthfulness. The claim is that when we try to imagine something perfect in every aspect, we arrive at the idea of God — and one of those aspects, of course, would be the perfection of existing. In this we would have the logical and perfect proof that God exists, although we have nothing more than an old sophism.

As we can see, the argument treats existence as a quality, as if there were some qualitative difference between a hypothetical perfection and a real perfection. In reality, there isn't, because non-existence is not a type of imperfection. To demonstrate it, we can use this same argument, but with an internal combustion engine:

> *I have the idea of an engine, of a perfect engine, in which there is full use of the fuel and no waste. Now, since there is necessarily more reason in cause than in effect, the idea of perfection can only proceed from perfection itself. This perfect entity must exist because, if it did not exist, it would lack the perfection of existence, and in that way it would not be perfect.*

It seems clear that the perfection of an imaginary ideal motor would be identical to that of a real perfect motor. The fact that it doesn't exist wouldn't make it any less perfect — less efficient — at all. So, supposing that a designer conceived such a perfect engine, and then built it, in what would the real engine be more perfect than the motor that was in his mind as an idea? In nothing, since the concept implicit in the real engine would not contain any perfection other than that present in the abstraction of the hypothetical engine.

Therefore, whether it exists or not, the content of the idea remains unchanged. That is the major flaw in the argument. However, even assuming that existence was a quality — therefore, that the concept of a real God was qualitatively superior to that of a hypothetical God —, this would still not prove anything, since imagination can conceive things that have no correspondence in reality. So it doesn't matter if God would be more perfect if he existed, because that doesn't imply his existence at all. The fact is that reality simply doesn't kneel before our syllogisms.

The Teleological Argument (Intelligent Design)

Proposition: *We see all the order and harmony that exists in the Universe, the myriad of species, the immense complexity that exists in every small cell of living beings, the intricate interconnection and interdependence that exists between them all. It's impossible to imagine that all this wonder exists by chance. That's because, if planetary conditions were subtly different from today's, life on Earth would be impossible. To say that the world we know came from an "explosion" (Big Bang) is as absurd as saying that a dictionary is the result of the explosion of a typography. There must be a mind behind our Universe, which planned, created, and maintains the order that we observe in it.*

Analogy: *Suppose that, while crossing a desert, I came across a watch. You would hardly think that it was always there or that it formed spontaneously from desert sand. By analyzing the complex structure of its springs and gears, we can only conclude that the watch must have had a creator, who must have existed at some time and somewhere, who made it for the purpose we see it fulfilling, who understood its operation and who designed it. The same can be said about life: it is absurd to think that there is no mind behind such complexity, which far exceeds that of a simple watch.*

If we were omnipotent, wouldn't we have been able to create a world that is better than ours? It is very strange to think that an almighty God would have deliberately created a world like this, with so many superfluities and imperfections, so many problems and diseases, when it was within his power to make it finished and perfect. However, let's get to the facts.

Undoubtedly, atheists also see this remarkable complexity and feel equally amazed by it. The difference is that they accept the challenge of trying to explain it in natural terms, without invoking the mysterious powers of the beyond. They rely on their knowledge of the world and of natural laws to formulate rational explanatory theories. Such hypotheses are not just sterile speculations that say "it was by chance" — here, chance can only be understood in the sense that there are no objectives. In reality, they are well-founded theories that incorporate the mechanisms of the very reality in which we live, and try to explain life in such terms.

It is true that we are not yet able to fully explain the complexity of life and the Universe, but that does not prove that there is a mind behind the world. This only proves that we don't have a definitive answer. Currently, there are several rational theories that attempt to explain the origin of life and its immense diversity — for example, Abiogenesis and the Theory of the Evolution of Species. Nobody believes them because of faith or personal preference. Scientific theories are not "invented", they are developed from meticulous research and investigation. We simply observe nature, collect the data and, interpreting that information, see where it points. Based on this, we build theories that seek to explain complex phenomena such as life based on the physical mechanisms that we know.

Science always evolves because it learns from its own mistakes. For example, ask a scientist if he believes that matter consists of fire, water, earth, and air, if they believe that the Earth is the center of the Universe, or if phlogiston is the fluid responsible for the combustion. Those misconceptions of the past were long ago overcome, because science is methodical, self-critical and, above all, it strives for truth, and that is why it is constantly reviewing its concepts about reality. On the other hand, ask a Catholic if we have a spirit, if the world and life were God's creations, if Jesus is his son, if the Trinity is formed by the Father, the Son, and the Holy Ghost, or if the Virgin Mary remains a virgin. This illustrates that, in terms of knowledge about reality, religion is in the diametrically opposite position, since it is structured on dogmas without grounds that can be verified — and this, consequently, makes it static. Within a hundred years, no doubt, much of our scientific understanding of the world will have changed, but the same will hardly be true for any of these religious dogmas. So, if we really want to discover, to understand something, the best path seems to be that of investigation, not that of belief.

The attitude of attacking the Theory of the Evolution of Species to demonstrate that it is impossible would be admirable, if it wasn't motivated by very unscientific behind-the-scenes interests. Even so, let us make no mistake about this: if anyone can demonstrate that the Theory of Evolution is wrong, scientists will be enormously grateful. What science wants is to describe reality as accurately as possible, and the Theory of Evolution is nothing more than a fruit of that attempt. In this sense, we should bear in mind that this theory has no importance in principle, except for the fact that it describes what we see happening in the world before us.

Of course, new ideas, at first glance, may seem strange, but they will not be discarded without prior analysis. Just as the very strange idea — at least at the time — of transmitting the human voice through metallic wires proved to be possible, and just as Einstein's Theory of Relativity overthrew Newton's classical physics — which, let's face it, is much more intuitive —, the Theory of Evolution can also be overturned by another theory, provided that we have real motives to accept it as true.

The Intelligent Creator hypothesis is not based on any evidence, but only on the human desire to have a certain "cosmic importance". If we had reason to think that life is the creation of a special being, we would undoubtedly defend that theory, but the fact is that we have none. The world in which we live shows no evidence of having been designed by a higher intelligence — unless that supreme mind aimed to create a reality "beyond suspicion", in which everything was carefully designed to deceive us, making it only seem that there was no creator. If that's the case, it's still true that he succeeded.

Furthermore, making analogies such as that of the "carpenter and the chair" and that of the "clock in the desert" doesn't explain anything, because the Universe doesn't work like the human mind, life doesn't work like a clock — after all, has anyone ever seen clocks creating copies of themselves? Undoubtedly, the complexity of these structures is remarkable, but to formulate an entire cosmology based on a failed analogy is really too much pretension. At best, an analogy serves as an illustrative metaphor that helps us to grasp the central idea that underlies the hypothesis. But the fact is, if the Intelligent Creator theory cannot present any positive evidence in its favor, how could we prove or refute its veracity?

Even if creationists refuted the Theory of Evolution, it would be ridiculous to think that this would authorize the Intelligent Creation hypothesis to occupy its space legitimately. The Theory of Evolution is scientific, that is why it clearly presents its assumptions, and the data on which it is based to justify its statements. The Intelligent Creation theory, quite the contrary, is not based on evidence, but on a question mark, on faith, and on the fertile imagination of its proponents.

The Religious Experience

Proposition: *We've never seen the wind, but we're sure it exists. And how do we know that? We feel the wind. Likewise, we do not believe in the existence of God because we see him, but because we feel his presence. Faith is like a sixth sense, and atheists are like blind people trying to deny the existence of colors. If an atheist is incapable of feeling God, that does not imply his non-existence.*

I close my eyes, I feel in communion with the essence of the Universe, and this proves that God exists. Simple as that. This naive argument clearly places subjective consciousness as a kind of criterion of truth, although this only proves that we like to daydream.

Our senses are imperfect, apprehending only a tiny portion of reality, and yet in an inaccurate way. Therefore, to begin with, it must be clarified that colors are not a "property of matter", since they do not exist independently of us. What really exists are electromagnetic waves that, when reflected by an object, stimulate our sensory organs, causing the subjective sensation of color. Our visual system is programmed to translate a certain range of electromagnetic wavelengths into visual sensations. Thus, it doesn't matter if blind people would be able or not to conceive what colors are, because they only exist in our heads anyway.

We, for example, cannot conceive of what happens in a bat's brain when it uses its sonar to locate itself while flying. Maybe it uses high-frequency sounds to create a mental representation of reality analogous to the one we create from electromagnetic waves — but how could we know for sure? Regarding bats, we are all "blind", as we cannot conceive what "sound images" would be like. However, although it is inconceivable to us what happens subjectively in a bat's brain, we know that, to guide itself, it uses high-frequency sounds, which are inaudible to us. Therefore, in the case of vision, reality is not in the subjective sensation, but in the external factor that causes the subjective sensation.

So, even though we don't see and don't hear many things, we know that they exist, because we can know their existence indirectly. For example, we can't see the air, but when you blow a balloon, it fills up. What is it filled with? With nothing? No, it's filled with a mixture of gaseous substances with certain properties that prevent it from reflecting light — at least not to a sufficient degree for our body to be able to detect it through vision. Many frequencies are beyond our visible spectrum, but that's not why we deny their existence. On the contrary, we can prove that they exist.

With all this in mind, the question we ask is this: how could one verify the theists' claim in an objective way? Can the theist prove that the "sensation of God" is caused by something external? Undoubtedly, it is much more likely that what they call "contact with God" is nothing more than an "oceanic feeling", as Freud called it, a subjective experience that can be achieved through meditation or prayer, but with no correspondence in objective reality.

Let's use a few more examples. As is well known, some mentally disturbed individuals hear "phantom voices", and sometimes even normal people hear them. This shows that our brain can construct mental representations that apparently have objective causes, but that in reality have both causes and effects that are purely subjective. The same can be said about dreams. How could we see all those images with our eyes closed? Of course, during dreams, our mind doesn't travel to capture the light of a parallel reality. Dream images are generated internally, by the brain itself.

Therefore, if the religious experience were to prove the existence of God through pure feeling, then the delusion of a madman would prove that he is Napoleon Bonaparte in flesh and blood — through pure feeling as well. The fact is that human subjectivity does not have any necessary correspondence with objective reality and, thus, cannot be used as conclusive evidence. Hallucinations, delusions, mystical sensations, and the like are not arguments.

In addition, there are several experiments that are very well accepted by the scientific community, which show that experiences of "closeness to God" can be induced artificially by magnetic fields. Apparently, mystical experiences are mainly related to the region of the brain called the temporal lobe, as Susan Blackmore explains:

Stimulating the temporal lobe (for example with electrodes or with magnetic fields) can give rise to out-of-body experiences, mystical experiences, sensations of floating and flying and also the feeling that there is someone there — even if you cannot see anything. The temporal lobe is especially active during some phases of sleep and so there may be a connection here with sleep paralysis. Also some people have much more unstable temporal lobes than others. What is called "temporal lobe lability" can be measured, and people who are high on this scale (with unstable or highly active temporal lobes) tend to be more artistic. They more often report déjà-vu, mystical, psychic, and out-of-body experiences, and more often have imaginary playmates as a child.

Logically, we should note that the fact that such experiences seem real is completely irrelevant, since colors also seem real, but they do not exist objectively, as something independent of our perception. This seems to strongly indicate that, like colors, gods only exist inside our heads. Hopefully no theist now wants to argue that it was God who placed in our brain a divine antenna, a "God-Receiver" programmed to capture metaphysical waves.

Pascal's Wage

Proposition: *Let us then examine this point, and say, "God is, or He is not". But to which side shall we incline? Reason can decide nothing here. There is an infinite chaos which separated us. A game is being played at the extremity of this infinite distance where heads or tails will turn up. What will you wager?*

In this argument, it is first postulated that it is impossible to prove the existence of God rationally, then the idea is basically this:

If God exists, and we believe in him, we will go to heaven. If God exists, and we don't believe in him, we'll go to hell. If God doesn't exist, and we believe in him, we lose nothing. If God doesn't exist, and we don't believe in him, we gain nothing. Therefore, the most advantageous option is to believe in God.

Therefore, God exists or doesn't exist. We need to bet, and reason has its hands tied. If God exists, whoever is wrong will go to hell. But if it doesn't exist, nobody loses, because everything was nothing more than a great fantasy. Given the options, it seems more reasonable to believe in God — except for the detail that it was a man who invented this bet, due to the lack of solid arguments.

Logically, its most "convincing" part is not explicit in the original argument, which consists of the supposed punishment that unbelievers would face in the afterlife, if they were wrong. Thus, coerced by fear, we are forced to choose between two incoherent positions — and we only consider the hypothesis of God because he intends to torture the infidels, something that seems more like a gun pointed us than an argument. So, to better understand how absurd this argument is, we only need to exchange God for the imaginary entity of our choice. For example, Santa Claus:

If Santa Claus exists, and we believe in him, at Christmas he will enter through our chimney to place presents under the tree. If Santa Claus exists, and we don't believe him, we're left without presents. If Santa Claus doesn't exist, and we believe in him, we lose nothing. If Santa Claus doesn't exist, and we don't believe in him, we get nothing. Therefore, the most advantageous option is to believe in Santa Claus.

As we can see, Pascal's bet is a great example of the argumentative fallacy called *false dilemma*, in which an attempt is made to restrict the number of possibilities when, in reality, there are many others. This argument makes it seem that both propositions — "God exists" and "God does not exist" — are equally likely to be correct, as if the existence of God were merely a matter of coin tossing.

But what if the true deity is Allah? Then they will both end up in Mohammedan hell! What if it's Huitzilopochtli? Or his brother Tezcatilpoca? Or Baal? Or Zeus? Or Moloch? Or the boogeyman, perhaps? After all, how could we find out who the true God is? On which deity should we bet? There are so many! If we're believing in the wrong god, the true one will fatally punish us.

The possibilities, in fact, are endless. This argument is nothing more than a cynical attempt to divert our attention — using the idea of eternal punishment — from the fact that it is a completely irrational attitude to believe in something without having a reason to do so. If, faced with the impasse, we still insist on betting on a particular god, we must admit that in the process we ended up losing something — common sense.

Furthermore, if God is omniscient, he will certainly know that the religious person believes in him only out of interest in going to heaven, and that the atheist is being honest with himself when he says that he has no reason to believe. So, if that God is also just, he certainly wouldn't condemn atheists, but religious people. It seems that logic sometimes leads us to ironic conclusions.

The pantheistic argument

Proposition: *God is the sum of everything that exists, he is the Universe as a whole. His will is the force that maintains the natural order of what exists, and his intelligence is manifested through the harmony and perfection of the Universe in which we live.*

Pantheism is typically used as a kind of subterfuge by those who wish to claim that they believe in "something higher", but without falling into all those webs of conceptual complications of a personal god. It would be a "God of rational people" who would be in accordance with science and with all the facts observed in nature.

However, this conception of divinity is littered with obvious mousetraps. If the "will of God" or "cosmic consciousness" is expressed by the set of laws that govern the Universe, we will invariably be forced to admit several things. For example, that the Earth is sacred, that every form of life is divine, that feelings are sublime, that nature is perfect, that genetic diseases are beautiful, that earthquakes are wonderful, that volcanoes are enchanting, that AIDS is our friend, and that the cancer that devours our bodies is a sublime and magnificent manifestation of the harmonious perfection of the Universe. The god of pantheism authorizes both pleasure and pain — he's as vicious as hunger, as ruthless as earthquakes, and as perverse as floods.

Besides, it's really strange that such a powerful God couldn't find anything better to do than turn itself into a bunch of miserable organisms that, in order to survive for a few years, have to devour each other. That God is, at the same time, the cruelty of the predator and the suffering of the prey! Couldn't the God of pantheism, with all his infinite splendor, have found a better pastime than playing at being born and killing himself in the form of living beings?

If we want to save the reputation of this God — which, otherwise, would be so absurdly contradictory that we would only be able to laugh at him —, we will inevitably have to rid him of any kind of interest in life. We must transform him into a strictly impersonal God, a *Deus Ex Machina*. However, reducing God's will to mere impersonal laws leads us to a dead end, because, in this situation, pantheism no longer says anything, since it is nothing more than an empty wordplay.

In fact, calling the Universe God doesn't mean explaining it — it just casts a veil of holiness over our ignorance, and its nature remains unknown. It is obvious that we are all amazed by the inconceivable grandeur of the Universe in which we live, but to deify it is a puerile attitude that makes us stop investigating it to simply worship it.

Furthermore, when equating God and the Universe, what is said is basically this: "the Universe is God; the Universe exists; therefore, God exists". We could also say: "love is God; love exists; therefore, God exists". But what pantheism really says is this: "the Universe is the world; the Universe exists; therefore, the world exists". That is *idem per idem*. Arthur Schopenhauer, therefore, was correct when he stated that the pantheistic God is nothing more than a superfluous synonym for the word "world":

> *Against pantheism I have mainly only this: that it does not mean anything. Naming the world God does not mean explaining it, but instead only enriching language with a superfluous synonym for the word "world". Whether you say "the world is God" or "the world is the world" amounts to the same. Of course, if one proceeded from God as though he were the given and the thing to be explained, and therefore said: "God is the world", there is an explanation of sorts, insofar as something unknown is traced back to something better known; still it is merely a semantic explanation. However, if one proceeds from what is actually given, hence from the world, and now says "the world is God", it is plain as day that nothing is said by this, or at least the explanation is of something unknown by something less known.*

So, it doesn't matter if we refer to gravity as "property of matter" or "will of God" — in the end, it remains the same thing. Calling the Universe God makes it divine just as much as calling a beetle monkey makes it a primate.

THE MORAL ARGUMENT

Proposition: *Every man has innate notions of good and evil, and they come from God. If there were no moral order in the world, there would be no fixed* *references for good and evil, and in this situation it would be impossible to achieve peace among men. Society would disintegrate and chaos would reign absolute on Earth.*

Another great example of an argumentative fallacy: this one is called a *slippery slope*. It is obvious that, if everyone were endowed with innate moral notions, there would be agreement on many issues that remain unresolved today, even among religious individuals — such as abortion, euthanasia, death penalty, chastity, homosexuality, monogamy and polygamy, and so on. Morality and customs have never been static. Quite the contrary, they vary from people to people, from time to time, from person to person. What in one culture is considered immoral and vile, in others is commonplace, or even lofty and sublime. This is not consistent with the idea that we have innate notions of right and wrong or of good and evil.

As we know, human beings have an inherently social nature, and not by chance — this is advantageous for the species. Not only humans, but also many other animals live in harmonious and organized groups. We find monkeys living in hierarchical groups, we find fish living organized in shoals, buffaloes in herds, lions in flocks, bees in hives, ants in a collectivist regime, and so on. However, is it true that "chaos" doesn't "reign" among them because they received from God an innate notion of what is right and wrong? And if they received it, then why don't they hesitate to use humans as food? Why do many animals commit infanticide? Much more likely, this social nature has a merely practical function, that is, increasing the chances of survival of the group via cooperation — and from that would come to the notions of right and wrong.

When we find out that collectivist behavioral profiles are not the prerogative of humans, we are led to the conclusion that all these innate notions that we have do not point to a higher mind, but to a lower mind, to the deeper and more primitive parts of our brain, which are not very malleable and, therefore, quite similar in everyone. We all agree on fundamental issues because, like other animals, we have a natural programming, which is linked to the survival instincts of the species. For example: living is good and dying is bad; pleasure is good and pain is bad; food is good and hunger is bad. Such references are instinctive, not divine, and much of our behavior is anchored in them.

Apparently, we mentally project the two basic motivations of our actions — pleasure and pain — into the outside world, as abstract evaluations we usually call good and evil. Thus, we tend to agree on fundamental issues because they are essential to our survival. However, when issues are less relevant, the degree of discordance becomes immense. Therefore, the tendency seems to be that, the lower the relevance of the issue to survival, the more frequent the occurrence of divergence. Hence the reason why discussions that seek to universally establish what is right or wrong, what is virtue or vice, are so fruitless, because each individual, being unique, finds pleasure and pain in different and equally unique things — but proportionally more similar the more fundamental they are to survival, as has already been pointed out.

Furthermore, reality shows us that both atheists and religious people are able to choose their own values independently, and both can live very well, even without following the same rules — or following the same rules for different reasons. Bertrand Russell also challenged this argument by evidencing what it quietly suggests. According to him, the reasoning behind the moral argument states is that:

(...) we ought to believe in God because, if we do not, we shall not behave well. The first and greatest objection to this argument is that, at its best, it cannot prove that there is a God but only that politicians and educators ought to try to make people think there is one. Whether this ought to be done or not is not a theological question but a political one. The arguments are of the same sort as those which urge that children should be taught respect for the flag. A man with any genuine religious feeling will not be content with the view that the belief in God is useful, because he will wish to know whether, in fact, there is a God. It is absurd to contend that the two questions are the same. In the nursery, belief in Father Christmas is useful, but grown-up people do not think that this proves Father Christmas to be real.

When we don't have enough education to create our own values and set our own limits, we need police and jails more than religions.

To live in society, we must fight against our natural selfishness, imposing limits on the freedom of the individual, which we do with shared moral values — and it doesn't matter if we believe that those values come from God or from humans. In this way, we see that the moral argument is an argument in favor of societies, not of the existence of supernatural moral entities. Believing that certain values have a divine origin only serves for them to be respected, but that's all. In any case, the fact is that, if such values were objective, coming from beyond, they would be the same for all societies — something that, like God, we have never observed anytime, anywhere.

Thus, we find no reason to think that morality is something transcendent. As far as we can see, it is nothing more than a reflection of our social nature. We are, therefore, led to the conclusion that the divine hypothesis is fully unnecessary to justify human morality and social behavior.

The Revelation Argument

Proposition: *We know that God exists because he manifested himself to men, revealing his will through the Holy Scriptures. It's the very incomparable perfection of the Bible that proves its truthfulness.*

If the Bible had been inspired by a kind God, it should be completely true; it should be the most perfect and sublime book; it should be unsurpassed in every sense; it should far exceed human production capacity; it should be in accordance with all the facts observed in nature; it should serve as a guide to promote peace, love, and happiness among humans.

So we open the Bible, and what do we find? Wisdom, virtue, elevation? Yes. But, mixed with that, we also find hundreds of bloody pages cluttered with ignorance, mendacity, injustice, killings, absurdities, contradictions, and prejudices. The inspired book doesn't just say that God loved us so much that he gave his only son to die for us, or that we should love our neighbor as ourselves. The infinite wisdom of the biblical God also supports slavery, says that homosexuals must be exterminated, and makes it explicit that women are inferior to men.

The Bible is full of passages that describe impossible and childish miracles. Can anyone in their right mind believe that God reproved Balaam through an Inspired Donkey? To stop the Sun from revolving around the Earth — did the lunatic who wrote this absurdity have any knowledge of Astronomy? And how fair is it to slaughter forty-two children for having laughed at Elisha's baldness?

In the case of Jesus, we read that he revived Lazarus and the son of the widow of Nain, walked on water, multiplied bread and fish, cured lepers, made paralytic people walk, cast out demons, transformed water into wine, rose again on the third day, ascended to heaven and, wow, cursed a fig tree. What is the proof of such miracles? The proof lies in the fact that some people — whose notion of the world was a flat Earth located at the center of the Universe — wrote several books in which they say that it was so.

In fact, not even the most fanatical Christian is able to follow it to the letter, since, besides the Bible being deeply contradictory, he would be arrested if he tried. For this reason, carrying the fear of Hell, believers perform all kinds apologetic gymnastics to try to justify its enormous incoherences. The Christian interpretation is, most of the time, so absurd that it would be easier to believe in the miracles themselves.

And, after all, what benefits have the "inspired books" of the Bible brought to mankind? Ask a doctor what diseases he learned to cure by reading the Bible — maybe he learned that the blood of birds in running water is medicinal. What contributions did the Bible make to the promotion of world peace? What contributions did it make to the improvement of our living conditions? What contributions did it make to the great discoveries and inventions? What contributions did it make to the progress of human knowledge? None. Quite the contrary, it was and still is an enormous obstacle, since it teaches man to despise reality in the name of the "kingdom of God".

Those who doubt whether the Bible is contrary to the intellectual progress of humanity need only ask themselves: what is the original sin? To taste the fruit of the tree of *knowledge* — "thou shall not know", that is the commandment that the Bible preaches. It makes research a sin and credulity a virtue.

When the Bible joined power, did we achieve an era of progress, of enlightenment, and happiness? It would have been great, but no — and it wasn't by chance that the Middle Ages were nicknamed the Dark Ages. The Inquisition was created, progress was practically paralyzed, intolerance reigned, and those who ventured to use their brains freely ended up tortured and burned — *ad majorem Dei gloriam*, of course.

Even today, this book incites a retrograde war, promotes irrationality, makes individuals despise proven knowledge, and hate science. It makes them attack scientific theories to defend primitive myths of a divine creation by some bearded god enthroned in the firmament, whose notion of justice was the savagery of "an eye for an eye, and a tooth for a tooth".

Those who say that the Bible is the most profound of books, those who think that Christ was the greatest of philosophers, have probably never read any work by great minds such as Nietzsche, Schopenhauer, Freud, Hume, Sartre, Rousseau, Heidegger, Kant, Aristotle, Darwin, Russell, to name a few. Those who say that it is the most beautiful of books have probably never read Shakespeare, Dostoevsky, or Fernando Pessoa. And those who say that it is a source of enlightenment have probably never studied science.

If he existed, God would convulse with his eyes turned upside down when people claim that he was the one who inspired this indecipherable amalgamation of myths. The Bible does not reflect the wisdom of a supposed God, but the exact ignorance of the people who wrote it.

Note: we discussed the Bible because it is the most influential book in our cultural context. However, there would be no difficulty in demonstrating that all the so-called "Holy Books" contain absolutely no hint of higher enlightenment. All these works are human productions and claim to be inspired by a higher power with the simple and obvious goal of ensuring their credibility.

III

ARGUMENTS AGAINST THE EXISTENCE OF GOD

And let everything break up which can break up by our truths! Many a house is still to be built!

— Friedrich Nietzsche

So far, we've looked at some of the main arguments that attempt to prove the existence of a god, and we've highlighted the reasons why they're invalid. As we can see, not even the best arguments presented even came close to what would be sufficient to prove anything. In this way, we clearly see that there are no logical reasons that justify the belief in the existence of a divine being.

Although mere refutation is sufficient to justify atheism, throughout this chapter we will continue our critical analysis, and with this we intend to demonstrate that the belief in God is not only unjustified, but also highly incoherent, contradictory, and full of unsolvable impasses.

Since the argument, from here on, will be openly focused on demonstrating the impossibility of the existence of God, this means that we will adopt the perspective of *critical atheism*, which is the philosophically most sophisticated and powerful category. First, let us remember that each religion characterizes its god in a particular way, and that's why it would certainly be irrelevant to state that the arguments presented here do not refer to "true divinity". There are thousands of gods catalogued, and it is impossible to make a detailed and individual analysis encompassing all possible conceptions of God, since the imagination can conceive infinite types of gods.

The arguments, therefore, do not refer to any specific god, so that the critiques and objections should be valid for any deities in which the attributes involved in the argument are admitted. In this sense, we will postulate the "standard deity" as being the typical personal god of theism, who created the Universe and who is normally described as possessing the following characteristics: perfect, omnipotent, omnipresent, omniscient, kind, just, immutable, true, eternal, unique, holy, immaterial.

As we noted in the previous chapter, the claim that human reason is insufficient to address the question of God's existence is a double-edged sword. Because, supposing this claim to be true, that is, that God is inconceivable to the human mind — say, in the same way that a human is something inconceivable to bacteria or the Theory of Relativity is unintelligible to a dog —, that would certainly make any effort to refute his existence futile. However, to the same degree, it would make the attempt to defend it futile. Therefore, in this case, the theist automatically loses the prerogative to affirm the existence of God, just as the atheist loses the prerogative to deny it. Both being human and, therefore, possessing a limited mind to the same degree, neither of them would even know what they are talking about when debating about things that are rationally impenetrable, such as gods.

However, if we bear in mind that there have never been logical reasons to believe in the existence of any god, then the allegation of the supposed divine unintelligibility certainly does not place both in the same situation, because, as we have seen, it is those who affirm something that have the obligation to prove it. Therefore, if the affirmative party cannot do so, their claim will automatically be relegated to an unjustified belief, to speculation. Not that, on our part, we have anything against the existence of a deity. This happens simply because we could assume the existence of various realities or unintelligible beings, and they would all be equally irrefutable and inconceivable. As Sebastièn Faure said:

It was you who first affirmed the existence of God; therefore, you must be the first to put forth your case. Would I ever dream of denying the existence of God if you hadn't started to affirm it? What if, when I was a child, they hadn't imposed on me the need to believe in him? What if, as an adult, I hadn't heard statements to that effect? What if, as a man, my eyes had not constantly contemplated the temples raised to that God? It was your affirmation that provoked my denials. Stop affirming and I will stop denying.

THE PROBLEM OF OMNIPOTENCE

Omnipotence is another strange quality that we find linked to supreme deities. In our daily lives, we are used to dealing only with finite powers, which are easily conceivable and measurable — they can be added, subtracted, canceled. However, when we bring this question to the realm of the ideal, that is, to infinite and absolute power, we see that it becomes hopelessly absurd and contradictory.

God, no matter how much he wanted, could not restrict himself from something without, at the same time, abdicating his omnipotence, which would make him stop being God. For example, could a God endowed with infinite power create something indestructible? No, because omnipotence itself, by definition, denies the indestructibility of anything, since "being able to do everything" includes "being able to destroy everything". However, at the same time, being omnipotent also includes "being able to create everything" — even indestructible things. This implies contradiction. We conclude, then, that "creating something indestructible" would not really be a creation, but in fact an abdication of the power to destroy something, that is, an abdication of omnipotence itself.

Could God create a rock so big that even he couldn't move? No. He could just create a rock and then arbitrarily renounce the power to move it. From then on, we are forced to admit that the existence of an omnipotent entity is logically impossible, since, being contradictory, such an idea crushes itself.

The impression we have is that attributes idealized as omnipotence were not actually created to be internally coherent or logical. Probably the various "omni-something" were attributed to God solely because of their aesthetic, subjective, and poetic value, because of the strong emotional influence they are capable of exerting on us, inducing feelings of reverence and admiration.

Logically, the "pure ideal of power" attributed to God is not something real, but simply an abstraction, a misguided flight of human imagination. So it's not surprising that conceptual absurdities like this can be found in the middle of this poetic idealism.

THE PROBLEM OF FREE WILL AND OMNISCIENCE

God is commonly regarded as omniscient; it is also commonly said that we have free will. It is not clear, however, how God could know everything and, at the same time, not know our destiny, so that free will could be preserved.

If God is truly omniscient, then for him there are no mysteries or secrets — he doesn't ignore anything at all. So, whether we like it or not, "knowing everything" includes knowing what will be the fate of his creatures on this planet. God, then, knows exactly what the future of each person will be like, their sufferings, their happiness, their desires, their fears, their shames, and so on, down to the most futile details.

Thus, at the moment of creation, God necessarily already foresaw the destiny of each individual. But if our destiny already existed in the form of an idea before we were even created, it follows that it is impossible for man to have free will, since his entire history was already mapped out beforehand, contained in the mind of God. Thus, it is impossible for human free will and divine omniscience to coexist, since they are mutually exclusive.

The only way to solve such a problem, at first sight, would be to claim that God, in this case, deliberately wanted not to know what was the destiny of mankind, in order to preserve its sacred free will. We can imagine that the reason for this is the fact that it would be very boring to watch a long play of your own authorship — hence the idea of creating it and then forgetting the script, resulting in a certain degree of suspense. Entertainments of this kind possibly help God deal with the boredom of an eternal existence.

Irony aside, we see that free will would remain non-existent even if God didn't know what our destiny is. For human freedom to be real, in the act of creation, God would have to have made beings whose destiny is not only ignored by him, but literally impossible to predict, even if he wanted it, because any predictability implies predestination.

However, the impasse lies in the fact that, if God is the supreme and ultimate authority, then there are no rules to which he must submit. Thus, he can choose not to foresee our lives, but he cannot forbid himself from this, he cannot make himself incapable of it. If, for any reason, God wanted to predict our lives like the screenplay of a movie, since he is omnipotent, creator of the heavens and the earth, he could do so, because there are no limits to what his will is capable of doing. On the other hand, if he cannot do so, he is not omnipotent — therefore, neither a god.

Therefore, regarding the present question of the incompatibility between the existence of an omniscient god and human freedom, we can say that Mikhail Bakunin was absolutely right when he stated that *The existence of God necessarily implies the slavery of all that is beneath him. Therefore, if God existed, only in one way could he serve human liberty — by ceasing to exist.*

THE PROBLEM OF CREATION

We human beings are imperfect. We have flaws, we have limitations, we have needs and, for that reason, we are always pursuing objectives to achieve what we lack. We are always striving to get as close as possible to the state that we consider "ideal". Likewise, on a daily basis, we have to face many adversities in order to survive — we must seek food, we must protect ourselves, we must always be supervising our health, and so on. In general, it is mainly factors of this kind that guide our actions.

From this perspective, as we approach our ideal, the gap that separates what we are from what we would like to be is diminishing. The closer we are to our ideal, the less things we want to change and, therefore, the fewer goals we have. For example, a happy person who lives in a peaceful society, in which there is equality and justice, who enjoys perfect health, who does only what he likes, who has a prosperous family, and who has everything he wants, is unlikely to find much to do, except to enjoy his fullness. He would have no desire to change anything, since everything is already exactly as he wants.

So, when we get to absolute perfection — which would be God —, it becomes impossible to imagine what reason there could be for him to have any goal. Does he need to do something to guarantee his own existence? No: God is indestructible and eternal. Does he have imperfections to be corrected, faults to be fixed, limitations to overcome? No: God is perfect and omnipotent. Does he need something external to complete himself? No: because, if he is perfect, logically he is also self-sufficient. Can he be improved in any imaginable way? No: he is the ultimate, he is the supreme, he is infinite perfection — he has and is everything, and lacks nothing.

The problem with this, obviously, lies in the fact that what motivates us to action is exactly the difference between what we are and what we would like to be. Our will is always "the will for something we lack" — because we cannot desire what we already have, we cannot have the "will to exist" or "will to live", because we already exist and are already alive. On the other hand, God is perfect in everything and cannot improve at anything; he is the ideal being par excellence. Therefore, in God, there is no room for the will. The fullness of perfection makes it static. A perfect being wouldn't do anything except exist.

So let us ask: why did God create the world and man? What could cause eternal infinite perfection to wish to step out of its self-sufficient balance and create an imperfect world with imperfect humans? If all that existed before God created the world was himself in his perfection, then there was nothing external to motivate him to any action. The tendency, naturally, would be for everything to remain eternally static and perfect. Not to mention that God, by definition, is an immutable being, and therefore it would be a contradiction if, out of nothing, he manifested the will to do something.

It does not seem possible to imagine any logical reason for the creation of man and the world. Was God bored? Lonely? Or could it be that, due to the idleness, God slept, and our reality is a dream in his mind? Could it be that God was bored with so much perfection, and thus decided to create some imperfect entertainment to divert attention away from himself, improvising a planet full of living beings with free will to contemplate as a pastime?

As we can see, this is an unsolvable paradox. The divine creation is a great mystery because it is a great contradiction. No philosopher or theologian has ever been able to explain why a perfect God would be motivated to create all the "imperfect filth" that is the material world — at least in comparison with his "ideal spirit".

The Problem of Imperfection, Goodness, and Free Will

Man is certainly a very sophisticated being, of almost impenetrable complexity. However, he's not perfect. Without a doubt, we have countless limitations, and that is an undeniable fact. The only being endowed with perfection would be God, who, by definition, is perfectly free, since he is perfectly powerful, so that nothing can oppose his will. Assuming that God was powerless to do a single thing, he would no longer be perfectly free, since his impotence would be a limiting factor for the actions he is capable of perpetrating.

Naturally, since man is not omnipotent like God — in fact, very much inferior to him —, it follows that the human creature has a very narrow free will, since it has many limiting imperfections. Let's say that man is free, but only to play with the cards that God has given him.

If we were created like this, imperfect, limited, and partially free, this fact implies that God, in the act of creation, deliberately chose to give us freedom in some aspects, and to hinder us in others. He could have made us winged beings, but he didn't; he could have made us peaceful beings, but he didn't. This illustrates that we are not perfectly free beings, but only relatively free.

In the view of theists, the alleged human free will is a necessary condition so that we are not simply puppets in the hands of God. However, we must admit that, to the same extent that we are inferior to God, we were manipulated, determined, and molded by him, because that inferiority implies impotence, which in turn implies restriction, that is, the absence of freedom — of which God, being omniscient, was fully aware of when creating us. The fact is that God could not create us perfectly free, because he would have to create us as gods, since only omnipotent beings enjoy absolute freedom.

The problem to which this leads us is just one: if God is good and has made us impotent and limited in countless ways, and in that there was no problem from the point of view of our free will, then why hasn't he made us powerless to choose the path of evil? Why didn't he give man the ability to choose between several good paths, but none bad?

The argument of free will, in this case, would only apply if man were fully free. But we have just demonstrated that, in addition to the fact that man does not have such a degree of freedom, it is in fact impossible. Consequently, we can only conclude that God created man with the potential to choose evil because he deliberately wanted it to be so, and that fact is in direct contradiction with a divine attribute — goodness. A God who creates limited humans and then allows them to choose the path of evil cannot be good.

THE PROBLEM OF MULTIPLE RELIGIONS AND THE EVOLUTION OF THE DIVINE FIGURE

Each religion — or theistic individual with a particular concept of God — explains differently the creation of the Universe, the nature of man, the meaning of life, the divine attributes, the higher moral values, the absolute truths, etc. Many of the different conceptions diverge on issues so fundamental that it is impossible to reconcile them in order to find a kind of common factor, a shared foundation — except that they're all based on faith.

Since ancient times, countless religions, deities, and beliefs have been born and collapsed. Gods of all kinds have already been conceived by the human mind, being used to explain the world, to justify rules and values. However, over time, knowledge evolves, needs change, and the gods, as they are static, become obsolete, and ultimately end up unable to answer the new questions that eventually arise. In this situation, it is either necessary to adapt them to new needs and knowledge, or else they must be discarded as false deities.

A good example of this is the fact that the deeds and nature of the biblical God of the Old Testament, Yahweh, reflect exactly the cultural level of the people who worshiped him, that is, the Hebrews. Today much of what was considered a "divine truth" because it was in the Bible has already become a laughable mythical fossil. In addition, there were countless other gods, religions, and beliefs among ancient peoples, and all of this was slowly discarded and replaced by more "modern" versions, or else they were subject to reforms to remain compatible with their time. Nobody, for example, still believes in Zeus: this entity that, today, for us, is just mythology, was once a god of civilized individuals. It's no joke: Zeus was a deity worthy of respect like those that are fashionable today — and we have no respectable reason to think that our case is any different.

This immense number of different conceptions of God, of different religions and beliefs — contemporary or extinct — is a very strong evidence that "divine truths" have no roots in the transcendental. It seems obvious that, if God were something external — and not internal, subjective —, if our concept of God were the fruit of our interaction with nature, of our investigation of reality, it would be the same for all individuals and for all peoples — those familiar with the scientific method, at least —, as formal logic and knowledge derived from experimentation are the same for everyone. The physical equations apply to Brazilians, Americans, Chinese, Japanese, Egyptians, Germans, French, Angolans, and Norwegians. Why not the concept of God?

Because, apparently, God is a subjective concept forged according to our profound need to have explanations, to have the answer to the "great questions" of existence. Logically, to do so, we rely on the available knowledge about the reality in which we live — this to make divinity coherent —, so that, for this reason, the divinity itself ends up reflecting the cultural characteristics of the people who created it.

Thus, the thousands of gods ever created by humanity do not seem to embody the essence of a constant, unique divine entity derived from the "beyond", but rather the degree of development, culture, desires, and particular needs of the people who believed in it. As Mencken, a well-known iconoclast, told us:

> *Where is the graveyard of dead gods? What lingering mourner waters their mounds? There was a time when Jupiter was the king of the gods, and any man who doubted his puissance was ipso facto a barbarian and an ignoramus. But where in all the world is there a man who worships Jupiter today? And who of Huitzilopochtli? In one year — and it is no more than five hundred years ago — 50,000 youths and maidens were slain in sacrifice to him. Today, if he is remembered at all, it is only by some vagrant savage in the depths of the Mexican forest. (...) Speaking of Huitzilopochtli recalls his brother Tezcatlipoca. Tezcatlipoca was almost as powerful; he consumed 25,000 virgins a year. Lead me to his tomb: I would weep, and hang a couronne des perles. But who knows where it is? (...) What has become of Sutekh, once the high god of the whole Nile Val-*

ley? What has become of: Resheph, Anath, Ashtoreth, El, Nergal, Nebo, Ninib, Melek, Ahijah, Isis, Ptah, Anubis, Baal, Astarte, Hadad, Addu, Shalem, Dagon, Sharaab, Yau, Amon-Ra, Osiris, Sebek, Molech? (...) Ask the rector to lend you any good treatise on comparative religion: You will find them all listed. They were gods of the highest standing and dignity — gods of civilized peoples —, worshiped and believed in by millions. All were omnipotent, omniscient and immortal. And all are dead.

Nowadays, there is an almost inconceivable number of deities, and all of them are "unique" and "true" for their respective followers — but only for them. This is a rather absurd situation and, to solve it, the only way out seems to be to admit that gods are human creations. Not only does this make the issue much less problematic, but in fact it makes it perfectly obvious why gods always accompany human development. Thus, everything leads us to the conclusion that religions — with their gods, rituals, rules, and values — play an essentially social role, also functioning as an amalgam that fills the explanatory gaps of each era.

Moreover, especially with the flourishing of science, as knowledge rapidly evolved, almost all religious explanations for the reality in which we live were abandoned. All the question marks that religion answered were proved wrong when science was able to shed some light on them. Today, no doubt, many question marks still remain, but why should we believe that religions are right about them, if they never were about the others?

The problem of evil — Part I

The problem of evil is one of the most powerful arguments to be used to challenge the existence of personal gods. Such argument was made a long time ago. Epicurus presented it quite clearly and concisely in these terms:

Is God willing to prevent evil, but not able? Then he is not omnipotent. Is he able, but not willing? Then he is malevolent. Is he both able and willing? Then whence cometh evil? Is he neither able nor willing? Then why call him God?

This is the basis of the reasoning from which atheistic argumentation is developed in relation to the problem of evil. Basically, the problem lies in the fact that theists claim that their divinity has certain attributes that are logically incompatible with the reality in which we live, which supposedly would be his creation.

Let us note that, in principle, evil is not incompatible with the existence of an omnipotent, omniscient, and omnipresent God. Such a God, possessing unrestricted free will, could do whatever he wanted — including creating a world like ours, filled with suffering. There would be no incompatibility between God and evil if we were to suppose that God is an evil and perverse entity — in fact, it would make much more sense. However, since it is insisted that God is an entity endowed with perfect goodness, we do not see how it would be possible to make it compatible with the reality in which we are. The divine attributes — particularly omnipotence — seem irreconcilable with the moral attribute of goodness. If God is all-goodness and all-powerful, then why doesn't he remove unnecessary thorns from the path of his beloved children?

No theologian or philosopher to date has been able to explain satisfactorily the reason why God allows the creatures he supposedly loves to be needlessly afflicted by suffering. Assuming that the creative force that originated us is good, the presence of evil in the world seems inconceivable. In the case of the biblical God, there is no doubt as to what the source of evil is, because "God" himself affirms: *I am the Lord, and there is none else. I form the light, and create darkness: I make peace, and create evil: I the Lord do all these things* (Isaiah 45:6-7). However, here we do not intend to restrict ourselves to the biblical God, but to the general concept of a deity as possessing the attributes mentioned above.

Since some theodicies were presented with the objective of making divine goodness compatible with the presence of evil in the world, we will briefly analyze the most relevant arguments, aiming to demonstrate that all attempts, so far, have failed.

There's no such thing as evil — everything is good

Some simply deny the existence of evil, claiming that what we call evil actually results from an erroneous and limited interpretation of reality. Therefore, if we were able to see God's plans in a more "complete" way, we would see that, in truth, everything is good.

For our part, we can only say that it seems a rather naive attitude to turn a blind eye to the evident reality that shows us exactly the opposite. According to this view, a serial killer is not committing an atrocity by torturing and killing innocent people. However, since we cannot understand the reason why this is "good", then we could limit ourselves to assuming that, for example, the killer is simply following his "divine vocation".

It is also possible to ask some rather uncomfortable questions: Why do prisons exist if criminals are really just misunderstood philanthropists? If evil doesn't exist, what exactly would we be afraid of when someone tries to rob us? What would we be defending ourselves from when someone tries to beat us up? The good? Probably it would also be unsuccessful the attempt to convince a family man with terminal cancer that, in reality, the disease is for his own good. However, one thing is certain: if this were true, all the safe, alarm, lock and bolt industries would go bankrupt.

So, as we can see, saying that evil does not exist is not a solution, but an evasion that leads to a very dangerous complacency. Closing our eyes does not make evil cease to exist.

Evil is the absence of good

This answer is based on the idea that only good exists, and evil, in reality, is only a consequence of the absence of good — probably derived from the notion that darkness is just the absence of light. As it tries to defend that evil does not exist by itself, we can see that this idea is somewhat similar to the one presented above.

Without difficulty, we can demonstrate that such an answer is a meaningless wordplay that does not solve anything. Firstly, renaming evil as "absence of good" or darkness as "absence of light" does not make such things cease to exist, because here we are dealing with subjective concepts, not objective ones. Perhaps some examples will elucidate the idea:

"Sadness doesn't exist; it's just the absence of happiness".

"Love doesn't exist; it's just the absence of hate".

"Peace doesn't exist; it's just the absence of conflict".

"Pleasure doesn't exist; it's just the absence of suffering".

"Poverty doesn't exist; it's just the absence of wealth".

"Albinism doesn't exist; it's just the absence of melanin".

"AIDS doesn't exist; it's just the absence of immune system".

This makes it obvious how easily we can reformulate the way in which words are presented in order to place the existence of one thing as subordinated to that of another. We could also say that good is the absence of evil. This statement is equally well justified, since it is based on the same logic — and we certainly have no reason to judge that the first is more coherent, other than our remarkable liking of goodness.

Finally, we should not fail to notice that, when we define evil as the absence of good, this places us in front of a great impasse. For example, suppose four actions typically considered evil: 1) Stealing ten dollars from a bystander; 2) Torturing an animal for pleasure; 3) Beating a friend to death for a futile reason; 4) Killing one's own family with an axe. At least in our society, all of this is commonly viewed as something negative.

Now let's see: if evil is just the "absence of good", we are forced to choose between two hypotheses: 1) Technically, a person who steals ten dollars and another who butchers his family with an axe are evil in the same degree, since they are only "lacking goodness"; or 2) The actions get progressively worse as the "absence of good" increases, so we have to admit that there must be some degree of goodness present in the act of torturing an animal for pleasure — a degree that would be absent in act number four. We also have to admit that beating a friend to death is not an evil thing, but in reality just something "less good" than stealing ten dollars. Undoubtedly, both conclusions are abhorrent and absurd.

Character building

Some say that evil exists so that we can improve our character. Without evil, we could never really know what good is, since one doesn't exist without the other. Evil would be necessary to guide us, so that we could evolve our spirit on the correct path — the path of good.

Such a statement is only superficially coherent, as it is only compatible with normal people who experienced small doses of suffering and had the chance to learn from it. However, it fails to explain things like the reason why babies die at the age of two months. Now, they don't even have a character to be evolved, they don't even know what the word character means — not to mention that they will never have the chance to grow and then choose between good and evil.

This response is also not compatible with the existence of lethal accidents. After all, what is the purpose of a person having an accident and being instantly transformed into a red and misshapen blob? That doesn't make any sense. A bunch of twisted viscera has no character to be improved. Furthermore, it is simply unfair to allow an accident to take the life of an innocent person, making them a scapegoat, just to serve as a lesson to other individuals.

If we reflect a little more on that answer, we will see that many rather embarrassing questions begin to creep in: if God is omnipotent and kind, why doesn't he just create people with benevolent character instead of torturing them? Why didn't he invent a different method, in which character evolution could be achieved without suffering? Why is the suffering experienced not proportional to the degree character of the individual? Would we consider a father to be good if he was as indifferent, impassive, and authoritarian with his children as God is with us?

Good cannot exist without evil

This statement may be valid in the narrow sense that we tend to give more value to what's good after having bad experiences. From this perspective, it is an argument analogous to that of character construction, in which, due to the suffering experienced by individuals, feelings and values considered elevated appear in counterbalance — values of charity, benevolence, compassion, altruism, solidarity, etc.

But here an inconvenience arises: isn't it precisely *because* of suffering that such things are regarded as virtues? The reasoning is clearly inverted, because it is certain that we would consider insane a person who mistreated their friends only to allow them to practice the "virtuous action" that is to forgive. The reasoning that it is a good thing to inflict suffering so that virtue and goodness can be fostered does not seem logical.

The fact is that, without the existence of evil, the appreciation of humanitarian virtues — of good — has no reason to be, since these appear as its consequence. So, what we can conclude is not that good cannot exist without evil, but that good is not necessary without evil.

Furthermore, if we do not admit that good can exist without evil, we reach the conclusion that: 1) If God is not evil, he is also not good; or 2) If God is good, he is also evil. So, if we can admit the existence of an exclusively good God, who has no need of an evil correlated to his goodness, why should such a rule be different for humans, if God is omnipotent and good? Simple: it shouldn't.

Free will

In reality, we wouldn't even need to address this issue, because we've already seen that, if God exists, human free will is impossible. Let us therefore ignore the conflict that exists between omniscience and free will, and pretend that human freedom is somehow compatible with that attribute.

The free will argument, without a doubt, is the most common and, apparently, the most convincing. However, if we think a little bit about it, we will see that it is probably the most absurd of all. The idea behind it is this: God, when creating man, did not want to create robots; therefore, he gave him the freedom to choose his own destiny, to follow the path of good or the path of evil, by his own free will.

However, the claim that evil comes from free will only answers the question of the personal choice of evil. In other words, let's say that if someone wants to be mean, if they don't want to follow "God's Law", that someone has the right to do so — and no one can stop him, since he is free. That's all the free will response solves.

However, such an answer is clearly incapable of justifying the existence of evil when it is directed at the innocent. To argue that God does not oppose the presence of evil in the world in order to preserve human freedom only seems reasonable, but it is not. Let's look at a little story that elucidates the problem of evil directed at the innocent:

There was a family that was living happily, consisting of a couple and their three children — two boys and a girl. They were all good and followers of God's commandments. One night, a person entered this family's house; because he had free will, he decided to be mean and deliberately refused to follow God's commandments. That person broke down the back door and headed to the room where the children were sleeping. In the meantime, the father, who heard the break-in, picked up a firearm and went to check what was happening. The mother huddled in a corner of the bathroom out of fear. The attacker was carrying a knife and, with it, killed one of the children while sleeping. When he heard the other children's desperate scream, the father hurried to the bedroom and opened the door and was faced with the scene. But the criminal, being focused on his act, did not realize that he was being watched. So he went on, coldly killing another child with several stab wounds. Finally, there was only the girl left, which he didn't kill because he intended to rape her before. The child was helpless and paralyzed with fear. The criminal then tore her clothes and raped her. Finally, when the wrongdoer was about to take the life of the last child, she shouted "daddy, help me". The criminal, noticing the presence of the father, who was carrying a firearm, fled. After recovering from the shock, the daughter asked her father why he hadn't done anything to stop the criminal. The father calmly replied: "My daughter, you know that I love you with all my heart. I know that I could have prevented you from being raped and one of your brothers from being killed. But you must understand my situation: I'm not in a position to tell other people what to do with their lives. Human freedom, my daughter, is something sacred, and I had no right to intervene in the free will of the criminal who violated you. But know that I care for you deeply, and that although this incident seems purely negative, through it, you were unknowingly benefited: now your character will be stronger".

Who would be foolish or cynical enough to say that the father's inaction was based on his goodness? Such an attitude borders on complete insanity. However, that is exactly the position in which they place God when they affirm that, despite being capable and benevolent, he does not intervene in the world with the "just motive" of preserving human freedom. However, the fact is that no genuinely good person or entity would preserve freedom when this occurs to the profound detriment of justice.

The problem of evil — Part II

If God made this world, then I would not want to be the God. It is so full of misery and distress that it breaks my heart.

— Arthur Schopenhauer

Our last objection to the existence of a personal God is based on *the problem of free or natural evil*, which definitely cannot be imputed to humans. For example, if we have a healthy child, we should thank God. But if we have a mentally disabled child, who should we complain to? Why do harmful diseases plague kind, just, and honest people? If there is an earthquake that destroys millions of people or a volcano that incinerates thousands of lives, who is to blame? It would be irrational to attribute the cause of such natural phenomena to humans, for they have little control over their small lives, and none over the physical laws of the Universe in which they live, to which they themselves are subject. So whose fault are natural disasters?

Suppose that there was an environmental control center on Earth. Within that place, a person would be responsible for controlling all natural phenomena. It would control air streams, ocean waves, the movement of tectonic plates, rain, volcanism, and so on. Could we consider this person good if he allowed entire crops to dry up due to lack of rain while, somewhere else, a flood was taking place? Or if he let tectonic plates crash into each other, producing earthquakes? Or else, out of carelessness, wouldn't prevent the eruption of a volcano next to a village of peaceful, honest, and hardworking people? Or if hurricanes were allowed to take the lives of thousands?

What would we think about such a person? We certainly wouldn't consider him good. At the very least, we would say that he is completely irresponsible and negligent towards his fellow human beings. The creator of the heavens is exactly in that person's position. If God is omnipotent, he has the power to control natural phenomena. However, despite being good, he prefers to do nothing to avoid the catastrophes that constantly afflict humanity. In this situation, if God cares about his creatures, it is impossible to imagine any justification for his not intervening in natural phenomena.

Even if God's "policy" is the non-intervention in physical laws, it is certainly not possible to exempt him from the responsibility of having created them. All of them are a direct reflection of his will, they were completely determined by him, because physical laws are not living beings, they have no "free will" to be preserved. In this way, being omniscient, he knew, he could predict exactly what natural laws might cause — he knew what potential harm they would represent to his creatures when he made each one of them and every square meter of the Earth. This means that if we're living in the "best of all possible worlds", God is certainly incompetent.

Furthermore, this God — who is "eternally good" and "perfectly compassionate" — created an infinitely cruel nature, in which brutal violence is an essential factor for subsistence. In the world we're in, peace is not an option — and it will never be. We are born on a battlefield. The food chain is a global killing field: life feeds on life. Every second, countless fights are being fought. Everywhere, the suffering of one life is being caused by another, not out of malice, but out of necessity, by nature — to survive.

On our planet there is an army armed to the teeth — literally! A multitude of killing machines equipped with teeth, claws, fangs, and beaks, all finely designed to tear apart the flesh of other living beings. Countless highly efficient predators with specialized senses for just one thing: claiming lives. Others have weapons that kill in silence: snakes with modified teeth inoculate lethal poisons, which paralyze in seconds; insects that reproduce by paralyzing other beings with stings, and depositing eggs in their bodies, from which hatch creatures that devour them still alive; fearsome reptiles with infectious bites; violently venomous fish, frogs, spiders, and scorpions; electric eels; parasites that devour us alive; bacteria, fungi, and viruses that rot us from the inside. On the defensive front, there are also species that survive just because they are true biological fortresses, shielded by carapaces, by almost impenetrable shields — showing how brutal is the reality in which they must survive. And all of this is just a tiny sample of the almost inconceivable degree of cruelty that drives the wheels of life. Ingersoll presents us his reasoning in this regard:

If a good and infinitely powerful God governs this world, how can we account for cyclones, earthquakes, pestilence and famine? How can we account for can-

cers, for microbes, for diphtheria and the thousand diseases that prey on infancy? How can we account for the wild beasts that devour human beings, for the fanged serpents whose bite is death? How can we account for a world where life feeds on life? Were beak and claw, tooth and fang, invented and produced by infinite mercy? Did infinite goodness fashion the wings of the eagles so that their fleeing prey could be overtaken? Did infinite goodness create the beasts of prey with the intention that they should devour the weak and helpless? Did infinite goodness create the countless worthless living things that breed within and feed upon the flesh of higher forms? Did infinite wisdom intentionally produce the microscopic beasts that feed upon the optic nerve? Think of blinding a man to satisfy the appetite of a microbe! Think of life feeding on life! Think of the victims! Think of the Niagara of blood pouring over the precipice of cruelty! (...) these frightful facts deny that any God exists who has the will and power to guard and bless the human race.

Since its beginning, Earth has witnessed a war that continues today: Life versus Life. Only to the fittest, the most selfish, the best strategist, the most efficient murderer is given the right to exist — the trophy of survival! Who would be stupid enough to claim that this bloody and hellishly diabolic scheme was created by an infinitely good being who loves all his creatures? "Kill each other, and may the best ones survive and reproduce" — is there any trace of goodness in that? Where is the reason for the unnecessary pain and the gratuitous suffering present in nature?

In view of this situation, it seems very wise to advise the following to the defenders of the existence of a kind God: observe more and argue less — and, who knows, after a while, they will begin to understand the type of explanation that we are expecting from them, as well as the magnitude of the absurdity that they are trying to mask with their theodicies.

The fact is that, if any individual behaved like God, we would never consider him good — we would never consider good a person who, having the power to create a world free from pain, deliberately creates the opposite for "educational purposes". Nobody thinks it's wise to torture an individual to make him learn to be kind — but God thinks so, and we should find that "very good".

The situation is clear. It wasn't man who created the Earth, it wasn't man who created life, it wasn't man who created natural laws, it wasn't man who created diseases and all the other dangers that constantly haunt us. If a building collapses because it was poorly designed, or rather, because it was designed *to collapse*, killing its inhabitants, whose fault could it be, if not the master of contradiction, the supreme designer of benevolent cruelty?

In any just court, God would have to answer for all of that. According to criminal law, since the causal chain is infinite, the relevant segment must be limited by guilt and intent (e.g., a firearms manufacturer cannot be accused of murder, but only those who had intent or guilt in the crime). The causal chain of facts, obviously, refers to the first cause, which was an intentional and premeditated act, whose consequences were all previously known. The conclusion is obvious: if an omniscient and omnipotent God planned and built everything that exists, then there was intent in creation, in the first cause, that is, a desire consciously directed to obtain a criminal result or to assume the risk of producing it.

In a criminal trial, God would have to answer for all crimes — although presenting the defense for the charges of infinitely qualified homicide and failure to provide help would be sufficient to occupy the heavenly lawyer for a few thousand years. Apart from this minor detail, according to current laws, when interpreted in this perspective, God should be rotting in a maximum-security penitentiary, where the most heinous criminals are locked up. Of course, if the penalty for his crimes were to prove some of the poison he created, he would certainly rather have never existed — and disappear in the snap of a finger!

The presence of this type of evil makes the existence of any type of "higher force" that cares about life on Earth something profoundly incompatible with the reality in which we live. Omnipotence and benevolence remain immiscible like water and oil. Until now, the only excuse capable of saving God's reputation is that he doesn't exist — but, if he did, he would only deserve our deepest contempt.

IV

RELIGION AS ALIENATION AND SOCIAL CONTROL

Religion is excellent stuff for keeping common people quiet.

— Napoleon Bonaparte

As we have seen, the primitive and naive anthropomorphic notions of personal deities are irreconcilable with the current level of knowledge. Although the various internal contradictions that exist in the concepts of a personal god are strong arguments, the main reason for discrediting this type of entity remains the problem of evil, which frontally contradicts the logical possibility of its existence and, therefore, dismantles the idea of a supposed Benevolent Providence that is concerned with the fate of humanity.

On the other hand, we also saw that there are the concepts of natural gods, who would be responsible for the order and harmony inherent to the Universe in which we live. But the fact is that, if we cannot grant such "cosmic intelligence" any degree of personality — so as not to fall into the irremediable absurdity of personal gods —, they end up relegated to mere blind impersonal forces, and thus become indistinguishable from the physical laws that govern the Universe. *The idea that God is an oversized white male with a flowing beard, who sits in the sky and tallies the fall of every sparrow is ludicrous*, said astronomer Carl Sagan, *but if by "God" one means the set of physical laws that govern the universe, then clearly there is such a God. This God is emotionally unsatisfying... it does not make much sense to pray to the law of gravity.* Impersonal gods are nothing more than wordplay, metaphors. They are completely unnecessary concepts that don't explain anything.

Thus, even if we search every corner of our understanding of reality, we are unable to find objective justifications for the belief in any god, superior force, moral world order, or any kind of transcendental reality. However, it would certainly be a naive mistake to think that the mere contestation of the logical possibility of the existence of God would be sufficient to dispel the belief of a religious individual — at best, it causes a subtle tremble, from which he soon recovers.

The irrationality of belief is clearly not an obstructive factor to faith. Thus, even without any rational or empirical support, without any objectively plausible reason to do so, legions of religious individuals are convinced of the existence of their respective gods. It doesn't matter how many inconsistencies we point out in their beliefs, it doesn't matter that we refute all the arguments they present to justify their faith — in its essence, it will remain untouched, without suffering a single scratch.

As we have observed, faith and rationality can coexist in the same individual without much problem, so long as one does not invade the other's terrain. One interesting thing to note is that the same reason, the same logic, the same critical sense that guides believers throughout their lives, when pointed to the analysis of issues justified by faith, end up completely blunted — they lose their strength, their sharpness, their sobriety, and this happens only in matters related to such issues. Thus, when it comes to the existence of God, it seems that even mathematicians become unable to calculate a simple change. It is an apparently strange phenomenon, but whose reason is not very difficult to understand. As Sagan noted: *You can't convince a believer of anything; for their belief is not based on evidence, it's based on a deep-seated need to believe.*

By now, anyone with common sense must have figured out where we are going: the idea that the motives for the belief in something "higher" are not based at all on reason or reality. The cornerstone of all religions, of all religious beliefs, without a doubt, is emotion. In our personal lives, we can clearly see that emotions are powerful and dominant forces in humans. "Passions", so to speak, can generate the most varied types of beliefs and ideals that, justifying objectives, greatly enhance human determination and motivation — and in this equation rationality only comes as an accessory.

Therefore, since it is not the soil of rationality, but that of emotion, the one on which religious belief is developed, when a theistic individual tries to rationally justify his belief, it has already been established beforehand, so that, in its origin, reason did not influence it at all. This leads us to the hypothesis that such beliefs are anchored in strong subterranean emotional factors, being unconsciously generated by mechanisms that operate in a way that is alien to the individual will — in other words, the belief satisfies emotional needs. Human emotions, as we will see later in detail, have a nature that is dangerously independent of reason, since they operate at unconscious brain levels.

As we can see, the enigma is not in the *existence* of God, but in the human mind, in the *belief* in God — in why so many individuals believe in his existence, even though there is no evidence to justify it. Gustave Le Bon closely analyzed this phenomenon, raising many questions that are quite pertinent:

> *Why do we observe, at the same time, in certain spirits, beside a very high intelligence, very naive superstitions? Why is reason so weak to modify our sentimental convictions? (...) How do illustrious scholars, reputed for their critical spirit, accept legends whose childish naivety arouses smiles? (...) Without a theory of belief, these questions and many others remain insoluble. With the aid of reason alone, they could not be explained. (...) Reason generally influences beliefs as much as hunger or thirst. Elaborated in subconscious regions that intelligence could not reach, a belief implants itself in the spirit, but it cannot be argued. (...) Reason has no power against the most erroneous beliefs. (...) Since the mystic's faith is limitless, no rational absurdity could disturb him. He is impervious to reason, observation and experience. The failure of his predictions proves nothing to him, for supernatural powers are by definition capricious and subject to no law.*

Therefore, it is worth remembering that our emotional needs are not just a "detail" of our personality. Rather, they are something inseparable from human nature and, contrary to what we would like to believe, they occupy a much more fundamental level than rationality itself — and can even suppress it temporarily. For that reason, *A view of human nature that simply shrugs off the power of emotions,* says Daniel Goleman, *is sadly myopic. The very name* Homo sapiens, *the thinking species, is deceptive in light of the new appreciation and vision of the place of emotions in our lives that science now offers. As we all know from experience, when it comes to shaping our decisions and our actions, feeling counts every bit as much — and often more — than thought. We have gone too far in emphasizing the value of the purely rational.*

The comments above will be helpful in making this chapter easier to understand. However, it does not deal directly with these issues, which we will continue later.

Before addressing the issue of religion as alienation and social control, we will make a short digression whose purpose is to understand human nature a little better and, with that, possibly begin to see it more objectively.

We, human beings, cherish the illusion that we are, by nature, civilized animals, predominantly rational, lucid, capable of answering for our actions and, deliberately, exercising control over our decisions, opinions, and beliefs. Without a doubt, it's good for our ego to think that *Homo sapiens* is such a free and civilized species by nature — it may feel good, but it doesn't make sense.

Our supposed civility is not innate. On the contrary, much of it lies in the fact that we have great cognitive potential and great behavioral malleability. For example, assuming that an individual with the genetic constitution of modern man was born in the Paleolithic, let us not think that he would be anywhere near civilized and intellectualized like modern humans. Without a doubt, he would be just another savage that, despite having a modern genetic code, would hardly differ from other individuals.

Thus, being subject only to the pressures of a rustic and wild environment, his reasoning would be tied to pragmatic and simple notions. The development of his capacity for abstraction would be quite small. His expressiveness would be very reduced — he wouldn't know how to read or write. As clothing he would wear some pieces of leather. He would make his weapons, tools, and utensils from bone, wood, and chipped stone. His daily bread would probably be achieved by something like a club, or else he would collect fruits and roots, because at the time we were all nomads, as agricultural techniques did not yet exist.

So, as we can see, it was only our *civilization* that overcame this phase, not our species. We didn't become more sophisticated because our species underwent some kind of raging biological evolution from the mentioned time to the present. Organic evolution occurs at an incredibly slow pace, measured in geological time, so it would be impossible to justify the advance of our species solely by means of this evolutionary mechanism.

Making an analogy, we could say that the genetic code — which contains all the information related to the constitution of the human body — is a kind of biological informational legacy that synthesizes, at the molecular level, all the "biological wisdom" that was selected for its usefulness for survival. This DNA, therefore, represents the end result of millions and millions of years of trial and error experimentation. Let's call this organic evolution at the genetic level "macroevolution", which is hereditary and works in the very long term.

Biological instincts, because they adapt to the environment in the very long term, are not very versatile, that is, they have little malleability. That is why they are inefficient in dealing with the constant and countless changes that occur in the environment. Its weak point, therefore, lies in its rigidity.

Contrary to instincts, we know that the human intellect is a superbly versatile tool. This versatility works in such a way as to allow us not only to follow our biological legacy blindly, like instinctive and brute animals. In this situation, the instincts present in us do not work as determinant tendencies, but as general rules that are diffuse, relatively loose and unspecific. Let's say that instincts only tell us what is the objective, the need to be satisfied, leaving the means to do it up to our intelligence.

Thus, as we can see, intellect was the solution "found" evolutionarily by nature to overcome the impasse of instinctual inflexibility, functioning as a means to increase human adaptability to the environment through a greater behavioral gap to be filled by experience. As a result, man gained a lot in malleability and, therefore, in potential specificity. From then on, the ways of satisfying fundamental instincts, being mediated by intelligence, began to be able to be adapted, in the short term, to the specific pressures imposed by the environment — and let us always remember that, the greater the capacity to harmonize its behavior with the environment in which it lives, the more adapted the species is.

This could be termed our "card up the sleeve" in relation to the other species. Since the intellect is capable of incorporating many new information about the environment in which it lives and then using it to adjust behavior in favor of survival, man, with it, begins not only to follow a rigid instinctive legacy, which is easily decontextualized, but allows him a kind of non-hereditary adaptive "microevolution" that takes place at the individual level.

In the Paleolithic period, the knowledge acquired was probably based only on personal experiences and on a few parental or tribal teachings, learned through observation or oral tradition. In other words, the cultural legacy, from generation to generation, was quite small. Later, most of the knowledge acquired was lost with the death of the individual, and this was a major obstacle to the development of culture.

However, after the advent of writing — around 4000 BC —, people became capable of recording the knowledge acquired during the period of their lives, so that, slowly, it accumulated and became more sophisticated. Thus, with the advent of writing, the individual "microevolution" became hereditary and began to be passed to future generations. The trial-and-errors of the past, in this way, became cumulative. So, to conclude our analogy, just as at the genetic level there is the slow process of cumulative natural evolution, writing gave rise to the process of cumulative cultural evolution.

This worked so well that, currently, the available cultural legacy is so monstrous that the intention of absorbing it all over the period of a lifetime would be laughable. But the most important fact is that, due to our intellectual capacity, we can absorb a reasonable portion of a hard-won cultural legacy — an amount of knowledge that would be impossible for us to elaborate individually. For this reason, if we hadn't absorbed part of the cultural legacy left by many, many brilliant minds, we would probably be living in barbarism instead of reflecting on the essence of human nature.

Undoubtedly, this is an enormous progress, but with an inconvenience:

much of what we learn does not come directly from our personal experience, but from the belief in the testimony and knowledge of others. For example, we would find ourselves in serious trouble if someone were to ask us how we can be sure that all the things that we accept as obvious truths are in fact true. How could an ordinary individual prove that there are atoms and, within those, the protons and, within those, the quarks? What about the myriad of chemical reactions that produce ATP in the mitochondria — do they actually occur, as biologists say? How could we know for certain if all the historical facts that the books mention occurred?

Most people have no idea how the components that make up computers work. We know that they process information, we know that they use electricity, semiconductors, but we never thoroughly investigate them to see if they really work as they tell us — we simply believe, because we have no time to find out and no reason to think that they are deceiving us. Likewise, we all believe that the Earth is round and revolves around the Sun — not because we concluded this personally, but because we absorbed in five minutes the final conclusions of someone else, who took a long time to infer this from countless observations, calculations, and reflections.

Anyone who insisted on self-sufficiency would find themselves in trouble when they became ill. Being sick, you would need to be treated, but how could you trust the doctors' diagnosis? What if the active ingredient in the prescription drug had been poorly investigated? Refusing to rely on the testimony of doctors and scientists, he would have to graduate in medicine and carry out independent research in the medical and pharmacological fields in order to constitute his own knowledge. Such an individual would probably end up dying of old age before even discovering what his illness was. This illustrates what would happen if we were overly skeptical about knowledge.

On the other hand, becoming a passive receptacle for information doesn't seem like a viable solution either. Instead, we could use some simple filters. For example, as Dawkins suggested: *Next time somebody tells you something that sounds important, think to yourself: "Is this the kind of thing that people probably know because of evidence? Or is it the kind of thing that people only believe because of tradition, authority or revelation?"*

In any case, the fact is that, at the current stage of our civilization, it is simply impossible to dispense with the belief in the knowledge of others to guide our lives. Because of the enormous amount of knowledge available, even if reluctantly, we are forced to be a bit gullible and to harbor some prejudices for the sake of practicality — and, of course, also for the sake of survival.

Now let's bring these conclusions to the subject that interests us here. We can see that religion works on two levels. On an individual level, it satisfies emotional needs. As Freud stated, it has a threefold mission: *they must exorcize the terrors of nature, they must reconcile men to the cruelty of Fate, particularly as it is shown in death, and they must compensate them for the sufferings and privations which a civilized life in common has imposed on them*. This means satisfying things such as the need for special explanations for the reality in which we live — the origin and raison d'être of the world, the meaning of life, etc. — providing a moral and ethical framework, that is, a kind of "guide to the correct way of living" and, of course, also some kind of hope, even if *post-mortem*. On the other hand, at the collective level, religion plays a social role, helping to promote the integration and cohesion of the whole. The generalized communion of fundamental ideas makes society function as an organism, in a more predictable, orderly, and consequently more maneuverable way.

Of course, from the perspective in which we are analyzing this issue, the so-called "sacred books" are nothing more than the cultural legacy of a people translated into religious terms — a body of knowledge that represents the sum of the experience, customs, wisdom, and ethics that a people acquired over time, that is, the "correct way of living" in their view.

Objective knowledge is demonstrable. For example, the veracity of a mathematical theorem, a physical law, a biological mechanism, etc. However, it is practically impossible to demonstrate the veracity or superiority of a moral, a principle, a maxim, a custom. Rational reasons and justifications have nothing to rely on to defend a moral doctrine, since there are infinite ways of looking at and interpreting reality in terms of rights and duties, morality and immorality, right and wrong, good and evil. That is why it is extremely difficult to present some "wisdom of life" as true knowledge, and not just an opinion.

To be obeyed, such "wisdom" must be presented in an imperative tone, it must be seen as something above any question. In other words, to be accepted, it must be stated not as an opinion, but as a law — and every law needs the sanction of an authority. That is exactly the device used by the authors of "holy books" to make people submit to the rules presented in them. It goes without saying that such authority comes from the creator of the Universe — God. Once authority has been established, then it is often joined by tradition, with which it gains much more weight. Nietzsche presents, in his way of understanding, the conditions for the creation of a holy book of definitive laws:

(...) the thing that is to be avoided above everything is further experimentation — the continuation of the state in which values are fluent, and are tested, chosen and criticized ad infinitum. Against this a double wall is set up: on the one hand, revelation, which is the assumption that the reasons lying behind the laws are not of human origin, that they were not sought out and found by a slow process and after many errors, but that they are of divine ancestry, and came into being complete, perfect, without a history, as a free gift, a miracle...; and on the other hand, tradition, which is the assumption that the law has stood unchanged from time immemorial, and that it is impious and a crime against one's forefathers to bring it into question. The authority of the law is thus grounded on the thesis: God gave it, and the fathers lived it.

By placing such truths in the mouth of God, they cease to be seen as simple "human truths" subject to challenge, which were created and slowly improved through the process of trial and error. They become divine laws that were miraculously revealed to mankind already complete, perfect, and finished. They will necessarily represent the pinnacle of wisdom, which no person has "enough height" to challenge.

The Bible was inspired by God — do we now understand what this means? One more small step, and we will also understand what is the true intention behind concepts such as "sin", "eternal damnation", "curse", "expiation", "will of God", "salvation", "value of faith", "devil", "temptation", and so on. God — that cosmic spy who even knows what we think — is a fiction that represents the factor of authority used to justify ideological imperatives whose main function is social control.

Richard Dawkins, from a different perspective, sheds some light to aid our understanding of the religious phenomenon, explaining one of the reasons why it is so persistent over generations:

A human child is shaped by evolution to soak up the culture of her people. Most obviously, she learns the essentials of their language in a matter of months. A large dictionary of words to speak, an encyclopedia of information to speak about, complicated syntactic and semantic rules to order the speaking, are all transferred from older brains into hers well before she reaches half her adult size. When you are pre-programmed to absorb useful information at a high rate, it is hard to shut out pernicious or damaging information at the same time.

Religion, by imposing general rules of behavior, making individuals massively accept a line of thinking from childhood, lays standardized foundations for the construction of mentalities. As we saw above, people are predisposed to absorb the knowledge of their cultural context almost passively and, therefore, tend to internalize, as their own, the moral rules and beliefs of the society in which they are born. In this way, they begin to believe in God and in the religious traditions of their social context as the "great answer" to the reality in which they live, using it as a support for their willpower, thereby justifying their dreams, their objectives, their efforts, that is, their lives.

However, religion is not widely accepted solely because of tradition. Its contagiousness is strictly linked to human nature, perfectly meeting its profound emotional needs: *Mental contagion constitutes a psychological phenomenon whose result is the involuntary acceptance of certain opinions and beliefs. All manifestations of psychic life can be contagious, but it is especially the emotions that spread in this way. Contagious ideas are syntheses of affective elements.* And, continuing, Le Bon makes it clear that emotional beliefs do not have any necessary link with reason. By nature, they can be established in a way that is unrelated to evidence, logic, and will:

The strength of beliefs is well understood when it is observed that they escape any rational influence. (...) Belief, as an invincible necessity of our affective nature, cannot, and in this sense it is like any other feeling, be voluntary and rational. Intelligence does not form or govern it. Whatever the race, the time considered, the degree of intelligence or culture, man has always expressed the same desire to believe. Belief seems to be mental food, as necessary to the life of the spirit as material food to the nourishment of the body. The civilized could not do without it, and neither could the savage. (...) If beliefs were accessible to the influence of reason, we would have seen all those that are absurd disappear long ago. Now, the observation shows its persistence. We are therefore forced to admit that there are no absurdities for a believer and that man does not have the freedom to believe or to disbelieve. Since all these beliefs are elaborated in the unconscious, they escape, not only our reason, but also, necessarily, our will.

Contrary to science, religion is not cold and indifferent, it does not consider only purely rational and objective factors in its explanations. Religion makes man the supreme creation, gives subjective meaning to reality, explains the world in human terms, as if everything revolved around our navels. And, without a doubt, it does so in a very astute way, in order to satisfy the most intimate emotional needs of each person, making the individual literally fall in love with such ideas and embrace them body and soul, in the illusion that they have found "what was missing" in their lives. Religion, thus, in addition to existential comfort, gives reason, importance, and meaning to their lives — but in return, it takes away their freedom.

From this perspective, Nietzsche was able to clearly identify the factor that makes religions, especially Christian ones, extremely attractive to our ego:

"One thing only is necessary"... That every man, because he has an "immortal soul", is as good as every other man; that in an infinite universe of things the "salvation" of every individual may lay claim to eternal importance; that insignificant bigots and the three-fourths insane may assume that the laws of nature are constantly suspended in their behalf — it is impossible to lavish too much contempt upon such a magnification of every sort of selfishness to infinity, to insolence. And yet Christianity has to thank precisely this miserable flattery of personal vanity for its triumph — it was thus that it lured all the botched, the dissatisfied, the fallen upon evil days, the whole refuse and off-scouring of humanity to its side. The "salvation of the soul" — in plain language: "the world revolves around me".

Despite its rational incoherence, religion undoubtedly works and will continue to work, since it operates on an unconscious level, which is independent of reason. Religion knows how to exploit very well a typical weakness of humans, which is the profound need to "believe" in something, to have some ideal higher than themselves — something that works as an independent reference for locating themselves in the world in which they live, that is not subject to their will and according to which they can weigh the value of all things with a precise and infallible perspective. With this, individuals find meaning in their lives and, as a result, feel important and necessary, as part of something "bigger than themselves".

Not only the unenlightened, poorly educated, but especially the insecure, weak-willed, who are incapable of psychological independence, fall into this trap. Such people are inept in setting their own goals — they need to receive instructions, they need some objective to believe in, because only then, as servants of a cause, of a higher purpose, can they achieve the determination necessary to carry their lives forward, and that is why they gladly believe in sacred lies. Their lack of psychological firmness persuades them to hold on to unshakable and unquestionable truths. Thus, the person who cannot live with doubt must consider it something evil, a sin — having faith, from this point of view, literally means surrendering oneself, giving oneself up to an idea, cause, or principle. It means abdicating independence and impartiality in exchange for an ideological backbone that supports the individual's willpower.

In this way, because they can only achieve well-being as followers, as believers, they end up making themselves slaves to their beliefs and, consequently, slaves to the interests skillfully imbedded in such beliefs. Without a doubt, this is exactly where the enormous power of religion as a tool for social control lies — that is, the art of making individuals follow and believe in the ideals of others as their own. Of course, religious hypocrites, unscrupulous politicians, and deceivers in general know this better than anyone. In the words of Seneca: *Religion is regarded by the common people as true, by the wise as false, and by the rulers as useful.*

It's no wonder, then, that History has taught us to fear for our freedom every time religion seeks to extend its hands to power and every time the current power raises the flag of religion to justify itself. Religion, being based on dogmatic factors, has an inherently inflexible and authoritarian nature — it is the symbol of partiality and intolerance per excellence. Thus, with a little shrewdness, it becomes possible to use it as the perfect trick to cast the sublime veil of holiness upon the most disgusting pretensions. In this sense, the thinker Ludwig Feuerbach correctly asserted that *Wherever morality is based on theology, wherever the right is made dependent on divine authority, the most immoral, unjust, infamous things can be justified and established.* Two regrettable examples of this fact: the Inquisition and the Crusades.

In the Middle Ages, the Catholic Church, thirsty for power, used the Inquisition to impose its will on the masses with iron fist. To this end, it created the *Index Librorum Prohibitorum*, a catalog of forbidden books, in order to avoid the incursion of "heretical" ideas into the herd, which was kept in complete ignorance. It incinerated countless "wicked" libraries, depriving us of an enormous part of the cultural legacy of Antiquity. It tortured countless individuals with absurd cruelty — using instruments that would shock the heart of a hyena — and burned countless individuals publicly, usually on extremely dubious charges of "witchcraft" or "heresy", and soon began to confiscate their assets — to increase the assets of the Holy Church, obviously.

The Crusader movement, on the other hand, using the religious excuse of "saving from the infidels" the Holy Land where Jesus was supposedly born, served to attract the population surplus out of Europe — which was overpopulated at the time — and to conquer new lands. It also served, of course, as a pretext for looting the riches of the East, and resulted in the reopening of trade in the Mediterranean.

Let's see: looting, violence, and oppression in the name of God — would it be necessary to add something more to realize that, when religion is united with power, the "will of God" becomes "the will of those in charge"?

Some think that the times when religion was pernicious are over, since everyone currently has religion freedom. However, this is nothing more than an illusion, another fraud by religious propaganda. Even today, it promotes injustice — and its mechanism, as we have seen, consists of involving ideological factors of mass manipulation in its comforting views.

The basic mechanism is very simple: if doubts appear, we resort to threats — the fear factor plays the role of keeping the individual always suggestible.

Moreover, by explaining the inner essence of reality in purely mystical and metaphysical terms, religion manages to distort it to the point of absurdity. In this way, it functions as an extremely efficient tool to alienate the oppressed from the reality of their oppression, making them see inequality, misfortune, suffering and poverty as part of a "natural order" that is the design of a god who is supposedly "evolving their character" or "testing their faith".

Logically, it is not difficult to understand that this is the reason why religion always emphasizes, under the mask of virtue, things such as humility, faith — that is, blind credulity —, submission, resignation, hope, optimism, patience, pacifism, simplicity, hope, perseverance, and contempt for materialism. The idea can be put in these terms: *the materialists, the greedy, the rich, and the powerful are foolish. What's the importance of a brief and ephemeral earthly happiness? Let's follow God's will. Let's be honest and humble workers. Let's accept the toil as our fair share. Salvation comes through faith! God will reward us for our virtue!*

Nietzsche was able to make a fair analysis of the hidden factors behind this perversion of reasoning that transforms impotence into a virtue, with the purpose of justifying and embellishing one's own weakness:

> *When the oppressed, downtrodden, outraged exhort one another with the vengeful cunning of impotence: "let us be different from the evil, namely good! And he is good who does not outrage, who harms nobody, who does not attack, who does not requite, who leaves revenge to God, who keeps himself hidden as we do, who avoids evil and desires little from life, like us, the patient, humble, and just" — this, listened to calmly and without previous bias, really amounts to no more than: "we weak ones are, after all, weak; it would be good if we did nothing for which we are not strong enough"; but this dry matter of fact, this prudence of the lowest order which even insects possess (posing as dead, when in great danger, so as not to do "too much"), has, thanks to counterfeit and self-deception of impotence, clad itself in the ostentatious garb of the virtue of quiet, calm resignation, just as if the weakness of the weak — that is to say, their essence, their effects, their sole ineluctable, irremovable reality — were a voluntary achievement, willed, chosen, a deed, a meritous act.*

(For those interested, a famous example of this type of inverse argumentation can be found in the Sermon on the Mount. [Matthew, chapter 5])

We have long overcome the illusion that religion — or God, faith, and the like — is necessary to explain our reality. Religiosity was once an honest but naive attempt to explain the world. However, now, it is nothing more than a social tool, used to keep us under control. Religion, then, has nothing to teach us about the world. However, even so, it is important that we understand it in depth, not to understand the world, of course, but to understand the human being, the human mind.

Nowadays it is science that guides human knowledge, and religion, now restructured, exists only as a tool for domesticating and oppressing the masses — and, we must admit, its role is played with indisputable competence and objectivity. The eternal happiness promised in the paradise of the afterlife — where only the souls of "true believers" go — is the perfect scam. With such rhetoric, the individuals' eyes are diverted from the reality in which they live, and their expectations are moved to a beyond; at the same time, simplicity and humility are promoted as virtuous things. With this, it is possible to transform them into puppets for the purposes of those who pull the strings behind God's figure. And, also including the abject rhetoric of the "dignity of work", they manage to create a caste of slaves who see their labor force as their greatest asset and, precisely for this reason, give rise to the perpetuation of their exploitation, as if exhaustion were, in itself, honorable, and idleness a kind of shameful situation. The "dogma of work" remains, hand in hand with religious tyranny, one of the most efficient ideological tools ever created so that a paradoxical self-imposed shackling is seen as something natural — and not only natural, but also valuable and noble.

In spite of everything, for some, religion may still be a necessary evil. As long as the conditions of society are perverse and unequal, individuals will be unable to endure existence as an end in itself, since, in this situation, any unnecessary suffering becomes almost unjustifiable. Sacrosanct opium continues to be sought as another way out to cushion all the suffering and injustice that they are forced to endure. And, without a doubt, all the brain-washing they suffer is not limited to religion, but also includes various other media: lustful, automotive, sports, television, carnival, narcotics, and so on.

Every type of escape ends up becoming an absolutely necessary crutch to take their minds off the miserable reality in which they are inserted. To quote Bakunin on this issue: *People go to church for the same reasons they go to a tavern: to stupefy themselves, to forget their misery, to imagine themselves, for a few minutes anyway, free and happy.*

Finally, take away from a simple and honestly religious man the belief in God and the hope of a future reward, and then let's ask: what do you have left — if not fear, suffering, despair, and impotence? In other words, you have absolutely nothing. Now, let's give the word to Nietzsche:

> *The man of faith, the "believer" of any sort, is necessarily a dependent man — such a man cannot posit himself as a goal, nor can he find goals within himself. The "believer" does not belong to himself; he can only be a means to an end; he must be used up; he needs some one to use him up. His instinct gives the highest honors to an ethic of self-effacement; he is prompted to embrace it by everything: his prudence, his experience, his vanity. Every sort of faith is in itself an evidence of self-effacement, of self-estrangement... When one reflects how necessary it is to the great majority that there be regulations to restrain them from without and hold them fast, and to what extent control, or, in a higher sense, slavery, is the one and only condition which makes for the well-being of the weak-willed man, and especially woman, then one at once understands conviction and "faith". To the man with convictions they are his backbone. To avoid seeing many things, to be impartial about nothing, to be a party man through and through, to estimate all values strictly and infallibly — these are conditions necessary to the existence of such a man. But by the same token they are antagonists of the truthful man — of the truth... The believer is not free to answer the question "true", or "not true", according to the dictates of his own conscience: integrity on this point would work his instant downfall.*

It seems clear as day that such individuals have no choice: they believe out of necessity, they need their beliefs to be true, they must make them unshakable for the sake of self-preservation — without a god, their world would collapse. Furthermore, the pain of opening one's eyes after a lifetime in metaphysical darkness is so excruciating that few are able to do so. To make matters worse, this opening of the eyes is not to a pleasant and beautiful reality, but mostly hard, rough, arid, and sordid. And even those who do not have a life of misery live like prisoners who, having spent their entire lives in a comfortable ideological prison, now feel horror and anguish at the face of freedom, hindered by the fear of glimpsing the harsh reality behind the veils of illusion. They became cowards before their existence, and that is why they take refuge in the ideal, seeing themselves as the center of attention of a divine beneficial force, never surpassing the childish fantasy of an affable "cosmic daddy" who looks after them. Precisely in this regard, Sigmund Freud says that religion is:

> *[a] system of doctrines and promises that, on the one hand, explain the enigmas of this world with enviable perfection and that, on the other hand, guarantee that a careful Providence will watch over your life and will compensate you, in a future existence, for any frustrations you have experienced here. The ordinary man cannot imagine this Providence in any other form but that of a greatly exalted father, for only such a one could understand the needs of the sons of men, or be softened by their prayers and placated by the signs of their remorse. The whole thing is so patently infantile, so incongruous with reality, that to one whose attitude to humanity is friendly it is painful to think that the great majority of mortals will never be able to rise above this view of life. It is even more humiliating to discover what a large number of those alive today, who must see that this religion is not tenable, yet try to defend it inch by inch, as if with a series of pitiable rearguard actions.*

The enlightened among us cannot be seduced by such indecent lies. Religion, in a broad sense, has been a great misdirection to humanity. Historically, it has benefited only a minority. Waged a war of death against the intellectual emancipation of man, paralyzed his brain, hindered his freedom, forcing into his mind a stupidly static, imaginary, falsified vision of the world, full of fantasies, souls, miracles, powers, and fictions, preventing a clear and objective understanding of reality.

With its dogmatic moral values, imposed by authority and the threat of divine punishment, religion robbed man of true moral conscience, alienated him from the genuine origin of the concepts of good and evil, right and wrong, which must come from the understanding of human nature itself, from the recognition of the real motives and the advantages of acting in a moral and social way. Every lucid and conscious individual knows that the purpose of morality and laws should be the promotion of general well-being, and not the satisfaction of the caprices of a tyrannical god.

When awareness of the role of values and rules in promoting our well-being gives way to respect for authority, which transforms them into an impersonal obligation, it is quite obvious that, without a god to compensate us for such deprivations, such regulations could only seem odious to us. In this view, if people understood that regulations, in theory, should not be designed to dominate and oppress them, but, on the contrary, to serve their collective interests, they would gladly obey them instead of secretly harboring hatred towards them. Creating this awareness is a fundamental step so that, without God, instead of destroying them, we seek to improve them. To that end, it is vital to have them as a flexible body of rational notions, not a tablet of commandments fallen from heaven.

Thus, after religion has corrupted, alienated, and perverted all of man's faculties, of having implanted artificial and unnatural moral values into their minds, of having forged and declared a completely fictitious reality as the only true one, of having made man almost illiterate of himself, in short, after having made man's will take root on the infinitely false and harmful soil of theology, they say that religiosity is necessary to maintain the order of society. We are told that lying has value because it serves a purpose. They want us to believe that religion and the belief in a "moral world order" are the cost of maintaining a peaceful society.

However, the fact is that some people cannot live without religion because, since they were children, their intellectual freedom was violated by the imposition of imperatives of all kinds, on the basis of which they learned to justify their lives — which is why they find any other system of thought inconceivable. Only from these can we fear some kind of "vigorous reaction" in the face of disbelief. However, how can individuals who had a non-religious education — an education for reality — be outraged at the non-existence of something that they never thought existed?

In any case, today, it is undoubtedly true that religion is still needed: after all, how could it not be dangerous to open the eyes of slaves who will discover that their own condition of existence is a divinely masked injustice? There is no doubt that, as long as this type of unfairness is present in our society, religion will continue to be cleverly used to justify it, as a kind of *post-mortem panem et circenses.*

To better illustrate this point, let's look at Nietzsche's analysis of the psychology of the slave who, strangely enough, was induced to accept his abject situation and, on top of that, to feel satisfied with it:

> *(...) against this condition of depression, a different and certainly easier training is tried far more often than such a hypnotic collective deadening of the sensibilities, of the ability to experience pain, for this method requires rare powers, above all, courage, contempt for opinion, and "intellectual stoicism". This different training is mechanical activity. There's no doubt whatsoever that this can significantly alleviate a suffering existence. Today we call this activity, somewhat dishonestly, "the blessings of work". The relief comes from the fact that the interest of the suffering person is basically diverted from his suffering, that some action and then another action are always entering his consciousness, thus leaving little space for suffering. For it's narrow, this room of human consciousness! (...) Mechanical activity and what's associated with it — like absolute regularity, meticulous and mindless obedience, a style of life set once and for all, filling in time, a certain allowance for, indeed, training in, "impersonality", in forgetting oneself, in "incuria sui" [no care for oneself] — how fundamentally, how delicately the ascetic priest knew how to use them in the struggle with suffering! Especially when it involved the suffering people of the lower classes, working slaves, or prisoners (or women, most of whom are simultaneously both — working slaves and prisoners) what was needed was a little more than the minor art of changing names, of re-christening, so as to make those people in future see a favor, some relative good fortune, in things they hated.*

Furthermore, religion has always taught contempt for the "wisdom of this world", incited detachment from natural reality, advertised credulity as a virtue, using countless vile tricks to perpetuate itself. It is not surprising, therefore, that it represents one of the greatest obstacles to the progress of knowledge and civilization. Let us imagine all the progress that could have occurred from the Middle Ages to the present day, and that was hindered by the religiosity that dominated the minds of individuals, and by the oppression of the dogmatic monster that was — and still is — the Catholic Church and its sisters. In the medieval period, religion did not focus only on the "inner sense of things": practically everything revolved around God, who was used to explain the entire reality in which they lived. For this reason, every believer in God was satisfied in his ignorance and never bothered to investigate reality, because he was sure that he already knew everything there was to be known: the will of God. If it weren't for the heroes who had enough courage to oppose religious tyranny, sometimes even giving up their lives for it, we would still be living under the same conditions, with a herd-like population, submissive, ignorant, and dominated by the fear of the "wrath of God" that was reserved for the wicked — i.e., those who denied submission to current dogma.

To have a vague idea of the magnitude of this obstruction, we only need to note that, in the last two centuries, in which man began to distance himself ever more from myths and superstition, starting to emphasize reason, there has been more intellectual and material progress than in the entire history of civilization. All the advanced technologies that we have — information technology, telecommunication, transportation, etc. All the progress in medicine that was made possible by the study of the anatomy and physiology of man. All the remedies and treatments that have been developed to prolong and improve our quality of life. All the theories that explain life and our place in the world. All the incredible discoveries in Physics, Astronomy, Biology, and Chemistry. All of this, among many other things, appeared almost in the last century. This stupendous scientific advance only took place after an intellectual elite emancipated itself from the shackles of superstition.

For too long religion has kept man in the dark. But now that we have been able to throw off the yoke of the sacred lie, we cannot allow progress to be paralyzed again by dogmatism. If, every time we encounter a mystery, we appeal to supernatural explanations, we will remain as ignorant as we were born. Only by understanding the true nature of life can we make the most of it. We must therefore educate future generations for reality — teach them to live for the real meaning of Earth and of life, without false promises, without fictions. We cannot allow them to continue to relegate our world to a disposable shell of another hidden reality that would be the "absolute" one.

Let the dogmatists dare to discourse on the "humanitarian benefits" of religion — this miserable mishmash of unnatural and enslaving dogmas that conspire against what is most human in life, that stall all progress that is already painful enough in itself, that turn upside down all the healthy notions of human morality, that throw fellow human beings against each other for reasons that say nothing, that alienate life from itself with metaphysical and anemic ideals, with necromantic ideologies that feed on human misery, that themselves invent misery in order to become immortal.

And the beyond — what does this "beyond" mean? The desire to escape and to deny reality on the part of those preachers of death — or of "eternal life", whatever they prefer —, of those rotting fruits on the tree of life, all driven by the cowardly need to falsify reality at all costs; this need for pathological self-deception, always accompanied by that repulsive smile of satisfaction due to the fact that freedom was finally banned and their "brothers", like them, turned dull, trained, domesticated as gregarious animals, resigned to a grotesque alienation that awaits, harmlessly, for death, so they can enter the "true world" — that is the perfect formula for the decay of the human species. These are some of the "humanitarian benefits" that religion has to offer us.

Some will even object that, without God, life has no value or meaning. But the truth is that it was the very seductive expectations sown by religion that have brought discredit against life and against what is earthly, with their exuberant promises of an idealized world — "bliss", "salvation", "eternal life" — that make life seem insipid in comparison, as if no other viewpoint could have value.

This, however, is nothing more than a misunderstanding. It is necessary to realize that, if there is no god, we are the ones who assign value to things — there is no one to tell us what to do. Life can only have true value and meaning when man is aware of his freedom. When man forgets the transcendental lie and begins to live for reality, for the present — only then will life have real value and meaning, that is, human ones. However, as long as a man considers it more important to please ultramundane ghosts — in exchange for an apartment with a view of Eden —, this will remain impossible.

So, let's not be fooled: *Religion can never reform humanity, because religion is slavery* — Ingersoll said it perfectly. Without this falsification, this poisoning of reality, this shift of expectations to a "beyond", life would not be relegated to a mere phase. Atheism simply brings the center of gravity of life back to life itself instead of slandering it in the name of a "beyond", in the name of *nothing* — and, if atheism represents a curse, it is undoubtedly the curse of freedom.

PART II

New ears for new music. New eyes for what is most distant. A new conscience for truths that have hitherto remained unheard.

— Friedrich Nietzsche

INTRODUCTION TO PART II

No, our science is no illusion. But an illusion it would be to suppose that what science cannot give us we can get elsewhere.

— Sigmund Freud

In the first part of this work, we sought to analyze the problems typically related to the dilemma of belief/disbelief in God, so that our observations have mainly revolved around the plausibility of the divine hypothesis as an explanation for our world. We have been busy explaining what are the conceptual problems present in such notions — both of personal and impersonal gods — and for what reasons they should not be accepted as true — or at least as rationally justified. We debunked some myths, challenged the most frequent arguments that attempt to support the belief in higher entities, presented a quick outline of the anatomy of beliefs, and explained why atheism should not be viewed as an extremism, but as something reasonable and lucid.

It shouldn't be understood that, by doing so, we have destroyed the possibility of the existence of a god. We only demonstrated that atheism, currently, is the perspective most corroborated by reality, and most capable of being rationally supported, since all the facts that we know to date point to a reality without a guiding mind behind it. However, we can never stress this enough: let's always keep our minds open to new evidence, to new theories that may emerge, because that's exactly what helped us get here. Thus, if we become atheists, or if we stop being atheists, this is something that, in a sense, must remain independent of our personal will.

Any sane individual, when declaring himself an atheist, doesn't do so looking for any kind of gain or personal satisfaction. The assumption of atheism must stem from his sobriety in the face of reality. Therefore, we should not understand atheism as an arbitrary choice, but as a reflection of an enlightened conscience, of being honest with ourselves. Precisely for this reason, we should always be willing to change our point of view — even if doing so is uncomfortable or painful — if there are good enough reasons to do so, that is, superior in strength to those that point to a natural world without gods. Therefore, if the hypothesis of a divine creation were to somehow become the most plausible explanation for our world, and most consistent with facts and knowledge, then we should forcibly give up our atheism — because, if we don't, we are giving up our rationality.

But, given the current situation, and all the colossal effort that has been made for centuries to support religious beliefs, we can think of such hypotheses, at best, as unfounded speculations, which have no reason to be taken into consideration. Simple fables and chimeras from the human imagination, which we could multiply *ad infinitum* with some free time and creativity.

In any case, it's of little use just criticizing the wrong views about the world, just pointing out mistakes. After the demolition work, it is wise to reflect on what was the trap that led us to error, in order to avoid being caught again. To this end, it is necessary to analyze the issue in detail, striving to understand what were the causes of these errors of interpretation. After destroying, therefore, it is necessary to rebuild: to overcome the error and then restructure our worldview so that it has a greater correspondence with reality.

In our society, for long centuries, the divine figure has played a central role. Many of the answers to the most relevant questions in our lives originated in theology. However, since such foundations, in our eyes, proved to be wrong, we consider it extremely important to reevaluate the elements that were most strongly influenced by religious explanations. We will thus begin a critical review of the most relevant aspects of human nature — this in order to understand them, analyze them, confront them with reason and evidence, and thus verify if our notions still have any consistency, some real content, or if they were nothing more than errors and ghosts, if they should be rejected altogether with the idea of a god.

This review is important because, even rationally, a veil of mystery has always been cast on such issues. Perhaps this is because they represent something very important to us, and so we imagine that their depth and complexity should match their relevance to our lives — hence they remain misunderstood and untouched, like "great mysteries". The fact is that, if a man does not rid himself of his prejudices, expectations, and desires before setting out on that objective, if he does not approach these issues in a disinterested way — understanding by "disinterest" the fact that he is not seeking any pre-established answer —, this will fatally lead to many errors of interpretation that will make such subjects incomprehensible.

Thankfully, it seems that humanity has found the path that leads to the most certain possible kind of understanding: the scientific one. We hope that we will still harvest a lot of fruit from this. However, it is quite true that our understanding is only in its infancy. Reality has only recently begun to show itself to our eyes with sufficient clarity. Based on the rudiments of this process, on the little that we know, we will try to construct a worldview that, although very incomplete, already has its foundations solidly anchored in a world that is natural, in which those fictions that populated our minds for so long do not exist.

In the following chapters, we'll address fundamental issues of human nature that, in general, have to be reviewed almost completely after the radical split with theism that atheism implies. As a starting point for this review, we will present the basic concepts of the Theory of Evolution, which is a is very well established theory in the scientific domain. This theory explains, in natural and logical terms, the origin of the diversity of life on Earth — of all species, including us — without invoking any "miracles". From then on, the evolutionary perspective will serve as a guide for our subsequent reflections, because, as it places man in his true context, this will make it possible for us to understand things that, until now, seemed like untouchable mysteries.

V

THE THEORY OF EVOLUTION

Given so much time, the impossible becomes possible, the possible becomes probable, the probable becomes virtually certain. One only has to wait; time itself performs miracles.

— George Wald

Evolutionism is the name given to the theory that explains the process that originated the myriad of species that exist or have existed, including us, humans. In general, it is accepted that the evolution of species through natural selection began from an ancestor common to all forms of life, which appeared in primitive seas about 3.5 billion years ago. Subsequently, it gained complexity, adapting and spreading geographically, colonizing different environments, finally taking over the entire planet in the most varied ways.

Although the basic principles of the Theory of Evolution are relatively simple, there are many widespread misconceptions that distort and distance it from its true meaning. For example, many say that Evolutionism is the "theory of chance". In fact, they don't lie, because chance is certainly present, and it's an important component, but it just means the absence of purpose — in no way this diminishes the efficiency of the theory. Living beings, in this sense, certainly evolve at random, but their selection is made by environmental contingencies that incorporate the exact antithesis of chance. Also, many mistakenly believe that it is the degree of intelligence what defines how evolved a species is. And the very name of the theory is misleading, since the term "evolution of species" is commonly understood as "the constant tendency to increase in complexity and sophistication of the living beings", when in fact it means nothing more than the adaptation of the population to the environment in which it lives through the selection of the fittest.

There are also the ever-frequent and dubious objections of creationists, who inadvertently make analogies and more analogies, almost always out of context, to support their dogmatic beliefs — and they must naively imagine that, if they can refute the Theory of Evolution, this will immediately establish the veracity of Creationism. Such idea is a mistake, as we explained.

When serious and impartial arguments appear, ones that challenge Evolutionism for the sake of intellectual honesty and with solid evidence, then we can take those objections seriously. However, those who fight scientific knowledge to preserve their beliefs in religious myths only show a regrettable partiality, which is incompatible with the true scientific spirit. It would be like defending Geocentrism because the Bible says so — regrettably, that was actually done, and those who challenged this "divine fact" were burned at the stake.

Thus, in order not to be deceived by the slick arguments with which they are prepared, it is necessary that we have a reasonable understanding of the concepts that underlie the Theory of Evolution, and that is a second objective to which this chapter is dedicated. So let the evidence speak for us.

TRYING TO CONCEIVE THE INCONCEIVABLE

Since the period of our lives is infinitesimal compared to the geological ages that were available for the selective phenomena of biological evolution to occur, when, after a beautiful lunch, we look at nature and see everything already finished, working in an extremely interdependent way, we are victims of the illusion that species are in harmony with the environment, and that "one exists for the other", or that they were created by some supreme intelligence as they are today. Intuitively, it seems absurd for us to think that all this magnificent profusion of species just "happened" by chance.

Certainly the species are in harmony with the environment, but not because one exists for the other or because they were created, but because the environment is a tyrant who mercilessly claims the lives of those who cannot survive under the conditions imposed by it. Of course, this explanation is not very intuitive, nor does it appeal to our poetic sensibilities.

This illusion is mainly due to our inability to conceive what that bunch of zeros that evolutionists use means in practice. Life began 3,500,000,000 years ago — no one can conceive what that means. The period of our lives, at best, reaches the first digit of the third house, and that's our *entire* lives. For this reason, it is completely illogical to limit ourselves to the ridiculously small amount of time in our lives to judge how things work in the long term, using only our direct observation to define what may or may not happen.

To demonstrate how small the range of our vision is, if we were to represent an entire millennium by the length of just one meter, what would be the equivalent in distance to represent the time since the origin of planet Earth? The immodest distance of 4,500 kilometers! A human would cover, on average, six to eight centimeters of this route.

Therefore, evolutionarily, it makes no sense to talk about periods related to the time of human life. Evolutionism speaks in geological language; it does not speak in years, decades, or centuries; at least, it speaks in millennia, and the most frequent units of measurement are millions, tens of millions, hundreds of millions, and billions of years. In comparison, our lifetime is nothing more than the blink of an eye.

THE ORIGIN OF LIFE

This subject does not belong directly to the scope of Evolutionism, but it is important to have a certain notion about it. The Earth is estimated to have appeared approximately 4.5 billion years ago, and the first forms of life 3.5 billion years ago. The exact process by which this occurred is still a matter of much debate, but currently there are already quite reasonable theories that explain how life could have arisen from non-living matter through natural mechanisms, explained by the laws of Physics and Chemistry.

The three most debated hypotheses about the origin of life are that of special creation, that of panspermia, and that of gradual spontaneous generation, also known as abiogenesis.

The first hypothesis — that of special creation — states that God created all species as they are today. Proponents of special creation theory are called creationists or fixists. Of course, it is not based on evidence, but on myths of religious nature. Since such hypothesis is based on an obscure miraculous singularity to explain the origin of life, it cannot be treated as scientific, since the primary criterion of scientific evaluation is based precisely on verification. If the theory does not present hypotheses that can be verified, it is not possible to compare it with empirical evidence so that its veracity can be proven or disproved. Science, therefore, has nothing to say about this hypothesis.

The second hypothesis — that of panspermia — defends that life originated somewhere outside our planet and, later, in some way, ended up being inseminated on Earth. For example, this could have occurred through spores brought by meteorites, which gradually evolved, giving rise to all the forms of life that we know today. We know that the Earth is frequently hit by meteorites, and organic substances have already been found in some of them, suggesting that the occurrence of such compounds is not as rare as was thought. The two main problems faced by this theory are: 1) When a celestial body, attracted by gravity, enters the Earth's atmosphere, it undergoes extreme heating due to friction with atmospheric air, and this would cause the total annihilation of any form of life contained in it. However, we should note that recent observations point to the possibility that, if the meteor is large enough, its heating could occur only superficially, allowing its still frozen core to reach the Earth intact; 2) This hypothesis, although logically consistent, only answers the reason why life exists on Earth, but it pushes the problem of the true origin, of the genesis of life to somewhere else, and thus the question of how life firstly originated would remain unanswered.

The third hypothesis is that of gradual spontaneous generation, or abiogenesis, which defends that life appeared on Earth through natural processes that consist on what's known as chemical evolution. It is the most plausible of the three, although its verification is somewhat problematic. One of the reasons for this lies in the fact that it is extremely difficult to reconstruct the exact profile that the Earth had several billion years ago. However, the attempts made by scientists to simulate Earth's primitive conditions proved fruitful, pointing to the conclusion that spontaneous gradual generation is theoretically possible.

The first defender of abiogenesis was the Russian biochemist Aleksander Oparin, author of the research that laid the foundations for detailed studies on the physical and chemical processes concerning the origin of life on Earth. According to him, the atmosphere of our planet, in primitive times, was composed of ammonia, methane, water vapor, and hydrogen. The Earth's crust, at that time, was still extremely hot, and that's why all the water was in the form of vapor. Little by little, this water condensed, causing rains that, when in contact with the crust, evaporated again, in an incessant cycle, causing a lot of lightning activity. Since in those remote times the ozone layer did not yet exist, the most energetic solar radiations were not filtered. This served, together with lightning strikes, as the activation energy for chemical reactions between components that existed in the atmosphere. These reactions produced, among various substances, also compounds of organic nature, such as amino acids, for example. These amino acids were carried by the rain to the Earth's crust; then the water evaporated, leaving the amino acids on the hot surface, which acted as a catalyst for the chemical reactions that combined them. It is currently known that amino acid chains are formed naturally by the process of dehydration.

After the phase in which the crust was above boiling temperature, primitive seas began to form, and the organic molecules synthesized on the surface of the crust were dragged into them by the rain. Once inside water, such simple organic substances began to react more intensely, forming molecules of greater complexity. These organic substances, in turn, formed larger aggregates, termed by Oparin as coacervates — a kind of very primitive pre-cell capable of performing some very simple functions. After interacting for a sufficiently long time in the seas, some coacervate would have acquired, in some way, the capacity to replicate in an organized way, and from then on life would have developed.

In fact, we have to admit that this is a rather far-fetched hypothesis, which depends on many factors occurring in harmony for the final result to be consummated. However, in science, no hypothesis remains in vogue by chance. There are several evidences that converge to support the theory of chemical evolution.

A fundamental point that is consistent with this theory is the fact that the elements that predominantly constitute today's living beings are exactly carbon, hydrogen, oxygen, and nitrogen, that is, the same elements that surround us in the environment. Let us bear in mind that the only difference between living matter and inanimate matter lies in its organization.

Various experimental studies were used to verify the hypothesis of gradual spontaneous generation. Stanley Miller, also a biochemist, simulated within a closed system the conditions predicted by Oparin of the early Earth. Inside the system there was a boiling water reservoir, which circulated the four substances proposed by Oparin. There was also a device that released electrical discharges, simulating solar radiation and lightning of the primitive atmosphere.

Leaving this system in operation for a few days, the spontaneous formation of simple organic molecules was later found. Currently, with similar experiments and more modern predictions about the probable components of the primitive atmosphere, it has been possible to synthesize many substances, such as nucleotides, ATPs, carbohydrates, lipids, fatty acids and amino acids.

Nucleotides are the basic components of genetic material; ATP is the molecule that carries life on its back, since it is from it that all organisms draw their energy to survive; carbohydrates, in general, are an excellent source of energy, and combine to form polysaccharides; fatty acids and lipids make up fats; amino acids are the basic components of proteins, an essential element in the constitution of living beings.

Thus, if the Earth's primitive conditions had been favorable, it was experimentally proven that they could have been formed, without any problem, by simple laws of Physics and Chemistry, the fundamental bricks that constitute life.

It is assumed that all of these substances were synthesized — mainly due to solar radiation, the heat of the Earth's crust, and the catalytic properties of clay — for an extremely long period, and were later washed away to the seas by water, where they continued to interact, forming increasingly complex substances. These seas filled with nutrients essential to life are what is normally referred to as "primordial soup".

Within the context of Oparin's reasoning, we notice that, if we throw a handful of amino acids into heated water, they are not randomly dispersed, but tend to constitute aggregates — called microspheres — that have interesting properties. For example, such aggregates of molecules are capable of being individualized from the environment through a film of water and proteins, conserving the internal aqueous environment — something that vaguely resembles the basic structure of a cell. These aggregates are capable of some rudimentary metabolic acts, such as, for example, the tendency to concentrate some substances inside. They are also capable of merging with each other, forming more complex structures. They can also divide and subsequently continue to grow individually.

In practice, it is thought that proteins and other organic molecules present in primitive seas would form colloids, as predicted by Chemistry, which in turn would be responsible for the formation of coacervates, which have, among others, the capacity to catalyze chemical reactions within them. Everything indicates that in the primordial soup there were many of them interacting with each other — entire oceans.

Although they were not really living structures, the coacervates were already under the action of a type of selection: of the most stable. Given the appropriate situations, coacervates tend to concentrate certain substances, eliminate others, absorb smaller droplets, etc. In this process, those that were more physically and chemically stable and more "aggressive" tended to remain.

Finally, this competition selected those that were more stable, organized, and efficient in their metabolic actions. At this stage, they are referred to as protobionts. However, this is still a long way from anything alive. In addition, they needed to acquire the ability to self-replicate in an organized way — that is, to create replicas of themselves. This capacity would have been provided by some sort of primitive informational molecule that is currently extinct — something analogous to modern DNA, which would function as a manager of the metabolic activities of protobionts, but with a much simpler structure. This molecule was probably made of RNA, which has catalytic and self-duplicating properties — and, in the primordial soup, there were certainly the substances necessary for its formation. It is worth remembering that, currently, it is already possible to synthesize RNA molecules capable of spontaneous self-replication in laboratory. A major difficulty, however, is to know how a nucleic acid would have taken control of the metabolic activities of a protobiont, so that it would then become a real living being.

Of course, we will never be able to verify this last phase experimentally in a realistic way, since we would need to know what were the exact primitive conditions and then build an Earth-sized laboratory, leaving the substances to react for a few million years. However, let us note that although such an event seems — and, in fact, is — very unlikely, it only needed to have occurred *once* to trigger the entire process — and there were entire seas full of these substances reacting incessantly, not for one, ten, or a hundred years, but for millions and millions of years. Thus, after the appearance of the first primitive living being, the path was practically unimpeded for the reproductive explosion of these new beings, who had all the food abundantly available in the primordial soup to grow, reproduce and, over time, diversify. As George Wald explained, *The important point is that since the origin of life belongs to the category of at-least-once phenomena, time is on its side. However improbable we regard this event, or any of the steps it involves, given enough time, it will almost certainly happen at least once. And for life as we know it, with its capability for growth and reproduction, once may be enough.*

How all this happened, and if it really happened, it's likely that we'll never know. But here the important thing is not to know exactly how it happened, but to realize that reality shows us that, without a doubt, life may have arisen naturally, through chemical evolution. To conclude this, we rely on simple physical and chemical laws that explain, step by step, the formation of life in a perfectly plausible and rational way, without appealing to any probabilistic miracle.

Thus, if we honestly want to understand the reality in which we live, and also our origin, we must always look in the direction in which the evidence points, never losing sight of the fact that science does not seek the chimeric absolute certainties — it seeks the most probable.

Darwin's idea

It was in the book *The Origin of Species* that Charles Darwin presented the main idea of Evolutionism, which is based on the selection of the fittest — to survival and to reproduction. The central thesis is goes in these terms: in a normal population of individuals, there are small natural differences between the members that, at first, would be of little relevance. But since that populations grows in geometric progression (1, 2, 4, 8, 16, 32, 64…), their members would soon outnumber the amount that the environment can sustain. In practice, this means that there is no longer food for everyone.

In this situation, the small differences between individuals come into play. Every living being, by instinctive nature, wants to live, but there are too many individuals, and the environment cannot sustain them all. What happens? A fierce competition for survival begins. The small differences between living beings, at this moment, can make all the difference — between those who live and those who die.

For example, let's imagine a population of lions. Suppose that their standard maximum speed is 60 km/h. In the environment they're in, there are gazelles whose maximum speed is 65 km/h, and it is only on them that they feed. Suppose that the only way to capture a gazelle is to beat it in a race. The lions will struggle to reach the gazelles, and the gazelles will also struggle to escape the lions. As there are subtle variations from individual to individual in every population, we will normally find faster lions and slower lions, and the same for gazelles. In this context, the selective factor is speed. The slower lions will not be able to reach any gazelle and, running out of food, will eventually die of hunger; the faster lions will reach the slower gazelles; and the faster gazelles will not be reached by any lion. Since, with each generation, only the best — in this case, the fastest — survive, the tendency will be that the predators become faster and faster. On the other hand, the same occurs with the prey: the tendency will be that only those who manage to escape predation will survive to reproduce, and so the fastest among them will be equally selected.

The example above serves as a paradigm for the Theory of Evolution through the selection of the fittest, which is driven by the refrain that, ironically, we find in the Bible: *life for life, eye for eye, tooth for tooth, hand for hand, foot for foot.* [Deuteronomy 19:21] Its driving force is the ruthless struggle for the right to exist. In the logic of life, therefore, the criterion of truth is survival.

INCORPORATING THE NEW DISCOVERIES: NEO-DARWINISM

Darwin created the Theory of Evolution based purely on his intuition and on his careful observations made around the world. However, since he lived in the 19th century, he still lacked the necessary technological instruments to understand the origin of variability between individuals in the same population. He admitted its existence, and also that it was through it that evolution worked, but he didn't understand the mechanism that originated it.

Currently, it is known that the presence of variations between individuals is due to genetic recombination and mutations, which can occur spontaneously, but that can also be induced by several other factors, such as ultraviolet rays, x-rays, radioactivity, etc. The improved version of the Theory of Evolution, which incorporates discoveries about the role of genetic material in promoting the phenotypic variability of species, is given the name of Neo-Darwinism or Synthetic Theory of Evolution — which, in parallel, also incorporates the theory of Continental Drift.

It is in this context that the question of chance in the evolution of species comes into play. Gene recombination and mutations undoubtedly occur by chance, that is, without any predefined objective — but to remain, they must pass through the rigorous filter of competition.

For example, if a certain mutation makes the individual better at surviving, the individual will be more likely to leave descendants, passing on such genes to the next generation. On the other hand, if the mutation is pernicious, the individual will be harmed, and this will decrease the probability of reproducing, making this mutant variety tend to disappear from the population.

To illustrate the mechanism, we can return to the example above. If a beneficial mutation were to cause a lion to be able to run not at 60 km/h but at 70 km/h, then it would be more capable of surviving in that environment. If, on the other hand, a lion were born with genetic material containing a pernicious mutation that would alter, for example, the length of its legs, and this reduced its maximum speed to 50 km/h, then it would be unable to reach its prey, and natural selection would rule that individual out — its unsuccessful genes would disappear from the lion population. In this way, we see that the adaptation of the species to the environment does not occur at the individual level. In reality, this phenomenon occurs at the level of population composition.

It's also important to point out that mutations work in small steps. We'll never see a chimpanzee giving birth to a man or vice versa — that's not how things happen. When large mutations occur, there is a great tendency for them to be pernicious, since it is very unlikely that a significant portion of genetic material will recombine at random in the exact proportion necessary to create a positive trait, since the number of pernicious combinations is much greater. Thus, what we can expect from a successful mutation is something quite modest, such as shorter or longer legs, lighter or darker hair, more or less dense hair, a modified digestive enzyme, sharper or harder teeth, and so on.

For this reason, a miraculous mutation would not be necessary to give rise to all of today's extremely specialized organs. It is quite plausible that they have arisen gradually, in several small steps. For example, it's astronomically unlikely that something like the human eye "sprang" out of nowhere, all at once, by sheer luck. But it's not unlikely that it was derived from something slightly less sophisticated, from a predecessor eye that was a little more rudimentary than today's, which didn't see so well. That rudimentary eye, in turn, would have come from an even simpler one, and so on, in an enormous and extremely gradual series, until it arrived at something like, say, a small crudely photosensitive structure, which would have been simple enough to have arisen by chance, from a single mutation.

Dawkins presents us with an analogy between stone arches and the functioning of evolution, explaining quite clearly how simple structures can serve as the basis for the emergence of specialized devices:

> *[An arch made of stone blocks, for example, is a stable structure capable of withstanding for many years, even if there is no cement to give it resistance. Building a complex structure through evolution is like building an arch using one block at a time, without cement. If we think about this task in a superficial way, it will seem impossible. When the last stone is in place, then the arc will be*

stable; it's just that the intermediate stages are unstable. However, it's relatively easy to construct the arc if we can add and also subtract blocks. We started by building solid foundations, then we built the arch on top of them. Then, when the entire arch is in position, including the main stone at the top, just carefully remove the bases and, with a little luck, the arch will remain intact. Stonehenge is incomprehensible until we realize that its builders relied on some type of framework, or perhaps slopes or gradients of land, that were removed. We can only see the final product. We have to infer what the setup was, which no longer exists.]

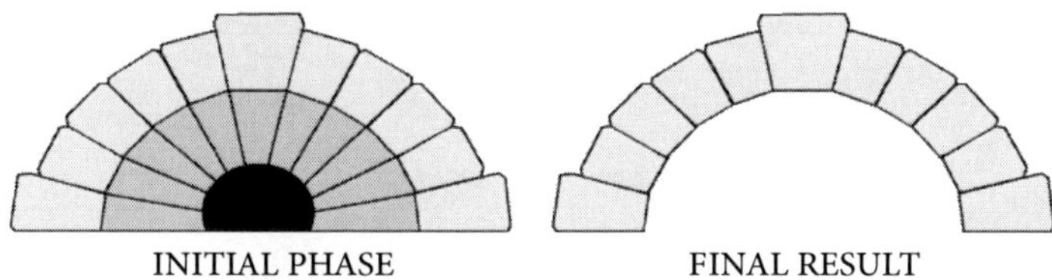

As we can see, the complexity of current life is incomprehensible if we do not consider its historical foundations, the way in which organisms and their characteristics emerged and changed during their evolution. That was one of the most important explanatory gaps that the Theory of Evolution answered.

Over countless generations, the most varied types of genetic mutations and recombinations occur, and the result is always forced to cross the filter of reproductive fitness. In this way, we realize that evolution is cumulative. The small favorable changes are selected and, little by little, they accumulate. Over time, they engender new features, devices, organs, etc. If the necessary conditions are met, new species may also appear, as we shall see below.

Simulating cumulative evolution

Mutations and adaptation

To get a better sense of how cumulative natural selection works in practice, let's use a simple example. Suppose that we represented the reproductive fitness of living beings by geometric shapes. In a certain environment, there is a species that we will call the "square species". We will remove this species from the environment in which it lives and place it in an environment that has a selective pressure for "roundness" — that is, the rounder the individual, the more adapted it will be to that environment.

Statistically, the probability of there being mutations, from generation to generation, is quite small. But to make the example didactic, let's suppose that they occur every generation. From the figure below, we can see that reproduction, in this case, is only asexual. To avoid complications, it was postulated in the example that each reproduction would produce only two individuals, and that of the two, only one would survive, and the selection, as mentioned, would be based on the individual's level of roundness.

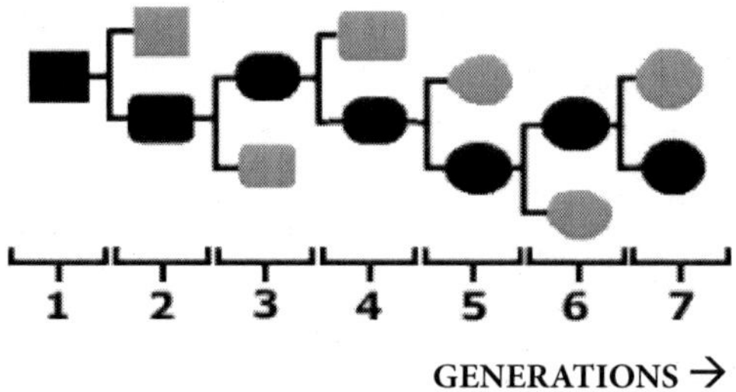

As we can see, in the first generation the being was a perfect square, since it was adapted to its old environment. The second generation has an individual like the parent and another slightly rounded, who mutated; the environment naturally favored the more rounded one, who survived. The same occurred in the third generation, and the rounder individual was selected; the other was discarded. In the fourth generation, we noticed that there was an unfavorable mutation, that is, one individual became squarer, while the other remained the same; the one that remained rounder survived. Following the scheme, we see that the tendency of individuals, by a factor of selecting the fittest in the long term, is to reach complete roundness, which means adaptation. As we explained, the rounder individual is more likely to survive and reproduce because the environment favors individuals that are more adapted to it.

This process illustrates how the small favorable changes that occur due to random mutations accumulate over generations, creating a tendency for the species to adapt to the conditions imposed by the environment. Complete roundness, in our example, means that the species is fully adapted to survive in that given environment — meaning the competition will become increasingly fierce and specialized.

This "complete roundness", in practice, could be illustrated by the animals that we commonly refer to as "living fossils", that is, species that, because they are extremely well adapted to the environment in which they live, remained practically unchanged for enormous periods of time. A good example is the Tuatara, a reptile that was contemporary with the dinosaurs and that lives on some New Zealand islands.

Adaptive convergence and adaptive irradiation

The mechanism called *adaptive convergence* explains the morphological similarities between species from profoundly different origins. For example, let's take two distinct species, one in the shape of a "drop" and the other in the form of a "diamond", and place them in the environment from which we took the "square species" used as the model above — an environment that has the "quadrature" as a selective factor.

Over time, it will happen that the two species will have the characteristics of their mutations selected according to the same criteria, so that they will tend to be similar in functional terms. Let's look at the diagram:

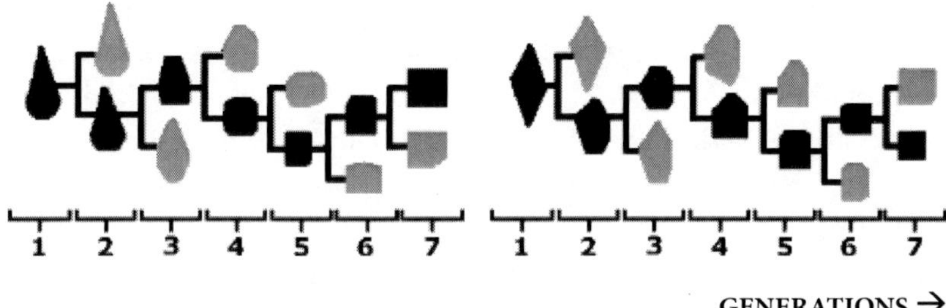

Living examples of this process are sharks and dolphins. The shark is a cartilaginous fish that breathes through gills, while the dolphin is a mammal that breathes through lungs. Sharks have fleshy fins; dolphins have bones. The functional similarity of their shapes is not coincidental — it is due to similar environmental pressures. In other words, since both were under the pressure of the same specific environment, over time they evolved convergently, since, through genetic selection, they found similar solutions to the environmental problems imposed on their survival as a species.

In the case of *adaptive irradiation*, what happens is just the opposite. If we separated a population of individuals of the same species into two distinct groups and placed them in different environments, for example, one in an equatorial forest and the other in a savanna, and assuming, of course, that both groups would survive to reproduce, it would happen that, over time, each group would progressively specialize in its new environment, and would eventually evolve in such a divergent way that they would become new species. Due to the different selective pressures of the environments in which they are located, they are differentiated through the progressive accumulation of differences that are adaptive to the specific environment in which they are. When groups reach a level of differentiation such that they are unable to breed, even if they are regrouped, it is said that a new species has emerged, a process technically called *speciation*.

A classic example of this process is Darwin's observation of finches — birds related to sparrows — inhabitants of the various Galapagos islands. Such birds were very similar to each other. However, they had different shaped beaks that, not by coincidence, were specialized in obtaining the type of food available on the island they respectively inhabited, strongly indicating that all varieties had evolved divergently from a common ancestor, who colonized the islands in an earlier period.

As we can see, all the diversification that occurred from the first form of life that appeared on Earth occurred through the process of adaptive irradiation. That is, as primitive life explored new environments, spreading around the world, it was confronted with challenges specific to each location. This profusion of groups of individuals, under countless different selective pressures, slowly and progressively, resulted and will continue to result in the emergence of the most varied species.

Some Evidence of Evolution

The Theory of Evolution itself makes sense. However, this wouldn't matter at all if there was no evidence to confirm its veracity. Does such evidence exist?

Yes, and it's very strong.

Paleontological evidence. Fossils are vestiges or remains of living beings that, in some way, have been preserved. They are great evidence of Evolution. It is through them that we can discover which beings lived before us, but are now extinct — dinosaurs, for example. By dating fossils via radioactive isotopes, we can reconstruct the evolutionary history of living beings and discover the ancestors of the current species, in what era they lived, and so on. The distribution of millions of fossils is at the exact depths expected if evolution had happened — the lowest layers of sediments with the simplest species and the most recent layers with more sophisticated and specialized forms of life, indicating that there was a gradual process of adaptive evolution. In addition, Paleontology has discovered numerous fossils in transitional forms, a fact that is in accordance with the ideas that underlie Evolutionism.

Genetic evidence. All living beings — with the exception of some bacteria and some viruses — use the same type of informational molecule: DNA, or deoxyribonucleic acid, strongly suggesting that all forms of life evolved from a common ancestor. Comparative studies between close and distant species indicate that the genetic kinship follows the patterns predicted by the Theory of Evolution. Modern laboratory analysis has revealed that we share approximately 99% of our genetic material with chimpanzees. Another evidence is the genetic material of wheat, which has varieties with 14, 28, and 42 chromosomes, corresponding to haploid, diploid, and triploid individuals, a fact that can only be plausibly explained through the occurrence of chromosomic mutations.

Cytological evidence. At the macroscopic level, individuals differ enormously, but at the microscopic level, we see that they are all made up of the same basic components: cells. These, in turn, are all basically composed of the same organic elements: proteins, lipids, carbohydrates, and nucleic acids.

Endosymbiosis. In eukaryotic cells, mitochondria and chloroplasts are organelles that have their own genetic material, and reproduce independently of the rest of the cell. If we destroy all the mitochondria in a cell, it will not be able to synthesize a new one — so, these organelles live as if they were "guests" inside our cells. It is likely that, long ago, primitive eukaryotic cells "swallowed" prokaryotic organisms, and in this situation both would have benefited, continuing to live in symbiosis. In the case of the mitochondria, this was advantageous because the eukaryotic cell became capable of breathing oxygen, greatly increasing its energetic efficiency. The only way to explain this fact plausibly is through evolution.

Homology and analogy. These are notions linked to adaptive irradiation and convergence. A clear and simple explanation, by biologist Sezar Sasson, will suffice to show its strength as evidence:

> *[Homology and analogy are] both used to compare organs or structures existing in living beings. Homology refers to the similarity of origin between two organs belonging to two living beings from different species, while analogy refers to the similarity of function performed by organs belonging to living beings from different species. Two homologous organs may be analogous if they perform the same function. The tail of a South American monkey and the tail of a dog are homologous structures (both animals are mammals) and do not perform the same function. The wings of a hummingbird (bird) and those of a bat (mammal), on the other hand, are homologous because they have the same origin and analogous because they perform the same function. On the other hand, the wings of a butterfly (an insect, arthropod) are analogous to the wings of a sparrow (a bird) because they perform the same function, but they are not homologous, since the origin of these structures is very different. Note that the homology cases reveal the operation of the adaptive irradiation process and indicate a kinship between the compared animals. On the other hand, cases of pure analogy, not accompanied by homology, reveal the occurrence of adaptive convergence and do not involve kinship between the exemplified animals. Thus, the anterior fins of a shark are analogous to those of a whale and both are the consequence of a converging evolution.*

Illogical project. Our optic nerve contains about three million wires that form a bundle that carries the information captured by the photocells to the brain, to be processed. Of course, it would be logical to suppose that the photocells should be facing the light, and that the wires that conduct the electrical impulses generated by them should leave from their back region, all in the same direction, converging to constitute the optic nerve, like a "pony tail" of photocells. But, strangely enough, what we find is the opposite: the wires start from the side closest to the light, and then pass over the retina until they are grouped together in a hole called the blind spot. The light, in this way, has to cross an obstruction consisting of a tangle of wires before reaching the photocells. Of course, this doesn't compromise our vision much, as we can see relatively well, but the fact is that, faced with such a design, a competent engineer would only laugh. This is further evidence that humans were not conceived by some intelligent designer, but are the fruit of evolution, like any other species.

Comparative embryology. Embryos provide very strong evidence in favor of the Theory of Evolution. At equivalent stages of development, vertebrate embryos are extremely similar — a very strong indication that we are related. Let's look at the figure:

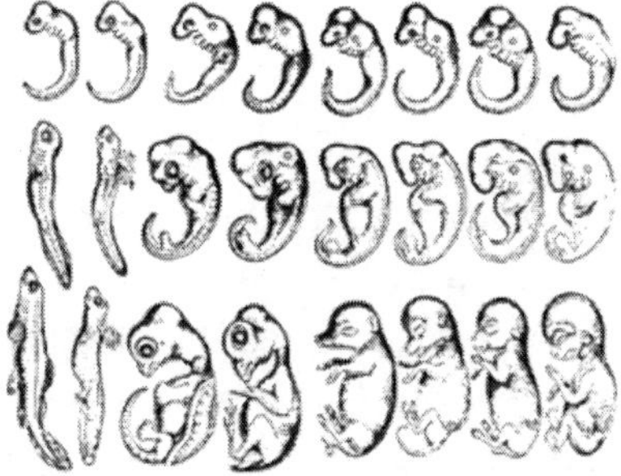

In the diagram we see, from left to right, fish, salamander, turtle, chicken, pig, cow, rabbit, and human embryos, in three equivalent stages of development.

We could cite several other evidences. For example, those of comparative anatomy, biochemical, geological, those of continental drift, vestigial structures, and so on. However, for our purposes, it seems unnecessary to go into so much detail. To conclude this point, Richard Dawkins briefly considers the solid foundation that the Theory of Evolution obtained through science, suggesting that the current evidence gives it a high degree of plausibility:

Millions of fossils are found exactly at the locations and depths calculated if evolution had occurred. A fossil that served as evidence against the theory of evolution has never been found: the discovery of a mammal embedded in rocks older than fish, for example, would be sufficient to refute evolutionism. The distribution patterns of animals and plants on continents and islands are exactly as expected if they had evolved from a common ancestor through a slow and gradual process. Patterns of similarity between animals and plants are exactly as expected if they were closely related to some and distantly related to others. The fact that the genetic code is the same in all creatures strongly suggests that we descended from a common ancestor. The evidence for evolution is so overwhelming that the only way to "save" creationist theory would be to argue that God deliberately planted enormous amounts of evidence to deceive us, making evolution just seem to have happened.

All the evidence available so far converges perfectly, indicating that organic evolution is not just a hypothesis, but a fact backed up scientifically by an overwhelmingly large amount of evidence. The problem now faced by contemporary evolutionists is not whether evolution occurs, but how it occurs.

Some evolutionary myths

Man, with his typical arrogance, almost always tries to close his eyes to his true nature. Always seeing itself as a "separate superspecies", he cannot admit that he has such a humble meaning — a mere means for the perpetuation of the species. This is probably because this truth does not inflate his vanity, does not magnify him before the world — and, therefore, tends to be put aside.

There are those who believe that man is the "goal", the "crown" of organic evolution. However, this is a tremendous misunderstanding of how life works. To begin with, the evolution of species has no fixed objective. The "goal" of evolution — if we can use that term — is anything that survives. Therefore, within ten million years, people will not be looking like aliens, all with extraordinary intelligence, gigantic heads, big black eyes, gray and slender bodies. There is simply no way to know what humans will be like in ten million years, as this will depend on the selective factors that are acting on the human species during that period. That's also why monkeys won't turn into humans if we wait long enough.

Many also think that man is the most evolved animal on Earth. The origin of such an illusion probably lies in our anthropocentric sense of importance. Man is not the measure of all things, and there's nothing special about it —

we're just a species like any other, struggling for survival. Nor is intellectual capacity that defines how evolved an animal is — our intellect is just an evolutionary tool, like our teeth. There is, therefore, no necessary tendency for the "intellectualization" of species over time.

The fact that the complexity of one animal is greater than that of another does not imply a greater degree of evolution. Some species may be more adapted to a given environment or have a greater degree of adaptability to different environments, but that does not mean, in any way, that this species is more "evolved". Man is more complex than bacteria, but he is as evolved as bacteria. In reality, there is no way to define the degree of evolution of any living being, since they have all been evolving for 3.5 billion years from the same common ancestor — bacteria, radishes, salmon, salamanders, cacti, elephants, humans, and everything else. Let us bear in mind that the fact that all other living beings coexist alongside man means that, like us, they are well adapted to the environment in which they live and, therefore, as a species, have nothing inferior to us.

Finally, we must undo one of the biggest myths: man did not descend from monkeys. That's a misunderstanding. Monkeys are monkeys; humans are humans. Both are just different species with the same degree of evolution. We are not an "improved" version of monkeys, and neither are they a "crude" version of man. In fact, monkeys are not our "primitive grandfathers", but something like our cousins. Both evolved divergently from a common ancestor that was neither monkey nor man, but a distinct species.

VI

OUR REPRESENTATION OF REALITY

"The world is my representation": this is a truth valid with reference to every living and knowing being, although man alone can bring it into reflective, abstract consciousness. If he really does so, philosophical discernment has dawned on him. It then becomes clear and certain to him that he does not know a sun and an earth, but only an eye that sees a sun, a hand that feels an earth; that the world around him is there only as representation, in other words, only in reference to another thing, namely that which represents, and this is himself.

— Arthur Schopenhauer

An extremely important point for understanding the place of man in this immense unknown called world is to have, first, a notion that is as crystalline as possible of the nature of the world in which we live, and of how we interact with it, so that we can understand ourselves within the general context, and not just as a small self-sufficient "miracle".

This, of course, is a rather confusing task, since such a distinction will never be strictly clear. We are faced with a paradox of incomprehension, which could be put in these terms: to understand oneself it is necessary to understand the world and, to understand the world, it is necessary to understand oneself. This makes the investigation, at first, confused, weakened by relativism. But later, as we advance in the inferences, in the intersection of information, some references and the force in our reasoning will be recovered. The rest, whatever gets lost along the way, the aborted ideas, the crippled theories, everything that was unable to survive on its own in the face of the facts — none of these interests us.

Therefore, if the goal is not to understand only the world or only man, we need to look not only within ourselves or only at the world around us, but to look especially at this fine line — and to do so with impartiality, with critical and sober eyes —, for only then will we discover the true distinction between the subjective and the objective, the internal and the external, the personal and the impersonal, the nature of man and the nature of the world.

Many people cherish the illusion that reality is as it is presented to us, as we perceive it, and that everything in it works as a whole because there is a "reason", repeating the old cliché that nothing happens by chance. They see the Universe as a great set of harmonious forces that interact in a purposefully exact way in order to allow this miracle — at the same time so magnificent and so fragile — called life to exist. It is believed that sunlight exists to warm the Earth and to allow us to see the beauty of flowers. It is believed that man's goal here is to be happy and to live in harmony with mother nature, and so on, in an endless series of fanciful explanations about the nature of life and the world. These ideas are particularly touching and pleasant, but unfortunately they find more support in our taste for poetry than in reason or evidence.

For example, "materialists" are often told that if the Earth's rotation were ten times higher or lower than the current, or if the Earth were more or less distant from the Sun, then life as we know it would be impossible. To which we respond: what's the problem with that? Where can one get the absurd idea that life must necessarily exist or, even more so, that it must exist as we know it? If Earth's conditions were inhospitable to life, it wouldn't have even arisen — just as it didn't appear on several other planets, such as Venus, Mercury, Saturn, Neptune, Jupiter, etc.

Explanations that try to make sense of random events *afterwards* are easy to debunk. For example, go to an open field, take a billiard ball in your hands and throw it. Then go to the blade of grass on which it fell and shout: "What a miracle! Of all the *millions* of blades of grass on which the ball could have fallen, it fell exactly on this one! How amazing! This can't simply be coincidental — there must be a special reason for this event to have happened!" At best, people around us will think that we're not doing very well in the head. The point is that the same applies to the existence of life. After everything has happened by chance over billions of years, we look back and say: "How amazing is the series of events that allowed life to exist! There must be a supernatural explanation for that!" It's the same logical error, but we don't laugh at this explanation, because the idea comforts us, since it places us as the objective of the world.

Thoughtlessly, many people imagine that life is the most important thing in the Universe, and that everything in it works in a similar way to life, that is, that everything revolves around us. For this reason, it is always common to see theories that try to explain the objective universe through analogies with the human subjective, without realizing any problem or incoherence in this regard.

Truly naive comparisons are made, such as that, among humans, there are legislators who make the laws that govern and regulate our behavior. Therefore, if the Universe also "follows" physical laws that allow life to exist, if it works in such an organized way, then it must have a "cosmic legislator" who created and maintains the harmony that permeates it. Thus, an analogy is drawn with the fact that there is a mind behind the "harmony of society" and it is concluded, from this, that if nature is similarly harmonious, then it must be controlled by some "supermind". Obviously, that supposed "supermind" would be God.

There is another common analogy, frequently used to support the intelligent design hypothesis. Proponents describe a carpenter and the entire process involved in creating a chair. Through this, they imagine demonstrating how it is necessary that, behind every creation, there must previously be a mind superior to the created entity. And so, starting with the analogy, they explain that to say that life did not have a creator would be as absurd as saying that such chair happened by chance, without a mind behind it. Therefore, there must be a "supermind" that designed and created life, because, otherwise, it would be inconceivable that we, who are much more complex than a chair, could exist. In this situation, the only "logical" way out would be to admit that everything was designed by a "carpenter of the Universe".

It is not difficult to see that such arguments always place life as something that incorporates the very essence of being. As if, for the Universe, life was something extremely important, as if it were the measure of all things, the essence and the ultimate point of existence. They are seductive arguments, but not to our brain, but to our ego, which loves to be soothed by anthropocentric delusions.

In the following pages, we intend to demonstrate that the attribution of human characteristics to the world always leads to necessarily false conclusions. That this attribution, in reality, is the result of a myopic anthropocentrism. As we shall see, most of the time, it is the confusion between objective reality and subjective reality that creates such misunderstandings.

To understand the error that exists in such analogies, we must first understand how we perceive reality. Thus, we need to outline what reality is separately from the human component, that is, the pure, uninterpreted reality that exists independently of us. To do so, we will use some examples that are easily understandable, and that make it quite clear how this mechanism responsible for the interaction between man and reality works.

First of all, we need to make it clear that man is definitely not capable of apprehending reality in and of itself, directly. What he does, in fact, is merely a *mental representation* of that reality through the senses and the intellect. We can use the example of colors to clarify this representation mechanism.

The visible spectrum, for us, ranges from violet — with a wavelength equal to 400 nanometers — to red — with 700 nanometers (a nanometer or *nm* is equivalent to one billionth of a meter, that is, 10^{-9} or 0.000,000,001 m). We see objects that are black, red, white, blue, yellow, etc. However, such objects are not really black, red, white, blue, and so on. What we see, in fact, is not the object, but the light that the object reflects. Black objects, for example, are those that absorb all the colors of the visible spectrum; white objects are those that reflect all the colors; red, blue, yellow, and green objects are those that absorb all the wavelengths, reflecting, respectively, only the red, blue, yellow, and green.

Normally, white light, which is the mixture of all colors — for example, sunlight or light from a lamp —, is used as the parameter to define the "real" color of objects. However, the fact is that no object has a color in itself, defined in advance. For example, if we illuminate a white object with a red light, it will be perceived by our vision as a red object. On the other hand, if we illuminate a red object with a blue light, in our eyes it will be black, since it will be absorbing all the light radiation that reaches it in the form of blue light. Thus, if the light released by the Sun and our lighting devices were just red, we would be used to the idea that all white objects actually "are" red. Of course, in our case, we use white light as a reference only because our species evolved a specialized vision to capture it, since it is very rich in information and is also the most abundant in our environment.

Our body, when it receives a stimulus from the environment in the form of light, physiologically translates the external stimuli as visual sensations, giving us the sensation of green, black, white, and so on. Our visual system captures information from the external environment, which arrives in the form of luminous energy, to construct, in the form of mental images, a representation of what reality is like. Our brain unconsciously processes and translates the information contained in the light, and then presents the finished result to our consciousness, without us understanding anything of what the machinery of our brain is doing below the level of our consciousness. The result of this is that we have the false impression that green objects are inherently green, and that red objects are inherently red — that is, our perception of reality, in addition to being incomplete, is also, in a certain way, misleading, because much of the process of sensory perception occurs behind the curtains of consciousness, to which we have no access.

From this perspective, we could ask some additional questions: why can't we see the ultraviolet frequency? Why do our ears only pick up a certain range of sound waves — between 20 and 20,000 Hz? Where do the "ghost voices" that torment mentally ill individuals come from? Why do train tracks seem to converge, even though we know that they are parallel to each other? Why, when detected by our olfactory system, hydrogen sulfide — which is released by decomposing food — is represented as an unpleasant sensation, that of a foul smell?

With this, we better understand that our sensory perceptions are not reality itself, but a partial and indirect representation of reality constructed by our brains. In other words, green, red, and blue are not real things, they have no existence of their own. Colors only exist for our consciousness, they are just the language into which the area of our brains responsible for vision translates reality, which speaks in "encrypted language", that is, it speaks in the language of "wavelengths". The sense of sight works, so to speak, like a biological transducer with certain conversion programs: "waves from 400 to 430 nanometers, translate to violet", "waves from 500 to 570 nanometers, translate to blue", and so on.

Regarding the way we perceive and interpret the world, psychobiologist Victor S. Johnson made an interesting comment:

[Our consciousness is a virtual reality. It evolved to impose a specific interpretation of the energies and materials that are around us. Nothing in the Universe is red or green in and of itself. What exist are electromagnetic waves of certain frequencies that are picked up by our eyes and interpreted to facilitate identification. Thus, objects that emit certain waves are called red and others, with hardly any smaller waves, are called green, just to facilitate identification. Over time, evolution has allowed us to adapt our emotions to what is beneficial to us. Likewise, the loss of a partner is sad, sugar (which provides energy) is tasty, and sex (which perpetuates the species) is pleasurable. There are no colors, smells, tastes, or emotions without a conscious brain. The world of our consciousness is a great illusion.]

In this way, it is understood that everything that exists for our consciousness, in reality is nowhere but in consciousness itself. The images we see are not the thing-in-itself — we don't see the real entity. "Seeing" is a mental phenomenon, an adapted translation, not an external reality. In other words, colors don't exist, they just *happen* in our minds. At first, this may sound strange, but if we ask another question, the idea will become clearer: where is the "running" when we're not running? Nowhere, because running is an action, an activity, it is the phenomenon of "running". Thus, running is not an object, but the action of an object. Likewise, colors, sounds, smells, and sensations in general are just mental phenomena, "brain acts", so to speak.

Asking where our consciousness is would be as erroneous as asking where is the image of a television. Both have no objective existence, but only phenomenal, subjective — they exist as the final result of a process carried out by electronic components, in the case of televisions, or by neural components, in the case of our brains.

Thus, everything presented to us by the senses is not something external, but internal — it is part of consciousness itself. When, for example, we observe an apple, this image isn't really outside our heads. It certainly seems external, it seems objective, but it's just an internal and subjective representation that our own brain creates based on the data it received from reality. Our sensory apparatus responsible for vision plays the role of a "mediator" between the light that the apple reflected and its image in our consciousness.

In this sense, if we think about it, we will notice that even what we see is not really the present, but the past. Light has to travel a distance until it reaches our eyes, to be processed by our sensory apparatus, and presented to the consciousness as an image — so what we see isn't exactly the present. Of course, for all intents and purposes, this detail is not very relevant, since the speed with which all of this occurs is almost the same as instantaneous. However, this temporal discrepancy becomes much more accentuated when we remember the stars — their light can take millions and millions of years to reach our eyes, and when this occurs, the star may not even exist anymore.

At this point, sometimes we get a bit confused, because we might have imagined that we could see something real or that our subjective "self" existed objectively — and wasn't just "happening". However, the fact is that our "I", our consciousness of the world and of ourselves, exists only in the form of a cloud of electrical impulses from a nervous system. The sensory world of colors, sounds, smells, textures, and flavors in which we live and that we think exists independently of us is, in fact, internal, mental, totally subjective. Everything we know, think, see, feel is just in our brain, and nowhere else.

That's why, with great propriety, we can call all feelings and sensations "fictions". It may seem aggressive and extremist, but it's not. All feelings and sensations are phenomena that have no existence of their own. They are merely classifications of mental states that, in turn, are a reflection of our brain physiology. In other words, all our feelings and sensations are just subjective mental fictions. Love does not exist independently of man, nor does vanity, pride, hatred, sadness, pleasure, suffering, sweet or sour. The so-called "time dimensions", as we conceive them, do not exist either: our past is not stored in a corner of the Universe — it only exists because we have memory and the future only exists because we have imagination. All of these are subjective realities that only exist in the context of the human body, all created by our minds, just like colors. Let us remember Schopenhauer's words: *The world is my representation.*

Now we have to take such conclusions one step further. Just as objects that reflect green light appear inherently green because of the way our minds work, life also seems to have inherent value. It seems to us that life is the most important thing in the Universe. But, of course, this is not due to the fact that we have a cosmic importance, nor to the fact that such objects are actually green.

This happens only because we are life itself and, thus, we are unable to see reality in any other way than through it. We must bear in mind that all the values and meanings that we attribute to the Universe do not belong to it, but derive from a point of view that is not impartial — the point of view of a living being with biological needs, which were forged by its evolutionary history. We are, therefore, naturally biased.

In fact, it is a fruitless task for the human mind to try to conceive what reality itself would be, in an impersonal way. Attempting it only leads us to the famous and frustrating conclusion: man is not capable of jumping over his own shadow — we cannot escape our human condition. It is precisely this inescapable partiality that gives rise to the illusion that the Universe revolves around life, when in reality life works like the rest of the Universe. Undoubtedly, life is not the measure of all things — however, it measures them as if it were. And since we are life, this measurement seems to us to be reality itself, when in fact it is just a subjective representation of it, which is the only way we have of conceiving it.

Looking at this idea from an evolutionary perspective, let's check James Alcock's interesting words:

Our brain and nervous system have evolved over millions of years. It's important to realize that natural selection doesn't select directly according to reason or truth, it selects according to reproductive success. Nothing in our brain apparatus places a special value on truth. Imagine a rabbit in tall grass, and give it a grain of conscious and logical intellect for a moment. He hears a gentle noise in the grass, and having learned in the past that this is eventually the sign of a hungry fox, the rabbit wonders if it's a fox this time or if a breath of air caused the noise. He waits for more conclusive evidence. Although motivated by the search for the truth, this rabbit doesn't survive for long. Compare this deceased rabbit to another, which responds to noise with a strong reaction from the autonomic nervous system and flees as soon as possible. This one has a better chance of surviving and reproducing. Therefore, seeking the truth does not always favor survival, and running away based on an erroneous belief is not always bad.

It should be noted that all the programing of the human body did not have its value defined by its veracity, logic, or coherence. Its value was defined solely by its efficiency, by its capacity to guarantee survival and reproduction. Originally, nothing in us is necessarily related to truth. We did not evolve so that our senses or intellect would necessarily apprehend reality in a more or less accurate way. Thus, in a nutshell, we can say that the body's "criterion of truth" is survival. If we could "ask" our DNA "what is good?", it would promptly reply: "good is everything that survives, and that is capable of reproducing". To the question "what's bad?", it would answer: "bad is everything that does not survive, everything that is contrary to the perpetuation of life".

As we can see, the fundamental purpose of life is merely to guarantee survival, to guarantee its own perpetuation — everything else being dispensable. It's hard for us to think that we are just that, ephemeral pieces of flesh destined to extinction and oblivion. This understanding comes to us as a corrosive reality, as a heavy blow against our pride and our sense of importance. From this perspective, what, in fact, are we? Robert Wallace presents us with an answer:

[Genetic guardians? Temporary chromosome accommodations? Slaves to tiny coiled molecules that operate us by remote control? Heavy robots, full of ration-

alizations, explanations, superstitions, and excuses, but blindly following the Reproductive Imperative? What about the fact that we are learning to play classical guitar? That we are we interested in tap dancing and can start taking lessons right away? Of being orderly and responsible, and having unusually good jobs? What if we read Camus and didn't pronounce the "s" in his name? If we have good friends, really good ones? Of being great people and our parents being proud of us? What to say about all this? Do chromosomes make us do that? "No", comes the mountain's answer, "but they don't mind you doing it" — as long as it doesn't interfere with their reproduction. Being a splendid person can even help you find a partner more easily and leave even more genes behind. "Don't they care what I do?" You scream. "Stupid coiled molecules that don't care? This one is really good! Man, you're crazy!" But it's even worse than that. The molecules aren't even stupid. They're simply indifferent. They don't even know they exist.]

At first, this seems a bit radical to us, as it hurts our poetic sensitivities, and strips our dreams and ideals of any real importance. However, as we have seen, the reasons for making such statements are simple and solid: those who do not act according to such rules simply disappear from the Earth within a generation, as they die without leaving any descendants, and those who worried about surviving and reproducing will take the place of those who did not give any importance to this. In other words, if we are here, this happened because we are the children of human beings who tend to act as good reproducers — not because this is good or natural, but because those who don't do it disappear. This is how nature selects the fittest: measuring their value by their ability to survive and reproduce, without taking anything else into consideration. Surely that's why we have this irrational and passionate attachment to life — because those who didn't have it didn't fight to preserve it and, in this way, disappeared without leaving any descendants. The same can be said about our fear of death.

With that, we realize one more thing: that our representation of reality has a specific objective — to promote survival. Since we are living beings, this already implies a perspective that is equivalent to a position in relation to reality, a position that weighs all things in the scale of utility for life. For example, food seems to be something of utmost importance. However, it is made up of clumps of atoms, just like anything else. A pile of rubble or a pile of food are also made of matter. However, for us, food is not just a "clump of matter", because it is from food that we draw energy to survive. For this reason, in our eyes, it presents itself as something important, as something distinct from matter that does not serve as food. However, if we were to feed on some other type of substance — say, on pebbles —, then we would look at all the organic compounds that serve as food with the same indifference with which we look at pebbles on the street, as they would not have any fundamental use for us.

It is precisely the fact that life has been shaped by the imperatives of survival and reproduction that makes us victims of the illusion that everything revolves around us. For life, the important thing is just life itself. But, for the Universe as a whole, life is not important. However, life is not impartial. Quite the contrary, it is endowed with an almost megalomaniacal egocentrism, weighing the value of things and interpreting the world always according to itself.

Now it's certainly easy to understand why putrefying food smells bad. Not because the H_2S molecule it releases is "inherently fetid", but because our senses were shaped within a survival-oriented system, and thus interpret reality according to those biological guidelines, which were programmed by evolution in our brain circuits.

As a result, it is obvious that our body will interpret and translate reality in terms of utility for survival. Thus, our body tells us, through an unpleasant sensation, that hydrogen sulfide gas is a sign of danger, since it is released by decomposing food, which would be toxic if ingested. But, on the other hand, we can suppose that the smell of carrion is something "intoxicating" to a vulture, since it was in this type of food that its organism — that is, its DNA — evolutionarily specialized.

Taking into account everything we saw above, we are able to understand something more. We can say that, *a priori*, there are no objective truths — let alone any subjective truths. Of course, this means that truths don't exist by themselves, independent of us, like humanly intelligible ideas hanging over our heads — until a brain captures them in some insight.

Independent of us there are only facts, phenomena, being, effectiveness. Thus, it is the interpretation of facts and reality — in terms that are understandable to the human mind — that is commonly given the name "truth", which, however, is only a human perception, and not truth itself, understood as objective reality. Therefore, no one has ever found or will find any truth. What we do is only an intellectual interpretation of the facts, and when the judgments that emerge from this interpretation can be verified and correspond to reality, we call those judgments "true" or "truths". In this sense, by a lie (intentional) or error (ignorance) we would understand some proposition that has no correspondence in reality.

Of course, the notion of true as a judgment that corresponds to reality, like the various other characteristics of human subjectivity, is something that exists only in our minds. "Truths" could only be classified as objective in the strict sense that they refer to the objective world. However, all of them are entirely contained in the subjective world created by our brains, never in the objective reality outside our minds.

The most common objection to this idea is that truth exists independently of us, just waiting to be discovered. But since when truth hides itself? Perhaps since the we realized our limitations and, trying to justify our ignorance, blamed reality. If, in this case, the word "truth" is equivalent to *reality* and the word "discovery" means *interpreted* or *translated*, then calling it an objection makes no sense. However, taken at face value, this objection is reminiscent of Plato, since it presupposes the independent existence of some kind of "world of ideas" tailored to humans, which is absurd.

Friedrich Nietzsche was correct in stating that *there are no moral phenomena, but only a moral interpretation of phenomena*. In this context, we could also say, with the same certainty, that there are no mathematical phenomena, but only a mathematical interpretation of phenomena. Undoubtedly, it is a mistake to think that reality speaks in "human language". None of reality is apprehended in itself, directly, but only through indirect associations and inferences, of intellectual nature. What we are capable of conceiving are merely descriptions, theoretical models, and representative formulas of how reality apparently works.

Therefore, we can say that the proposition "1+1=2" is just a numerical representation of reality, not an "indisputable truth", as many say. It expresses an apparently irrefutable idea because we obviously invented mathematics in accordance with the facts, and thus it is quite difficult to imagine a situation in which this proposition would be false.

For example, to quantify oranges, we take them as a unit reference and then, by counting, we intellectually convert an objective reality into a numerical abstraction, using mathematical symbols to construct expressions that represent a real thing, which behaves according to objective laws. For this reason, we can conclude that all the logical rules that guide mathematical operations are not only intended to maintain the internal coherence of the reasoning, but mainly to keep them in correspondence with the real world, since it would not make sense to invent some strange mathematics that follows internal rules that, although coherent, have no correspondence in reality, since such mathematics would be something profoundly useless. To challenge the proposition "1+1=2", therefore, is not simply to challenge mathematics, but what it represents, that is, nature itself, the functioning of our reality.

Likewise, water doesn't boil at exactly one hundred degrees Celsius at sea level — it boils when its molecules receive enough energy to volatilize. It was humans who invented the thermometric scale that goes from zero to one hundred, with the value "100" corresponding to the temperature that causes water to boil and with the value "zero" linked to the temperature at which it melts — this at sea level — and then started to use this as a reference, by convention. Likewise, when in free fall, the acceleration of bodies under the action of Earth's gravity does not "obey" the formula 9.8 m/s^2. Gravity is just a consequence of the properties of matter. But humanity, with its thirst to rationalize everything, devised an abstract formula that represents its effects mathematically. The meter, the kilo, the liter, the second, the light-year, etc. — all of these are inventions.

In science, abstraction has a very important character, since it seeks to predict the behavior of a reality that is objective. For example, it tries, through controlled experiments, to infer laws inherent to nature that are fixed and constant. Because of this fixity, it is possible to formulate general theories, that is, global explanations capable of encompassing a whole variety of apparently different natural facts, but which experience can demonstrate to be subject to the same laws and principles.

In the production of this type of knowledge, the notions of deduction and induction are essential. *Deduction* is a simple form of reasoning that goes from the general (premise) to the specific (conclusion). For example: *every atheist is boring; Charles Chaplin was an atheist; therefore, Charles Chaplin was boring* — which reminds us that not all logical reasoning is necessarily true, that is, consistent with the facts. *Induction*, on the other hand, starts from specific cases to general rules, and consists of generalizations and abstractions made statistically reliable by the uniformity of experimental results. For example, we can arrive at the general conclusion that all metals expand when heated by heating all metals over and over again and finding that they always expand. The concepts of natural laws, chemical reactions, instincts, conditioned reflexes, etc., involve both notions: they are constructed inductively, but can be used deductively to investigate specific cases.

Combined with controlled experimentation, deduction and induction — although the latter is implicated in one of the greatest conceptual problems in science — make it possible for us to formulate general rules on a ground that is sufficiently solid to allow the construction of a reliable knowledge, capable of extending itself to detailed predictions. These notions were extremely important for scientific knowledge to acquire the magnitude it currently has.

As it turns out, much of science is based on generalizations. They enable, for example, a more far-reaching vision of the future — Genetics, Meteorology, Astronomy — and about the past — Geology, Archaeology, and Paleontology. Furthermore, Physics and Chemistry are also based on abstractions; Medicine is based on the generic model of a human being. However, we should never forget that all human knowledge is nothing more than an intellectual representation of reality. Knowledge is an inference that we construct *from* reality based on experience. Thus, in addition to the fact that any theory is always subject to error, reality always takes precedence over ideas — in such a way that, if a theory and reality come into conflict, reality wins.

Therefore, should an individual appear telling us that he can logically demonstrate that "1+1=3", perhaps by some mathematical sophism this may even be possible, but we certainly could not attribute greater value to mathematical abstraction than to reality itself, because, when put into practice, we see that such a proposition does not represent any reality. An orange plus an orange, no matter how mathematically demonstrated otherwise, are two oranges. The proposition will be true if and only if it is describing how reality works. Mathematics also bows to the actual world, since it is nothing more than its numerical representation.

In short, we use our rationality to translate reality into ideas, and then we represent them by symbols — such as the words written on this paper — which, by convention, are associated with that certain idea. As we know, the capacity to conceive abstract ideas is only a peculiarity of human nature. Thus, even in the most "objective" truth, there is still much of the subjective, and the claim that truths have an independent existence can be easily dismissed as a humanization of reality.

As for our conventional systems of symbolic representation — such as mathematics and alphabetical language —, on the one hand, they allow us to record and communicate information in a very dynamic way, but, on the other, they do not seem to be very functional on daily life without incorporating elements that end up undermining its objectivity — and the domain of practical life is something that is definitely not committed to truth.

Language carries a whole series of words considered antonyms which are nothing more than subtle gradations of a continuum. For example, hot and cold are apparently antagonistic sensations. In reality, they only exist in relation to body temperature that we have to keep constant in order for our physiology to remain in order. Similarly, several false dichotomies inhabit our vocabulary that language incorporates as objective, when, in fact, they're a mere reflection of our anthropocentrism.

It's really nothing new to say that we project into the objective world the characteristics and peculiarities that only relate to life. Organic and inorganic, low and high, positive and negative, real and imaginary, logical and illogical, rigid and flexible, rational and irrational, good and bad, rough and smooth, light and heavy, alive and dead — all of these are false dichotomies. It's no wonder that Nietzsche said: *I am afraid we are not getting rid of God because we still believe in grammar.* The unconscious detachment that we suffer from objectivity by using a language addicted to an anthropocentrism that seems completely natural to us — that's just the tip of the iceberg. There are numerous, perhaps innumerable ways in which we delude ourselves without realizing it.

And here we come to another very important point, which may clarify some much-debated issues. Because of the distinction we draw between the objective world and human subjectivity, we can say that many questions considered profound seem completely nonsensical when viewed from the present perspective. For example, we can say, without hesitation, that it makes no sense to ask what is the "raison d'être" of existence, of physical laws, or of life, because asking "why" does life exist would be like asking why the Earth's gravity "wants" objects to fall or what is the personality of a stone — in other words, they are inquiries that presuppose a similarity between objectivity and subjectivity that doesn't really exist. This kind of poorly worded question is called *fallacy of presupposition* or *complex question fallacy*. Evidently, there cannot be a "reason for being" for the world itself because reason is a human characteristic, not a characteristic of the world — it is not something that is embedded in reality and, therefore, it makes no sense to think that reason is something that governs it.

Investigating questions at the level of reality is something very different and requires greater theoretical distancing. Firstly, it is necessary to reduce the notion of intentionality proper to life to that which is proper to reality — none. Our why-questions do not apply to the world, since they were created by us with assumptions that are incompatible with this type of investigation. "Why are there beings instead of nothing?" is a very different question from "why did they paint this house blue?". Interrogating the being itself directly using human reason does not lead us to any conclusion — we cannot obtain information from that. The being does not speak: we are the ones who speak for it with our interpretations, which always revolve around descriptions that are answers to questions that begin with *how*. How do objects fall? How is blue blue? How does metal fuse? How does thinking occur? How do bodies interact? This type of questioning leads us to situations in which the being presents evidence that can be investigated, since we will be turning our eyes to the phenomena of being. That is our way of understanding the world.

Since we are unable to apprehend naked and pure reality as a thing-in-itself, we have to resort to experimentation, and the use of experience involves practically unavoidable problems, which distance us a lot from the ideal of knowledge. Every understanding implies an interpretation, which is always a partial approximation made by the subject in relation to the object to be known. This impossibly neutral interpretation involves many specific variables — from methodological to physiological — which determine our exact way of interacting with the world. And many of these variables are not even understood — they actually elude us, making object and observer inextricable, inserted in an obscure relationship. The margin for error, of course, is immense, since our perception only allows us something like poking the "black box" of the being with a stick to see what happens. In this situation, it seems fatal that all knowledge will necessarily entail distortions and falsifications at some level.

As if that were not enough, we also have no guarantees of the veracity of the assumptions on which we build our knowledge, of what we admit about the characteristics of objective reality — that is, of the effective existence of an independent objectivity, with properties that, although not fully determinable, remain constant in their forms and procedures. Who guarantees the veracity of these foundations, of these premises? Nobody. Only having indirect means of investigating the world, we have no reliable references on which to establish solid notions of what objectivity is — nor the means of obtaining them. Our knowledge is nothing more than an elaborate assumption. Thus, if a theoretical brick is placed in the wrong place, if a premise that we use to interpret the facts is false, this will compromise the entire edifice of knowledge. That is why those who question the veracity of the fundamental premises feel an enormous weight on their shoulders.

This issue does not allow definitive solutions, but neither is it impenetrable. We deduce particular facts based on how objectivity works and we induce how objectivity works through the observation of the facts. This induction, in this case, refers to the foundations of material reality, creating a general rule that is a necessary and universal law, such as the law of Action and Reaction, for example, which is presented in these terms: *For every action, there is an equal and opposite reaction.* This means that if we push a wall, the wall will push us with the same force, in the opposite direction. To illustrate, let's imagine an iron cube on a table. It is being attracted by the Earth's gravity, thus exerting a force on the table — that would be the action. The table's reaction would be to apply a force equal and in the opposite direction to that of the cube. As the forces cancel out, it stays where it is. In another case, when a stone is thrown against a window, the bodies interact, exchange forces, and there is a physical result: the window breaks. The force exerted by the stone, in this case, exceeded the resistance of the glass structure to deformation. The reaction, here, will not nullify the forces — which would occur if the glass were strong enough —, it will only slow down the stone.

Action and reaction? Maybe that's an illusion. Is there really a direct relationship? It may be that, between action and reaction, there are imperceptible stages of equally necessary nature, but we only perceive the final result and, through temporal contiguity and experimental uniformity, we establish that there is a direct connection between action and reaction. However, it could be that the thrown stone, upon contact with the glass, would react in random directions; it could happen that the stone would stay stationary, stuck to the window, and a reaction would occur in 35.91 seconds, at an angle of 90 degrees; it could happen that the reaction would be a force ten times greater than that applied by the stone. That's not impossible, we've just never observed objects behaving in such a way. Every time we threw a rock against a window, the result was the same — if the result was always, let's say, a random little dance and then its melting, and if that phenomenon somehow applied to the entire natural world, that would also be a law. The important thing is that, until now, we have been able to observe that action-reaction phenomena occur with universal regularity and constancy, and that it applies to the way of being of the entire known reality. From this, the law of Action and Reaction was inductively formulated and, since it describes a universal constant, it is considered a natural law.

At least we were astute when we gave our investigations a predominantly experimental character, since reason, considered in isolation, has its hands tied on these issues. We were able to see that our only way of linking judgments to reality is pragmatic: we assume that, if the conclusions inferred by experimentation are consistent and constant, if they work, if they are in accordance with the body of knowledge acquired — or if they complement or exceed it —, then they are true. It is provisional knowledge, of course, like any knowledge. However, being human, it's the best we can do.

When we admit such limitations, to remain coherent, we have to limit our investigations to what is most probable, abandoning daydreams about impartial, absolute, and pure knowledge. Even so, the fact that any knowledge about reality must rest on assumptions that can be challenged is not an objection — if our knowledge lacked assumptions, it would be a dogma, it would have no prospects, it would have neither a starting point nor a destination, it would be doomed to stagnation. The fear that our knowledge may be disproven in the future and labeled as retrograde is what makes this idea seem so disturbing. Yet we should not have this fear, for what sense is there in lamenting the fact that a theory may succumb to the very thing we seek to eradicate — error?

It should already be quite clear that we, in fact, do not explain reality, but merely describe how it works. Human beings have reason only as an intellectual faculty that allows them to understand how existence works, and that's all: here, the temptation to ask *why* reality works in this particular way would already be the expression of our incurable anthropocentrism trying to inject reason into existence. For example, Isaac Newton's gravitational constant says that bodies attract each other in the direct proportion to the product of their masses and in the inverse proportion to the square of the distance between them — that's a description, not an explanation. Why do bodies attract each other in the direct proportion of the product of their masses and not in the direct proportion of the *sum* of their masses? Nobody can explain why. Although it's entirely possible to imagine that it could be so, the fact is that it simply isn't. Again, we see that the error would lie in the fact that we are directly interrogating the being, which is not even a bit chatty. Since we never found changes in natural laws so that we could collect data from this type of event to formulate a theory, we wouldn't even know where to start, and for a good reason: because, at first, this question is wrong in its assumptions, making the investigation useless.

In this sense, David Hume clearly demonstrates that no knowledge of reality could be inferred *a priori* from pure reason, since our notions of how reality works necessarily pass through experience, a fundamental condition of human knowledge:

> *But to convince us that all the laws of nature, and all the operations of bodies without exception, are known only by experience, the following reflections may, perhaps, suffice. Were any object presented to us, and were we required to pronounce concerning the effect, which will result from it, without consulting past observation, after what manner, I beseech you, must the mind proceed in this operation? It must invent or imagine some event, which it ascribes to the object as its effect, and it is plain that this invention must be entirely arbitrary. The mind can never possibly find the effect in the supposed cause, by the most accurate scrutiny and examination. For the effect is totally different from the cause, and consequently can never be discovered in it. Motion in the second billiard ball is a quite distinct event from the motion in the first, nor is there anything in the one to suggest the smallest hint of the other. A stone or piece of metal raised into the air, and left without any support, immediately falls: but to consider the matter a priori, is there anything we discover in this situation which can beget the idea of a downward, rather than an upward, or any other motion, in the stone or metal? (...) In a word, then, every effect is a distinct event from its cause. It could not, therefore, be discovered in the cause, and the first invention or conception of it, a priori, must be entirely arbitrary. And even after it is suggested, the conjunction of it with the cause must appear equally arbitrary, since there are always many other effects, which, to reason, must seem fully as consistent and natural. In vain, therefore, should we pretend to determine any single event, or infer any cause or effect, without the assistance of observation and experience.*

Thus, doubly undetermined, our view of the world is merely mental. It consists of abstract ideas and notions — false or true — inferred from reality.

Within what we call reality, "rational" is what our intellectual apparatus can concatenate into logically consistent terms. In the scientific model, because certain events follow a certain operating pattern that we have already been able to understand, we label our notions about such events as rational. "Plastic melts with heat" is a rational notion. As we see, reason did not determine reality, but only our understanding of reality.

The constant perspective errors in which reason is presented as something objective are probably due to our incompetence in discerning, through intuition alone, what is the true distinction between the objective and the subjective. But the fact is that reality is not subject to reason — we are the ones who employ reason in an attempt to understand reality. Therefore, the being has no reason, we have reason. This implies that the world, in its essence, is irrational and meaningless — if we search for a humanized essence in it, of course.

As far as we know, the essence of all things is their own existence. Being, by itself, carries no reason, value, or meaning embedded at its core — so neither do our lives. Apart from itself, life cannot be recognized as something important, nor necessary. Being here is a purely contingent fact, so that, if we are not looking from the human perspective — that is, pouring our judgments into reality —, nothing can differentiate a rock rolling down the mountain or a life being born. For the impersonal universe, external to us, to our subjective reality, life is indistinguishable from a clump of meaningless matter. To be here, alive and thinking, is something totally void of any objective significance.

Apart from that, we can do whatever we want, decorate our existence with whatever clothing we prefer. We can say that life is everything; we can say that life is nothing; that it is a blessing with thorns or without thorns; that it is a complete or incomplete curse; we can invent rules to define and judge other beings; we can pester others with theories about how we should behave and what we should believe, etc.; we can shout our opinions or remain silent. None of this will arouse the interest of atoms. As humans, the essential nonsense consists in believing whatever we invent — and pretending that reality was on vacation when we decreed the absolute truth.

Obviously, from afar we can already hear the whining voices rising up with their reproaches, mechanically reciting pompous clichés that exalt the value of life. But the fact is that the speech doesn't really matter: they're useless words. And if they're not hypocritical, then they're naive, because no one is claiming that life is good or bad, or that it's not worth living, but just that being alive, universally, doesn't mean anything.

Our emergence was a fortuitous event in a universe governed by impersonal laws, without a human background, whose innards work like cogs of an impassive machine. If the matter that makes up our bodies, instead of being organized as living beings, were floating through space in the form of dust, that wouldn't make any difference — to whom could it make any difference, if life wouldn't even exist? The inanimate matter floating in the void of space doesn't care about us. To it, it doesn't matter if we're happy or sad, whether we have children or not, whether we die young or old, and it doesn't matter if the Earth explodes into a billion pieces and life is extinguished. The Universe is indifferent to all of this because, being impersonal, it has no objectives.

The only distinction between inanimate matter and living matter is the way in which it is organized. Life happened and remains a material process that has self-sustaining and self-replicating characteristics. Death, from this point of view, represents only the rupture, the end of this process, as an equation that loses its balance, for whatever reason. The matter in our bodies, then, begins to be organized in another way — what we consider "being dead" and, after a while, "turning to compost". Therefore, death is nothing, for life is also nothing to grant it any status.

From this perspective, it is clear that we cannot consider life as something that exists objectively, since it is nothing more than a categorization that we made of a specific state of organization of matter. Life doesn't exist, it's just happening — and, in and of itself, it has no value, no reason, no meaning.

After this extensive digression, we must return to the problem that led us to these reflections and investigations. What we were trying to demonstrate was why the analogies between the human laws and the laws of the Universe were erroneous.

The error, of course, consists in the implicit admission that the nature of life and the nature of the Universe are analogous. Since life is inherently self-centered, using subjective intuition as a method of investigating the objective world frequently leads to this type of misunderstanding, making it seem that objective reality is based on the same foundations as our subjective reality.

When we understand that the mysterious transcendental world, in fact, is born from the projection of our subjective characteristics into the external environment, the origin of the misconception from which all the metaphysical speculations about a "moral world order" and about all the personal gods — who seem to have been made on demand for human needs — becomes almost transparent. Such deities are undoubtedly reflections of our anthropocentrism. Xenophanes, who was aware of this phenomenon, stated with some irony that *If cattle and horses, or lions, had hands, or were able to draw with their feet and produce the works which men do, horses would draw the forms of gods like horses, and cattle like cattle, and they would make the gods' bodies the same shape as their own.* They would give the Sermon on the Pasture, who knows? Blessed be the ruminants...

From this perspective, we can conclude that deities in general — personal gods, legislative gods, carpenter gods, etc. — are nothing more than reflections of a hypertrophied ego, but with a short sight. The same error can also be found in pantheism and similar when deifying the Universe, transforming into "God's will" the set of physical laws that would be "conspiring harmoniously" for our existence as living beings. Regarding this characteristic of the human mind, our innate tendency to anthropomorphize reality, Freud says that:

> *The humanization of nature is derived from the need to put an end to man's perplexity and helplessness in the face of its dreaded forces, to get into a relation with them and finally to influence them. (...) Primitive man has no choice, he has no other way of thinking. It is natural to him, something innate, as it were, to project his existence outwards into the world and to regard every event which he observes as the manifestation of beings who at bottom are like himself.*

The extremely anthropocentric explanations of human beings can be understood as a consequence of their first efforts to explain the world, but, at the same time, without having any kind of preparation for it. Their misunderstanding of the world and of themselves end up leading to a knowledge that confuses both spheres, resulting in a worldview based and centered on man, not on the world. Perhaps that is why practically all civilizations, in their explanations about the world, invoked chimeric answers, filled with deities and based on supernatural notions that always focus on the human perspective. In this state of ignorance about reality and life, this type of phenomenon, this "innocent falsification" of the world, may be considered, in a certain way, as natural in us, given the natural egocentrism of life.

But what about the also universal notion of a dualistic world and of the belief in a *post-mortem* existence? What kind of explanation could there be for the existence of belief in this type of illusion? They're certainly appealing ideas, and that explains why they're so popular. But we must, in addition, find the cause, the reason they arose independently in so many civilizations. Since our mind is prone to polarized thinking — pleasure and pain, real and false, body and soul, etc. —, Nietzsche explains, in a very ingenious way, that such beliefs probably had a strong influence from the misunderstanding of dreams:

> *In the dream, mankind, in epochs of crude primitive civilization, thought they were introduced to a second, substantial world: here we have the source of all metaphysic. Without the dream, men would never have been incited to an analysis of the world. Even the distinction between soul and body is wholly due to the primitive conception of the dream, as also the hypothesis of the embodied soul, whence the development of all superstition, and also, probably, the belief in god. "The dead still live: for they appear to the living in dreams". So reasoned mankind at one time, and through many thousands of years.*

Undoubtedly, such misconceptions follow the same general rule that we have been stating: we always tend to interpret the objective world according to our subjective. Ideas of conscious deities, of physical laws with objectives, of a moral world order, of transcendental realities, etc., are really just projections of the characteristics of life in the interpretation of objective reality, which has no commitment to life in its essential functioning — because the Universe, as we have seen, presents no evidence of a governing mind, but rather a complete impersonality, which is completely indifferent to the existence or non-existence of life.

This erroneous interpretation, due to its partiality, invariably leads us to that exalted anthropocentrism that makes us think that life is some kind of precious stone embedded in the forehead of the cosmos — an illusion that gives us a feeling of an importance that really we don't have. Of course, in any case, it is an undeniable fact that they are truly seductive ideas, given the thirst that everyone has to possess eternal, real, objective importance — and beliefs of this kind are perfectly compatible with the satisfaction of human vanities.

Religiosity, from this perspective, is nothing more than an expression, a facet of our anthropocentrism, since, in the end, every deity is nothing more than man looking at himself in the mirror of his beliefs. Thus, clearer than the day, is the fact that, in everything that man does, creates, believes, and sees, there hides the reflection of his own being — of his inescapable humanity.

VII

ON THE FOUNDATION OF MORALITY

Let us consider how naive it is to say: "a man should be like this or that!" Reality shows us an enchanting wealth of types, an abundant profusion of play and changes of form — and a miserable servant of a moralist comments: "No! Man should be different". This pedantic saint even knows what a man should be like: he paints his portrait on the wall and says: here's the man!

— Friedrich Nietzsche

In the field of morality, atheism is typically accused of immorality; theism, on the other hand, is constantly accused of dogmatism. Morality is certainly a problematic area, because there is no way to demonstrate or rationally verify the validity of the proposed ideas. Moral theories don't talk very well with each other. Therefore, if certain fundamental premises are not admitted, if we are not in agreement on some basic points — such as the origin and nature of moral values —, then any discussion on the subject is fatally reduced to a sterile and useless digression.

However, our intention here isn't to present solutions to moral dilemmas. We'll only try to outline the human foundations of morality, to understand what exactly morality *is*, and what is its function, so that we can think more clearly about such subjects. The best effort will be made to avoid "coloring" the study with personal preferences. We will not attempt to defend or embellish any moral values, emphasizing any specific point of view over another. The only emphasis will be on objectivity. Therefore, there is no room here for sensitive ethical concerns regarding the potentially pernicious consequences of knowledge, nor about its possible benign consequences. We are only interested in its veracity, its consistency — the rest being up to what each individual deems appropriate.

We know that much of what humans use to guide their actions derives from the idea that there is a "superior force" supporting certain values, considering them positive or negative, constituting something that could be termed a "moral world order". However, those who dispense with the belief in a personal god cannot back up their notions of morality in this type of fiction. If we need moral notions, they should be rational, useful, palpable, not inflexible as divine crystals. In this situation, those who understand what are *human* values can easily dispense with any help from the gods, myths, or mystical "gurus of good living" to guide their actions. We can dispense with all those metaphysical fictions of "good in itself", which are just chimeras of the human imagination, remnants of a past era in which we were unable to understand sufficiently well the reality that surrounded us and our relationship with it.

Firstly, we raise the question that, in the context of morality, the assumption of atheism — or, more specifically, the transition from theism to atheism —, in our view, implies certain inescapable consequences, but which are often not considered — a very common misconception among those who would like to *abolish God with the least possible expense*, as Sartre put it. With the disbelief, the divine authority that was used to legitimate the values ceases to exist. The whole castle of moral beliefs that had been built on dogmatic foundations crumbles — and now we must get rid of that rubble. The situation would be like that of a tree that, having its metaphysical roots removed, can no longer sustain itself or feed its branches with "nutrients from the afterworld".

In this situation, all absolutist valuation systems collapse, the rigid divine unity crumbles, transfiguring itself into multiplicity and becoming. The evaluative judgment that God "made" for us now every man must make for himself. The freedom that atheism brings with it is simply the result of the rejection of all external references in relation to which we could stablish ourselves in a universally secure way. In fact, if the entire distance that separates theism and atheism could be grasped in one fell swoop, the vision of the enormous abyss that lies between these two antithetical perspectives would be truly dizzying: on the one hand, the sublime ideal heights, with its unity and fixity; on the other, contingency and relativism.

As we defined before, a proposition is true when it corresponds to reality. However, without the belief in a personal god, there is no longer an independent "moral reality" to which statements of this nature could refer. Thus, strictly speaking, there are no moral truths and, therefore, any moral statement made impersonally is false, since it cannot find any support in objective reality.

Let's try to illustrate this point better. If, by means of abstract thought, we distance ourselves from reality for a moment, if we imagine ourselves elevated to the top of a mountain and we calmly observe the scenes of life from there, we are placing ourselves, in a sense, beyond good and evil, seeing the moral scene objectively. From this angle, the perspective we are presented with is something quite different from the reality in which our ordinary life is immersed. Alienated from our practical concerns, we see our situation, our personal positions alongside countless others, without any distinction. We are free not to need opinions, not to have to take a position before anything; we are there only to observe. What is being revealed? That morality only exists and only makes sense as a subjective set of human values, a position in the face of the reality in which we are inserted. That there is no predefined good or evil, right or wrong, virtue or vice; that there are no absolute values to guide our lives. All that refers to morality and ethics — virtue and vice, right and wrong, duties, principles, values, etc. — are points of view, and nothing more. Moral judgements can only have subjective value — they cannot exist except as the expression of the standpoint of the person who created them. Indeed, if we were not personally committed to any value, to any perspective, why should we think that good is itself more valuable than evil, or vice versa?

Now let's imagine a universe devoid of any life, totally barren. Suppose that, on a planet in this universe, there is a volcano located in an area of great seismic activity. We, as fragile human beings, tend to associate a negative image to active volcanoes, since they represent an enormous potential danger to our lives. However, would it make any difference if that volcano were to remain quiet or to spew ash and magma furiously and swallow up the surroundings, if there were no lives being consumed? No, there would be no problem at all. Stones don't mind being toasted by magma, water doesn't mind being evaporated, the earth doesn't mind being covered with ash. That planet could even be destroyed by a colossal wandering meteor, but still none of this could be considered an "evil" if there was nobody being harmed.

Do good and evil exist in this situation? No, because there is no type of reference against which we could establish them. However, if we placed an individual endowed with will — the will to survive, for example — on the surface of that planet, and granted him some intelligence, then that individual would position himself *in relation* to the natural phenomena of that planet, declaring them good or bad depending on whether they're favorable or unfavorable to his objectives.

Now let's suppose two different contexts. In the first, a man is a man is out at sea on a fragile boat, fishing to support his family. In the second, a poor farmer is on the brink of losing his harvest due to lack of irrigation. If there were a storm that hit both simultaneously, would that mean that the storm is a good thing or a bad thing? To say that the storm is good would imply that goodness can wreck an innocent individual's boat for no reason while remaining good. On the other hand, to say that the storm is inherently bad places us in a situation where evil saves us from misery and provides us with abundance — and that, by any reasonable definition, would be something good, not bad.

As we can notice, it does not seem possible to answer this question without first defining some *reference*. So, we would probably answer: good or bad for whom? This displaces the question of whether something is good or bad for the subject. From this perspective, all objective facts, in and of themselves, appear to be devoid of any moral value or significance. Of course, most situations do not present themselves to us in such a crystalline way, but such examples are certainly useful in order to understand how to proceed in an investigation in search for the origin and nature of our moral values.

In this way, a phenomenon simply happens, and whether it represents something good or bad depends only on the subject's eyes, the situation, and the judgment of the subject. At the heart of the objective world there are no judgments, no rewards or punishment: there are only physical consequences.

Such considerations demonstrate something of utmost importance: that every judgment is always subjective, and that objectivity is always impersonal and amoral. Therefore, we conclude that there is no objective basis for subjective evaluations, and also that values always arise and disappear linked to a will. To value things is a characteristic exclusive to life, implying the impossibility of existing of any value apart from life. Trying to suspend any kind of value above life as something supposedly independent is a consequence of that sad myopic anthropocentrism that cannot see the distinction between objective and subjective.

If values only exist subjectively, and always in relation to a will, then, in terms of valuation, everything necessarily unfolds on a personal level and solely on a personal level. However, humans are social beings. That is why, without a doubt, there are conventions between us. Furthermore, the intellect is capable of some abstraction of the facts related to human nature, giving birth to generic formulas that represent something that could be called a "general rule of human subjectivity". Regarding morality, all of this is certainly valid, but only from a pragmatic and statistical perspective. To expect that abstracting from the human being some general rule would demonstrate any objectivity, any self-sufficiency of that general rule — that would be simply nonsense.

Realizing all this relativity that exists in the moral field, we see that we are facing a somewhat problematic impasse. It is in the face of this type of impasse that we often resort to an "absolute reference" called "God's will" — or something like that. Inventing a higher consciousness endowed with will is a way of trying to establish absolute values. This god would be like an idealized human consciousness, that is, infinitely wise, representing a higher reference of values according to which we could locate ourselves.

In this situation, the ideal is presented as something objective — the real, subjective. This inversion allows the ideal to be used as a reference to guide actions with great solidity. In the ideal, there is no relativization — it is not viewed as a perspective. Thus, ideal values are equivalent, in terms of consistency, to objective reality.

This "moral world order", being independent of us, pushes the validity of values beyond the reach of our questions and our will, in the same way, let's say, that physical laws are beyond our questions and our will. Through this idealization, we create an "objective subjectivity", a "pure abstraction of human will" in which we can anchor our goals impersonally, suppressing the distressing problem of the lack of reference points.

As we can see, the trick consists of creating a pure and impersonal abstraction of something subjective, in order to grant it credibility. Based on the denial of the subjective nature of these values, the ground is ready to transform them into principles, principles into laws — and these, in turn, justify, in an impersonal and objective way, the values that determine human conduct. It is a circular fallacy so simple as to be laughable, but that is always used to satisfy the insecurity of irresolute egos, who need an external backbone to structure their lives.

Of course, this whole story of "God's will" is nothing more than a daydream and an excuse to give supreme authority to our own opinions, attributing them to God and then "forgetting" that we're the ones who created him — a subterfuge used to transform human opinions into divine laws. Thus, we see that any objective value is based on dogmatism, on the idealization of a personal value, gilded by authority. By the way, it is from this perspective, as we have seen, that we can understand where the great coercive power of religion resides, which works as a method of social control.

Fortunately, we know that all this just a bunch of chimeras. For this reason, we are aware of the complete impossibility of finding rational references to guide any value system that is universally valid. However, it is common to encounter individuals who affirm, with a supposed air of understanding, that "people should be more like this or less that". In fact, there is no way to express sufficient contempt for this type of attitude — such an individual is nothing more than a moralist with megalomania. Defending any kind of supposedly universal human ideal is a task that should be left to poets or those in mental asylums.

A proposition subject to an end is one thing. Saying "train if you want to win!", for example, places training as a means to achieve an end to which we arbitrarily assigned value. We deliberated on whether the victory would be interesting for us and, based on that, we decided that we are going to train. On the other hand, any kind of unconditional "thou shall" is a windmill on the grounds of dogmatism. It would be like just saying this: "train!" — an order as an end in itself. But training for what? And why is training good? Good for what, for whom? It's obvious how absurd is any kind of "universal imperative".

Assuming that someone could formulate universal moral premises, just like the universal premises of Aristotelian logic, the construction of an absolute moral system would be as secure as a syllogistic inference. This would consist of a series of logically consistent inferences, which could probably serve as an intellectual pastime for some bored thinker, but without any real use. In this regard, Frederick Edwords clearly demonstrates the impossibility of reconciling absolute morality with the dynamic and multifaceted human reality:

> *The most glaring problem with absolutist systems, such as the Ten Commandments, is that when there is more than one absolute rule, it is possible for conflicts to arise between them. Thus, one might wonder if it is appropriate to murder to prevent a robbery. Is stealing allowed to prevent murder? Should we lie if we had good reason to believe that the truth would cause the individual to die of a heart attack? Is it appropriate to lie to avoid being murdered? Is it lawful to break Holy Saturday to save someone's life? Would it be correct to steal a car if we knew that it would prevent its owner from working on Holy Saturday or killing someone? Should we honor the will of our parents if they asked us to break any of the other commandments? Should we rob our parents if, in doing so, we might be preventing a murder? All kinds of dilemmas like these are possible. (...) This shows that we cannot live based on absolute and abstract principles. We need to relate them to life and human needs.*

Absolute morality is as unsustainable as the existence of the tyrannical ghosts of creation. They are ghosts that shackle our freedom. This type of idea must be combated and attacked with all weapons, not by what it actually defends, because that doesn't matter, but by what it represents: a shackle, a tyranny of impersonal values. To declare that we must live according to "ultimate reasons" of moral nature misguides life in what should be a practical concern.

Perhaps it can be said that this vehement condemning position is arrogant, because who can say what is truly right or wrong? Nobody. However, our intention here is not to say what we should be. We intend the exact opposite. We are precisely defending the impossibility of finding an objective foundation capable of justifying any impersonal duty — hence we defend its non-existence. Therefore, this condemnation should be viewed as a counter-arrogance — against arrogant claim that man should be "such or such". From this perspective, if we defend that man should be something, it is simply this: man should be free to value whatever he pleases.

Thus, when it comes to values, the only thing that must be stated is that, *a priori*, none exist. Respect for the universal average is nothing more than respect for the universal average. Customs and traditions are not special values, they are old values. We don't need to defend our chosen principles, but only our right to have them — and never lose sight of the fact that it's simply a matter of choice and invention and personal taste. To forget this is to forget freedom.

Of course, most atheists would agree with this view, at least in principle. However, as the idea develops a little further, many become progressively embarrassed and hesitant with what they see, as the implications of this vision are all-inclusive, encompassing anything that we can imagine in terms of valuation, inevitably leading to amoralism, at least regarding the possibility of universal values.

Nothing that we do — for ourselves or for others — has any inherent value. We have no necessary commitment to humanity, nor does it to us. We don't owe any specific type of conduct to anyone or anything. After all, why do we have to behave morally? We don't have to. Against this obvious finding, the only objections that have been raised are penitentiaries. This may sound controversial — and it almost always does —, but when it comes to being moral, let's not forget that our history — this endless fight-for-yourself — was never an example of the philanthropic virtues that are fashionable today, and neither was the natural world — or did anyone learn about a recent hunger strike by predators out of respect for their prey?

From this perspective, the authority of all principles that are traditionally dear to humanity, such as the principle "thou shalt not kill", falls apart. The intentional murder of another human being is no longer necessarily a condemnable act — and indeed it never was: let's think of the death penalty and self-defense cases. The idea that we should do good and cause no harm ceases to apply. Love thy neighbor — who said that's necessary? Be fair — why should anyone? Don't steal — well, why not? Don't lie — what if it's helpful? Not committing adultery — even if there is consent? Don't copulate with relatives, animals, children, or the dead — will a rock fall on our heads if we do that? Not using drugs for recreational purposes — what if we want to? None of this is mandatory, none of this is forbidden. Objectively, raping a person or breaking a matchstick signify the same thing — nothing.

If we had been taught to greet each other with spit or to sacrifice our relatives when they reach 50 years, we would think that this is the right thing to do. Becoming conditioned to the values of the society in which we live is a natural tendency. The problem arises when we forget to explain why, the function of those evaluations, of those prohibitions and praises for certain types of behavior. In particular, the Christian ideals that permeate our society have succeeded in falsifying our values system in such a way that an authentically human perspective or a biologically honest commentary sounds like a monstrosity.

When reasons are lost and habits continue irrationally, due to their tradition and authority, this generates chaos within us. How can we follow contradictory values that don't make sense and that, in their application, have no trace of utility? But even to that, we adapt: for conflicts, we create a collection of different social masks, each appropriate to specific situations that require a persona from us. Fake it a bit to get some benefits — what's wrong with that? Nothing. Nobody needs to be truthful — as long as no one knows. It is ironic that, in a society of facades, the impostors that society itself created are execrated because they are not different from what everyone else is. Who knows how long we will continue pretending not to realize that beautiful ideal values are a hindrance to real life.

Despite such problems, it is obvious that some of the principles mentioned above can be useful in a society that intends to be pacific. Although we are a substantially selfish species, paradoxically, to live in society, we must behave under a collectivist regime, based on opposite values. Selfishness is typically seen as a defect because, when exacerbated, it promotes behaviors that, if everyone followed, would bring disastrous consequences to society. Thus, individuals who think of using the collective to provide themselves a great benefit at the expense of a small harm to the collectivity end up having their selfish interest curbed by the fear of punitive laws, which serve to discourage selfish and antisocial actions and thus promote the maintenance of order and general welfare. These are the "restrictions imposed by life in society" that Freud mentions, which generate the discontent that basically consists of the conflict between our nature and the nature of the civilization we created. This discontent is the price we pay to enjoy the benefits of a civilized life.

Let us note that, even if we were talking about moral values that guide an entire society, that would still not be good values in and of themselves or universally good, but good for a given objective — which in general will be to promote peace and order in that society. It is essential to be aware that such principles are just social conventions between individuals who have similar objectives, and nothing more.

Unfortunately, not everyone can live with this obvious idea and its logical consequences. For this reason, even among atheists, the unfortunate belief that these or those ideals should be cultivated, on the grounds that they are superior values — in general, humanitarian ideals. Obviously, those ideals are prejudices — but that's not the problem, because ultimately all our moral values are moral prejudices. In reality, the objection is primarily directed at the claim that they are better and superior because they have an altruistic and cooperative nature. The mere fact that a principle promotes the happiness of other individuals does not make it something higher — after all, what does happiness have to do with truth? In a word: nothing. Objectively, not even happiness has value in itself.

However, let this position not be misunderstood — we are just being unbiased. We have nothing against the idea that goodness, humility, and altruism are superior to malice, arrogance, and selfishness, as long as that idea is placed in its proper place, that is, it is viewed as a personal point of view, an opinion, having no more value, in its essence, than any other perspective. The fact is that being charitable, supportive, compassionate, and kind is a matter of personal choice, not a "principle of decency" or a "matter of humanity" — whatever that means.

Occasionally we come across well-meaning poets — with one foot in the clouds and the other in Wonderland — who claim to profess the "universal good". Although touching and certainly sympathetic, such an idea proves to be impractical. The origin of this illusion lies in the fact that individuals tend to think that everything that is good for them will also be good for everyone. However, the "universal good" is just another sterile fruit of moral egocentrism. After all, who is the universal good for? For everyone, really? But how is it possible to be equally benevolent to causes with conflicting interests? How could we help the wolves *and* the lambs? Doesn't helping the wolves mean harming the lambs indirectly? On the other hand, if we don't help the wolves because they are "bad", then the good is not universal, and it can be clearly seen that this supposed "universal good" starts from the point of view of what is universally good for the herd. So, faced with the impasse, perhaps it would be better to help both and run away, so as not to see the consequences and continue with a clear conscience? As we can see, impartial universality proves impossible. For a wolf, being universally kind is no virtue — compassion, for a predatory animal, would be its undoing. Likewise, for a peaceful and gregarious lamb, living on the cruelty of animal predation would be suicidal silliness.

The conclusion we are trying to reach is this: each individual has their own personal nature, and it is according to it that what virtue or vice is defined — not according to what some moralist with mental disorders thinks. Our values should exist only as a reflection of our intimate nature. Thus, after comprehending what we are, what we want, and our relationship with the environment in which we are, we distill from such knowledge the principles and rules that we follow for ourselves. The most important thing is to never lose sight of the fact that these principles are only a reflection of what we are — and only as a reflection should they have authority.

With this in mind, if we do not admit that many individuals base their moral thinking on prejudices, it is almost impossible to understand why they are proud to say that they act according to "such or such" principles, as if that would make them special and superior in some way — and still they condemn those who do not behave as they consider "correct", labeling them immoral, perverse, ignorant, inconsequential, etc. They make use of all the flamboyant rhetoric of goodness, humanity, solidarity, solidarity, dignity, decency, integrity, honesty, of love for others, and so on, to make it seem that these principles are good and have value in and of themselves, and then take a position in relation to them, justifying their pathetic self-flattery and condemnation of the unequal.

The problem with this attitude is that, considering all values as subjective, people cannot position themselves "in relation" to the values they defend, as if they were external; they must represent them, embody them. Seeing a value as if it were "outside", hanging over our heads, it can be used to judge and condemn others impersonally, because it is regarded as a truth, as a reference, as something that applies to everyone.

For example, a *person A* might do something that another *person B* reproves in their personal perspective. However, if *B* is able to realize that *A* sees nothing wrong with his own action, then *B* will have no grounds to justify any kind of reproval for the act of *A*. Thus, *B* could only say something like "I wouldn't do that" or "I disagree", but never "you're wrong", because *A* is simply acting according to his nature. It is the same issue presented above: different natures, different virtues and vices.

By the way, one of the advantages of free thinking is that, because it has no ingrained monochromatic prejudices, it has a suppressive effect on much of the intolerance toward different points of view. Through it, we overcome the one-dimensional, bipolar perspective of moral dogmatism and open our eyes to a spatial, three-dimensional view that allows for infinite perspectives. We begin to recognize life in all its diversity and originality, without false oppositions of values.

However, it's certainly not a good idea to try to say that benevolence isn't necessarily a virtue for any relatively conservative person. We are talking about values that are the sacrosanct cows of our modern civilization, which are so embedded in our society that they have become almost unquestionable.

Therefore, if we do not present such remarks in a very subtle and carefully justified way, they end up causing indignation and, not infrequently, we end up labeled as "immoral". This indignation is a typical symptom of those who are unable to relativize their vision sufficiently to realize that their supposedly universal values and convictions are nothing more than personal points of view.

This happens mainly because people tend to weigh the value of their own values against happiness, since for most people the real "litmus test" of moral values lies precisely in whether they lead to well-being. Of course, no one needs to be a scientist or a philosopher to have useful moral intuitions — everyone, in their own way, chooses or invents their own values, which come to be felt as something very intimate and personal. Therefore, when we call these values into question, we are also attacking individual notions of well-being, to which a great emotional value is attached. That's why inviting someone to impartially scrutinize the values on which their happiness depends is almost always an unfortunate suggestion.

But the fact is that, even if manifested on a personal level, the individual search for happiness converges on many points, such as biological and psychological well-being, good reputation, satisfaction of personal goals, etc. The most universal moral notions have their roots in such basic foundations, they express ideas valid for everyone or for almost everyone, they involve needs or characteristics that permeate our nature in a predominant way.

As we have already explained, life requires a position from us, life itself represents a position. Being alive and wanting to stay alive is an instinctive prejudice, but it's still a value. It is from this fundamental root — our very condition of existence — that we normally deduce most of the values that guide human action.

There's nothing wrong with outlining general rules that lead to well-being. Although individuality cannot be reduced to generalizations, these serve to establish its foundations. We could mention the universality of the notion that pleasure is good and that pain is bad. This is mechanically based on biological factors — hence the fact that everything that leads to pleasure and drives away pain is instantly termed "good". Nobody had to teach us that being happy is good — this is not a deliberate and free assessment, but an instinctive prejudice, our own evaluative shadow.

Up to this point, everything would be fine. But when we try to invert that reasoning, when we try to transform those general rules not into something that derives from us, but into something good in and of itself, then we are losing reality of sight. The mistake lies in attaching more value to abstraction than to reality, in trying to transform a reflection into essence. For example, if a certain principle widely regarded as virtuous and benevolent does not bring us well-being, if it is not in accordance with our nature, the most logical thing to do is to reject it, not to bow to its social authority. Every virtue must be *our* virtue. We must recognize its value personally, or it will be worthless to us.

Annoyingly, however, the common factor of human behavior is always interpreted as a morality in itself, as something objective. The harmful consequences of this crass interpretation should be obvious to any individual. A true castration of freedom in favor of generalized trends. The most monstrous crime against any structure is the one that attacks its foundations — the values that guide the action. Naturally, this type of name is not used to designate this mental leveling, this becoming-a-herd. They receive pompous shiny names — decency, dignity, humanity, honor, moral fiber — with the purpose of hiding the reality behind these unsustainable lies. All of these are chimeras that sacrifice the individual to the phantasmagoria of the "good for its own sake" — but even so, it would be naive on our part to think that moral principles are not involved in the games of social control.

There are also those who lie innocently: they offer the "formula of virtuosity" as an infallible solution, a path to be followed that works for anyone. They present us with the shadow of a ghost that they imagined whispering moral platitudes to them during a mystical catharsis as the solution to all moral problems. The fact is that, if we could visualize the roots of the impulses from which the most sublime moral doctrines are born, we would see monstrous egocentrism. In the leafy tree that is born from this egocentrism, is the idealization of oneself, the transformation of one's personality and one's personal tastes into higher principles. In any case, if that's done with enough charm, they may even be able to seduce a small flock in which to observe various imitations of themselves.

The same degree of foolishness is present in those who suffer in the name of the supposed virtuosity that someone else attributed to a moral principle — because for them that value was good —, and thus become involved in a harmful alienation. In fact, the influence of this type of lie on insecure individuals, who need to find some meaning outside themselves — and almost always find it by dissolving themselves in others —, is incredible. Self-alienation presents itself as the only way to feel valued.

Now let's distance ourselves a bit from this predominantly theoretical perspective and analyze the issue from a practical perspective. It is quite certain that we already have some innate programming of what is good and what is bad. This happens because we are animals with an evolutionary history and biological needs. Thus, with regard to life as an end in itself, we are always faced with the question of the value of pleasure — or, in its multiple facets: happiness, satisfaction, joy, well-being, fullness, fulfillment, etc.

Naturally, the value of pleasure seems predetermined to us because we only see reality through the eyes of life. Pleasure represents in us a kind of physiological reward within the context of the "reason of the body", whose criterion of truth is survival. This gives us the illusory impression that achieving happiness and satisfaction are the ultimate goals of our existence.

Looking at the issue closely, we will realize that pleasure and pain are closely linked to utility — and, considering the way we evolved, this could not be different. Pleasure and pain are mechanisms of psychological coercion. In fundamental matters, the feeling of pleasure in human beings works as a kind of "incentive for" or "reward for" actions that are in accordance with our innate instincts — learned evolutionarily through trial and error — of what leads to the perpetuation of life. Pain, on the contrary, is presented as a type of subjective punishment for events that are in some way pernicious to the fundamental objectives of life.

For instance, we certainly have sex in search of pleasure. However, pleasure is a facade, not an end in itself. Sexual pleasure is just a strategy, a "bait" that the body uses to induce people to copulate, as this leads to reproduction and the perpetuation of life. If intercourse were painful — say, like the amputation of an arm —, we would certainly avoid it at all costs. In that case, the human species would quickly disappear, with only the masochists left.

In any case, this could be a kind of answer to the question of what should be the references adopted to guide human values. That is, everything that leads to happiness must be cultivated and everything that prevents it must be avoided. However, the problem with this view is the fact that our innate programming was forged in our DNA by the pressures of a very different environment, and that occurred a long time ago. Most of our behavioral predispositions are completely decontextualized due to the frantic alteration of the environment that has been taking place recently, something that the slow pace of genetic evolution has not been able to follow, so that, in our current context, acting only in accordance to our impulses is not always equivalent to acting in the most appropriate way, both at the social level and at the level of survival. This invalidates the possibility of using only happiness or pleasure as a safe reference to guide our lives.

In fact, we're still armed with instincts for a life in the Stone Age. Our fundamental impulses are blind to reason and to the future of our world. As Steven Pinker explains:

> *The selection operates over thousands of generations. For 99% of human existence, people lived by gathering food, in small nomadic groups. Our brain is adapted to this long-extinct way of life and not to the very recent agricultural and industrial civilizations. He's not attuned to dealing with anonymous crowds, school, written language, government, police, courts, armies, modern medicine, formal social institutions, high technology, and other newcomers to the human experience. Because the modern mind is adapted to the Stone Age, and not to the computer age, there's no need to force adaptive explanations for everything we do. In our ancient environment, the institutions that today instigate non-adaptive choices, such as religious orders, adoption agencies, and pharmaceutical industries, did not exist, and that is why, until very recently, there was no pressure from selection to resist these stimuli. If the Pleistocene savannas contained birth control pill trees, we might have evolved to judge them as terrifying as a poisonous spider.*

Precisely because we are biologically decontextualized, we need to use intelligence to guide our instincts, to give them some vision and, with that, to be able to harmonize our impulses with the environment in which we live, at the cost of some administrative effort. Thus, rationality must work as an adaptive factor, as a mediator between our impulses and our actions, so that they are, at the same time, subjectively satisfactory and compatible with the environment that surrounds us. In the precarious situation in which we exist, and without being able to count on the voluntary assistance of nature, we should use our intellectual faculties in the most appropriate way possible, allowing our brief existence to be guided by strategic conventions that help us to live in a more fruitful, or at least decent way.

Therefore, as we have seen, it is possible to establish a human moral code based on our own goals and on our own nature. We don't have to resort to the wisdom of the gods. We just need to learn to rationalize our feelings, our nature, our needs, and our objectives, and then condense it all into behavioral principles that will serve as guides, making our mind compatible with modern reality. These principles will tell us when it is convenient to continue or stop, when it is convenient to give in to a desire or to repress it so as not to jeopardize a collective or long-term objective. Moral values, in this case, present themselves as a very useful tool for managing our impulses and adapting them, in a contextualized way, according to our interests, to the objectives we have in the short, medium, and long-term.

However, it is often objected that this type of "rational coordination" of morality leads to chaotic anarchism, since, for society as a whole, it would be impossible to justify principles that were based only on simple "mundane and relative opinions". Thus, without absolute morality, without a "higher reference", there would be no way to establish the validity of any principle, of any socially applicable notion. Of course, without this supposed "absolute reference", the first concepts to be discarded would be precisely the useless and the unnatural ones supported by authority, not those supported by utility. In any case, we don't need absolute reference as a guide, and we can use traffic laws to illustrate this point.

For example, if humans are unable to create their own rules and then submit to them, how could traffic laws exist? As far as we know, our traffic laws are not based on sacred imperatives of divine wisdom, which dictate *thou shall wait for the green light*. The fact is that not everything needs to be based on absolute notions — even better, nothing needs to. These laws are based on the reflections of humans who seek to reconcile the basic objectives of everyone. It is the question of the "general rules of human subjectivity". The premises of traffic laws are anchored in obvious things, such as the fact that no one wants to die in an accident on the way to work. So, if we want traffic to work, laws must be formulated to organize it in order to avoid universally unwanted consequences and, at the same time, maximize transportability, which is the objective of those who are trying to get around.

So, if we can create efficient traffic laws based on similar fundamental interests, why would the case morality be any different? We would only need to base ourselves on the assumption that we have many characteristics, objectives, and needs in common. From this, we would construct notions of morality capable of providing the organization and order necessary for life in society. By nature, it would be an organic, malleable, and rational morality. Something human constructed rationally to solve problems that are also human, consisting of pragmatic conventions that refer to the subjective reality of the human condition itself, not to any objective, immutable, or transcendental reality.

Therefore, we see that the mistake made by those who challenge the possibility of establishing rational morality lies in the attitude of judging that we are infinitely malleable beings. In purely rational terms, our morals are all arbitrary — but we are certainly not walking abstractions, we are not purely rational and arbitrary beings. We are human beings, not metaphysical souls. We have a nature that derives from our evolutionary history, which imprinted on us a common constitution, and that means that we are limited to the possibilities offered by our biological machines.

We have common needs in terms of survival, reproduction, nutrition, protection, socialization, affectivity, entertainment, etc. And let us also add that we are all on the same planet, and that there is no escape from this fact — we must face the hardships of the same environment. Furthermore, if we grow up in the same society, the needs will be even more similar.

There are lots of difficulties and characteristics that we have in common. In this situation, acting as social beings and behaving in a socially compatible way, organizing ourselves rationally through moral conventions to achieve common objectives, is not just a matter of personal choice, but a matter of mutual interest that seeks to maximize efficiency, something that, ultimately, will have repercussions for our own benefit. This does not mean, of course, that everyone must behave in a socially compatible way. We only demonstrated that it is possible to build moral values, both individual and collective, without resorting to dogmatism.

In this context, we must always bear in mind that moral values, in and of themselves, have no value — the value lies in the human purpose they are serving. Those who lose sight of this take the first step that transforms human values into pernicious fossils that stagnate humanity's moral progress. Frederick Edwords, in this sense, demonstrates the true function of moral values, as conventions that should always exist as means to our ends:

> *[Since the process of improving ethics is one of trial and error, then it makes sense to keep ethical principles flexible. After all, if a given principle is rigid and absolute, it tends to nurture a type of idolatry where people worship the rule rather than its purpose. Since good and evil are ultimately judged from the perspective of human need and interests, then it only makes sense that all moral principles work to satisfy human needs and serve human interests — as opposed to becoming an end in themselves. (...) When we realize that right and wrong cannot exist without beings with needs, and that human beings have proven capable of inventing and then applying their own rules, then there is no longer any way to deny that the pursuit of human interests — for individuals and for society, in the short and long term — is the main objective of laws and ethics.]*

Thus, from a social point of view, morality must be understood as a set of rules of conduct constructed by humans to satisfy also human needs, whose ultimate purpose is to promote our own well-being, both on a collective and individual level. As we have seen, pure reason will always be insufficient to guide our moral, social, and political notions. For this reason, we must always combine historical and experimental knowledge with reason, so that our moral perspectives are anchored in reality, in a constant process of evolution and improvement.

This conception of morality, as can be seen, is fundamentally pragmatic — and it could not be otherwise. It is based on the recognition that human beings have many needs, interests, and objectives in common — we share biological, psychological, social, emotional characteristics, etc. And it is based on the fact that we are able to rationally agree on moral values that are, at the same time, compatible with the maintenance of a life in society and with our private interests. So, it seems, we have to agree with Ingersoll when he asked: *So what is — or could it be considered — a moral guide? The shortest possible answer consists of just one word: intelligence.*

VIII

ON THE MEANING OF LIFE

The question of the purpose of human life has been raised countless times; it has never yet received a satisfactory answer and perhaps does not admit of one. Some of those who have asked it have added that if it should turn out that life has no purpose, it would lose all value for them. But this threat alters nothing. It looks, on the contrary, as though one had a right to dismiss the question, for it seems to derive from the human presumptuousness, many other manifestations of which are already familiar to us. Nobody talks about the purpose of the life of animals, unless, perhaps, it may be supposed to lie in being of service to man. But this view is not tenable either, for there are many animals of which man can make nothing, except to describe, classify and study them; and innumerable species of animals have escaped even this use, since they existed and became extinct before man set eyes on them. Once again, only religion can answer the question of the purpose of life. One can hardly be wrong in concluding that the idea of life having a purpose stands and falls with the religious system.

— Sigmund Freud

It would be nearly impossible to find any intellectually active individual who has never been confronted with the celebrated question of the meaning/purpose of life. What is this thing called the world? What am I doing in it? I'm alive, but what is this thing — life? At first glance, it seems logical to think that our life should have some kind of "point", since the world in which we live is so grand, so intricate, so curious, so rich in diversity, that all of this simply seems to *require* from us some kind of magnificent explanation, some special justification for the fact that we are here.

Obviously, countless explanations for what we are doing on this blue planet have come up and gone. Some are religious, some are metaphysical, some are poetic, some are moral, some are biological, others social, and so on. The human mind has devised countless types of explanation. Thus, if we were to ask several people what the real meaning of life is, the result would invariably be the same: discordant points of view and a purely subjective character attributed to the meaning of existence. Furthermore, most of the time, the explanation presented is so one-sided, subjective, and anthropocentric, so imbued with personal prejudice, that it is actually very, very far from the impartiality that this type of question requires.

Those who learn to look at reality courageously enough to be impartial in the face of their own expectations soon realize the error that almost everyone makes: when trying to explain life, they do not describe what they see, but what they feel. When they think of describing what they see, they are mistaken: in fact, they explain what they think of what they see. In this situation, they allow themselves to be overshadowed by the reverence that the grandeur of the world instills in them. They let themselves be carried away by the feelings of elevation that the most splendid hypotheses inspire in them. They begin to believe that "beautiful feelings" are an argument.

Thus, they create parallel realities and idealized fictional worlds that match their metaphysical inspirations, and then shift the center of gravity of life to that poetic and imaginary world. Then they call this completely falsified world "true reality", relegating material reality to a simple "appearance". On this unreal and subjective soil, anything can flourish, except the truth — it only flourishes on objective soils.

With critical eyes, we can see why such people will never find what they are looking for: you don't understand life by looking at the stars, and you don't understand the stars by looking at life. They search for the meaning of life, but they turn their gaze to beyond themselves, where life is not. Quite the contrary, what we are looking for is the meaning of life — of *this* life. The meaning of what we are in the reality in which we are — not the one in which we would like to be.

Looking at the world in depth and admitting that we see what we actually see: such lucidity requires something that few have — courage and intellectual integrity. In this arduous search, many succumb to dogmatic seductions that try to reconcile man with the indifference of the Universe. But we, as the astronomer Laplace told Napoleon, have *no need of that hypothesis*. We don't have to resort to the absurd, we don't have to derive our essence from a deity, we don't have to make ourselves the crown of a special creation to feel comforted. We don't need to falsify and distort reality to feed the whims of an anthropocentric arrogance. Quite the contrary, we know that we don't mean anything, that we don't matter at all.

Undoubtedly, the finite nature of human existence is one of the strongest indicators that we have nothing special. We enter existence, then we get out: *For you are dust, and to dust you shall return.* [Genesis 3:19] That's why so many rebel against death — and many even deny it, saying that it's just a "passage". In any case, they're not lying, since death is in fact a passage — back to the dust from which we came.

So, it is generally said that if everything ends with death, then human life has no meaning. The complaint is usually something like this: "If everything will be over when I die, why should I work, make efforts, achieve goals? It's all in vain, it's all ephemeral, nothing is worthwhile". This complaint, of course, has its reason for being, but it is launched against the wrong target. Let's suppose that science had discovered a way to make human beings immortal. Very well, now we no longer have to worry about death — we are everlasting beings. What, then, would be the meaning of the life of an immortal person? The same as for anyone else, because we would continue in the same situation, only indefinitely.

When they say that death is to blame for the absence of meaning, in reality this means that, if we're a simple limited and finite animal, if everything begins and ends here, then life has no meaning other than *itself*, that we do not belong to "higher planes of existence" — in other words, that we're not special. The idea that death represents our ultimate extinction can be frightening and discouraging, and that's perfectly understandable. However, it's not to blame for the lack of meaning in life.

As we can see, the question of the meaning of life has several possible interpretations. Therefore, it is necessary to clarify which perspective will be used in relation to the word "meaning". First, however, let us make it clear that we have no intention to moralize or to opine on the issues involved, since this is exactly the mistake made by most of those who try to deal with this subject. We will limit ourselves to highlighting the basics of the issue, without suggesting what to build upon them. Since this analysis is intended to be strictly objective and therefore materialistic, we will not consider answers that are grounded in human subjectivity. Thus, the following facts will be taken as assumptions:

1) However life may have arisen, this occurred naturally. Life wasn't intended or planned; it wasn't created by some "higher intelligence";

2) The physical Universe does not favor life at all, it does not conspire for it to exist. On the contrary, it is entirely mechanical, indifferent to everything and everyone, devoid of any purpose;

3) There is no "moral world order" or an "inner meaning" hidden behind material reality;

4) We are what we actually appear to be: biological machines. A form of life like any other. Our intellectual capacity is nothing more than an evolutionary weapon;

5) Our life is based solely on matter. Therefore, nothing will be left after death. We don't have a "soul" or a "spirit".

Just by clarifying these points, we realize that the classical meaning in which the expression "meaning of life" is used cannot be valid in a materialistic perspective. In other words, the problem of the meaning of life signifying "life's purpose" or "life's raison d'être" is a *false problem*. This is because, if life came into being as a result of the mechanical properties of an impersonal universe, then it wasn't planned. And if life is not an objective, if it does not result from a purpose outside of itself, then, in itself, it is devoid of any reason for being, of any objective purpose. In other words, its material existence contains its own meaning — none.

But there is another sense in which the expression "meaning of life" can be used, this one having a more literal understanding of the word meaning. Let's use a practical example: we take a cup of coffee in our hands with the intention of drinking it. What's the meaning of this cup of coffee? Its meaning is to satisfy our desire to drink coffee. In this case, the meaning of the coffee cup is subordinate to our will.

Now let's imagine an isolated coffee cup, floating lost somewhere in outer space. What would be the meaning of the coffee cup alone? None. Since it is an inanimate entity, devoid of will, needs, desires, etc., it can have no meaning in itself — for how could there be meaning without an objective? This conception of meaning, as we can see, is necessarily linked to the notion of will. However, the will does not exist in its pure form, because every will is always the will for something — and this something is the objective.

In this regard, let us note that this is the reason why, before life came into being, nothing had any meaning, since all that existed was non-living matter and, therefore, devoid of will, following physical laws that are essentially impersonal and aimless.

Let us now focus on the subject. When he manifests the will to drink coffee, what does that mean? It means that there was a reason for him to do so, that is, he started from a value premise that supported his will and justified his action of drinking coffee. For example: "drinking coffee is good". This value premise serves as a referential from which the individual traces his goal and launches himself towards it. Without referential values, that is, without value premises, the will would have nowhere to anchor itself in order to pursue something. In practical terms: why would anyone drink coffee if they didn't have a *motive* to do so? (motive, from the Latin *motivu* — "that moves").

Let's see this idea represented in a graphic diagram:

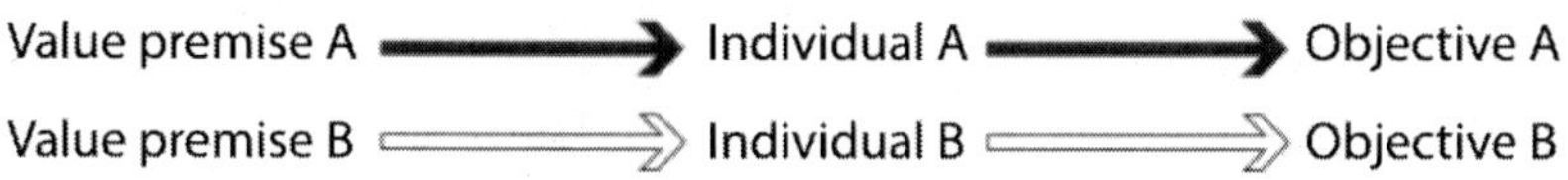

Value premise A ➔ Individual A ➔ Objective A

Value premise B ⇒ Individual B ⇒ Objective B

Interpreting the scheme, let's imagine the following situation. We place an

Individual A and an *Individual B* in the world. For *Individual A*, *Premise A* has value. For *Individual B*, neither *Premise A* nor *Premise B* have value — that is, nothing has value. From the *Premise A*, *Individual A* deduces that *Objective A* has value — thus arises in him the *Will of A*. Since nothing has value for *Individual B*, he does not aim at any objective, since his will has nowhere to sustain itself. Faced with the idea of conquering, for example, *Objective B*, he would ask himself this question: conquer for what? And this question would obviously remain unanswered. On the other hand, in the case of *Individual A*, the answer would be: "I want *Objective A* because *Premise A*" — or, changing the variables to make the idea clearer, we could say: "I want money because being rich is good". The "meaning of life" of *Individual A*, therefore, can be represented by the *Will of A*, that is, by his desire to pursue *Objective A*. In the case of Individual B, there are no referential values and, therefore, there are no objectives pursued. Therefore, his life is meaningless.

This makes it quite clear the sense in which the word "meaning" will be used: the one that refers to the idea of movement, as "towards something". Then, let's specify our central question in order to make our questioning more coherent. Let us ask the following: does life universally have any direction, any objective, any goal, any purpose? That's what we'll investigate from here on.

Let's first ask a basic question: why is a life with meaning better than a life without meaning? Now, isn't the "meaning" represented by the "will for an objective" exactly the only thing that distinguishes man from an inanimate object? Objectively, nothing distinguishes a 70 kg stone from a 70 kg person — both are made of matter. The only distinction that exists consists in the fact that the matter that constitutes the individual's body is organized in a very particular way called life, and this implies having a will, since a life without will would be a life in a coma.

But if everything is matter, then why is being living better than being inanimate? As strange as that sounds, it's not. However, it seems like it is. As we have explained, this partiality derives from the fact that we can only see reality through the perspective of life, because we are life, and so we think and weigh everything according to it — according to ourselves and our needs.

Therefore, everything that has value, has value only in relation to some subject, so that without a subject that valuates, there can be no values. It follows that if there is no life, there are no values. No value has the right to exist without an author, without a reference. That is why we can say that, in terms of valuation, life is the measure of all things — because it is only living beings that assign values to reality. If we were able to look at reality impartially, "from the outside" of life — say, from the indistinct point of view of a rock —, we would see that nothing really has value.

Of course, no one chose to value life. The fact that life apparently has an intrinsic value corresponds to a kind of instinctual dogma — something like an "embedded value", so to speak, aimed at self-preservation. Since our consciousness is based on such mechanical values, the value of life presents itself to us as something previously given, something intimately fundamental and unquestionable, as a profound instinct around which everything revolves. The value of life, therefore, is not justified by reason, but only by that kind of instinctive and involuntary passion programmed in us by our evolutionary history.

Thus, if the question of the value of our lives remains rationally unjustified, and if we base our actions on a dogma of self-preservation, it would not be true, then, that to live, what to act, that fighting for survival simply means to embrace irrationally, out of passion, the cause that was given to us by our own nature, by our evolutionary history — and with that we take refuge from emptiness, from nothingness, from death, from the paralyzing awareness of the very absence of meaning and value that is inherent to the human condition? And isn't it true that doing so amounts only to *believing* in that value, and not to a real value? It would be like saying that the dogma of life is to live. As if it were written on our genetic commandments tablet: *thou shall live!*

What is certain is that, in practice, we protect ourselves with all our might from the idea that we are responsible for the ultimate value of all things. Apparently, we are unable to reconcile evaluative arbitrariness with a solid will. Thus, we must always put on hold our skepticism regarding the value of our value premises in order to fight for the objectives that they support — as if, in order to act, we had to tyrannize ourselves, acting as if that premise had value in and of itself. In other words, if the will only exists on firm ground — on the soil of certainty —, in order to act, to pursue objectives, we must flee from everything that invokes relativism and arbitrariness. That is why our value premises are always surrounded by words whose meaning have an air of respect and authority: truth, ideal, dream, belief, virtue, conviction, doctrine, rule, law, norm, principle, etc.

From this point of view, evaluative dogmatism seems inevitable because, when we cast doubts about our real needs, we see that, in the end, there is no "I need...". When someone affirms that they have a need, they have already taken some premise as an assumption that justifies that need. As we go backwards in our assumptions, the "I need..." descends to increasingly fundamental levels, until we reach a point where we are forced to admit that our needs are all arbitrary. And then we can only say: "I don't need it; I just want it". Therefore, if our actions depended solely on philosophical and rational deliberations, we would never find reasons to do anything, because, in logical terms, human motivation is a kind of circular reasoning.

Thus, with regard to the issue of arbitrariness, the whole problem lies in how to convert an inescapable arbitrary premise into a "truth" that is capable of supporting our will. How do you do that? As strange as it may seem, this is done through the authority of belief, because value premises are unjustifiable, they are like dogmas. However, it is only through them that our lives can acquire meaning.

A practical example: the belief in the virtuosity of patience as a value premise. It seems intriguing that patience is considered a virtue until we understand its role in human motivation. Without a doubt, having patience is something that can become extremely difficult, requiring a great deal of discipline and self-control. But it's not about the value of *effort* that we're talking about, but about patience itself. If someone, for example, has a long-term objective and manipulates the many variables over time in order to converge their situation to the desired point, that individual could be praised as a good administrator and a good strategist. However, isn't it obvious that all the so-called "virtues" of a passive nature, such as patience, are based on the soil of impotence? We need to manage our small force and converge it with our objective to achieve it little by little, because it is too small to achieve it in one fell swoop. In this case, patience and perseverance are necessary as conditions that are imperative and indispensable. If we could achieve the objective all at once, we would naturally dispense with all the rhetoric of patience. It is only necessary for those who cannot achieve their objective immediately and, in their impotence, put on patience the mask of virtue to justify and hide their lack of power. There is nothing virtuous about the suffering that comes from impotence, but in order to endure it and to continue pursuing your goals, we must believe that such perseverance and such resistance are not a reflection of profound impotence in the immediate moment, but of a great force — the strength of those who know how to wait. Assuming that a person's objective was to buy a house and to do so had to save money for ten years, that patience, that knowing-how-to-wait would certainly be regarded as something virtuous. On the other hand, let us imagine that the individual, after having bought the house, decided to wait another ten years to occupy it, in a prodigious "demonstration" of the virtue through which he obtained it. In that second situation, that would be taken as something simply idiotic.

As we can see, that's a huge inversion. However, in practice, the individual, with the help of the belief in the "virtuosity of patience", was able to achieve his goal — and the fact that his belief was not objectively grounded in reality did not harm him at all. Thus, in terms of motivation, the belief in the veracity of a proposition is a fundamental point, in relation to which its own veracity can only occupy a modest marginal position. Efficiency doesn't depend on truth. Therefore, in a sense, we must admit that those who are able to make themselves believe, at will, in whatever they wish, are much freer than those whose intellectual integrity limits their beliefs to what their honesty allows.

The fact is that, in the game of life, we use all kinds of strategies to obtain the necessary motivation to keep our lives filled with meaning — in other words, to remain oblivious to the agonizing emptiness of reality. Certainly, our lives have no value in and of themselves. But even so, in order to live, it is as if we had to overestimate ourselves through irrational beliefs, for a simple matter of self-preservation.

Of course, luckily for us, most of our value assumptions are already pre-installed in our biological machinery, and their execution is done by our biology, not by our abstract reasoning. Le Bon, who was aware of the motives behind our actions, made the following observation in this regard:

> *The contrary impulses of the various logics [biological, affective, rational, mystical, collective] that lead us often make us hesitate about the procedure to follow. The simplest cases involve a choice between several solutions. The right choice must be made, because the necessities of life force us to act. How does our determination take place? An example will easily explain its mechanism. Let us randomly place any object on the plates of a scale. When the operation is finished, the needle, translating its movements, tilts to one side if the plates are unequally loaded, and remains vertical if they are equally loaded. Besides material scales, there are mental scales, whose mechanism is analogous. The weights are our motives for action. The needle represents the act that the fixing of the plate in its equilibrium position causes to be performed. These motives of action may sometimes be reasons, but the conscious motives of an intellectual order are more often than not joined by unconscious motives, which weigh heavily on one of the plates. In the final analysis, motives are energies in conflict. The stronger ones win. When the opposing energies have more or less the same intensity, the plates oscillate for a long time before settling down in a definitive position. Uncertain, hesitant characters. When the conflicting energies are very unequal, one of the plates immediately becomes balanced. Resolute characters, who move quickly to decision and action.*

Everything leads us to think that the most fundamental premises of the human condition are not really subject to the whims of our conscious will, but, on the contrary, are predominantly under the command of our unconscious and, at the core of that unconscious, we find the values determined by our own biological constitution. As we have seen, these would be something like "embedded values" in our genetic code, "biological values" that were evolutionarily adopted by our species due to their practical utility for survival.

From this perspective, it is quite interesting to note that the idea that there must be a meaning inherent to all things can be interpreted as a reflection of our need to remain alive. Possibly, the impression that life "must have a meaning" exists only because life needs to behave *as if it had meaning* for the sake of self-preservation. A meaningless life, from this point of view, would amount to a life in disarray.

Thus, we can suppose that most of the fanciful explanations about the meaning of life arose as an attempt to rationally explain all those instinctive, dogmatic impulses of life, that is, trying to justify our most profound needs rationally, as a means to certain ends that were presumed to be transcendental — and our fertile imagination is always available to invent them.

The mistake they make, obviously, consists of trying to interpret the vital impulses outside the biological context in which they appeared, as if they were disconnected from life itself or pointed to some objective other than their own — thus, "spiritual transcendence" is nothing more than an error of interpretation. In this great existential evolution, we can say that, in a certain way, life is eternal. However, it only transcends the individual, who is mortal, but never transcends itself.

These basic biological values probably serve well living beings devoid of conscious will, but they don't tend to satisfy rational beings like humans. When these impulses emerge from the depths of our unconscious, we feel the need to justify them, to rationalize them. From the short-sighted rationalization of such impulses, many theories, explanations, and meanings emerge that, obviously, due to our innate anthropocentrism, are always presumed to be inherent to reality itself.

Next, we will present four of the most common interpretations that seek to provide reference values for human life and, later, we will see what they have in common — and what can be inferred from this convergence.

The theistic premise: God's will

Here the central idea is to affirm that there are absolute values that are independent of man, since they are backed by the benevolent supreme will that created the Universe. In this case, the fact that God is infinitely superior to man would serve as the necessary authoritative factor to justify a belief without questioning. If God is omniscient, then it is not up to man, who is a mere mortal, to question what the value of the Divine Values would be — it's up to man only to follow them. There are also the sacred scriptures of the various religions. These serve as a guide, as an objective complement to the subjective belief in divine authority. These writings defend certain values, condemn others, explain the reason we exist and the ultimate purpose of all things. That's the whole truth — signed, God.

The reincarnationist premise: spiritual evolution

From the reincarnationist perspective, the claim made is that our material body is just a tool that the "spirit" uses to evolve. Supposedly, this would be achieved through the experience gained over several incarnations. All the learning acquired during life would be progressively accumulated, in some way, by the "spirit". To achieve this spiritual evolution, of course, there are conditions: we will have to follow certain moral guidelines — dictated by the so-called "higher spirits" — which would be inherent to the functioning of the "spiritual reality" itself, which would exist regardless of our material reality — a parallel reality in which our subjective exists objectively. The meaning of life, therefore, would be to live in such a way as to evolve our spirit.

The pantheistic premise: nature is divine

Pantheism affirms that the Universe itself is God, the sum of everything that exists. Thus, God's will would be the force that conserves the natural order of what exists. All life, all nature, the entire grandiose and intricate structure of the Universe would be a reflection of the will of that force. The meaning of life, in this case, would be to live according to nature, in harmony with the divine force that makes the Universe pulsate. Thus, we see that the solution presented by pantheism to overcome the fundamental impasse — that of the absence of will at the *origin* of life —, without appealing to the absurdity of a special creation, was to deify the Universe itself, its physical laws, making it all the will of God and God himself, which transforms life into something sacred, a divine event.

The objectivist premise: the escape from meaninglessness

This is an evasive solution, in which value is directly attributed to the objectives. Variants of this premise exist in many forms, and theories about the supposed "dignity of work" are a great example. Its internal mechanism consists in the fact that occupational tasks have the property of diverting our attention from ourselves, making us forget the anguish and questions that afflict us internally, suppressing the subjective colloquium that exists between the "me" and the "I", causing the superficialization of our consciousness. We can say that occupational tasks and entertainment are the two main methods in the task of self-forgetfulness. If idleness evokes thought, and thought without a goal makes us realize all the irrationality that permeates our life from end to end, we can infer from this the origin of all the horror that most people harbor toward the idea of loneliness and lack of occupations. Every individual who fully understands the nature of boredom and what it shows to our eyes also understands the subterfuge that responsibilities constitute to bring meaning to our lives. The observation that H. L. Mencken made in this regard is quite interesting:

> *Once I ventured the guess that men worked in response to a vague inner urge for self-expression. But that was probably a shaky theory, for some men who work the hardest have nothing to express. A hypothesis with rather more plausibility in it now suggests itself. It is that men work simply in order to escape the depressing agony of contemplating life — that their work, like their play, is a mumbo-jumbo that serves them by permitting them to escape from reality. Both work and play, ordinarily, are illusions. Neither serves any solid or permanent purpose. But life, stripped of such illusions, instantly becomes unbearable. Man cannot sit still, contemplating his destiny in this world, without going frantic. So he invents ways to take his mind off the horror. He works. He plays. He accumulates the preposterous nothing called property. He strives for the coy eyewink called fame. He founds a family, and spends his curse over others. All the while the thing that moves him is simply the yearning to lose himself, to forget himself, to escape the tragic-comedy that is himself.*

Thus, externalizing our attention represents the easiest and most common way to escape all this, from all that existential strangeness that invades us when we stop to think about our life. This subterfuge requires that we flee into some objective or situation that grabs all our attention, leading to an externalization of our consciousness, whose climax is to forget that we exist. Although this solution does not resort to absurdity to give meaning to life, it directly attaches value to the objective. That's why, when it is reached, the absence of meaning appears again, and so one lives constantly in an escape from oneself, in a trying-to-forget situation through the alienation oneself, always alternating occupations — amusement, work, etc. —, but never dealing head-on with the problem, ignoring the reasons that motivate life.

Let's see: why do premises that have no empirical support, that are rationally empty and unsustainable, end up being the most adopted? Simple: because they work. In practical terms, it matters little how true the belief is — it only matters that it works. Thus, the most pertinent thing about value premises is what they imply in practice. The important thing is that they are comfortable, functional, and sententious enough that they can anchor a will that is solid enough for life to remain justified in its meaning.

Let us also note that values, when assimilated — consciously or unconsciously — by our mind in the form of beliefs, whether by an internal or external factor, are felt as impulses to action. That is why religious premises are, without a doubt, among the most powerful, because clearly the role of every transcendental notion is only one: to generate a solid motivation through the idealization of an idea. In harmony with such reasoning, Nietzsche writes that:

> *Hope, in its most powerful forms, is a much more powerful stimulant to life than any kind of actual happiness. For man to resist suffering, he must have a hope so high that no conflict with reality can destroy it — in fact, so high that no achievement can satisfy it: a hope that reaches beyond this world (precisely because of the power that hope has to make sufferers persist, the Greeks considered it as the most evil among all evils; it remained at the bottom of the source of all evil).*

That is, in Pandora's box. Chimerical beliefs, exactly because they are intangible, exactly because they have no objective foundation, are untouchable as gods, as metaphysical ideals, as nothingness, and therefore have an air of "eternal truth". This gives them reliability, since they are beliefs that are independent of the material world, with an enormous potential to sustain the highest hopes and, therefore, to support solid motivations. Logically, this is why we always find the most splendid dreams wrapped in reasons that refer to the unknown and the intangible, where nothing from the "real world" can touch them.

Religions — freed from their component of social control — could therefore be understood as interpretations that express in a symbolic and intuitive way the most profound instincts of life, which arise in us as a diffuse and primitive feeling of self-affirmation, making us believe that life is something special, leading us to embrace its cause. Religiosity, in this sense, understood as an arm of the instinct of self-preservation, would work to justify our anthropocentric interpretations of reality, which would help to satisfy our basic survival needs. We can say that the logical scheme is something like this: if God created life, then life is divine, and everything in it has a reason for being, a very high reason. If life is the fruit of an infinitely wise mind, then there is certainly no reason to question it in its foundations — and this idea can be taken as a value premise that supports with maximum force the belief in the value of life, justifying, as ends in themselves, all the impulses of self-preservation that lead to biological, emotional, psychological, and existential well-being.

Nurturing a deep belief in the authority of life — as a value that cannot be disputed — sounds like an ideal way to nullify any doubt, any threat of jeopardizing the value of life, especially when we are faced with the anguish of problematic impasses. The idea of God, from this perspective, would work as the authority that assures the value and importance of our lives, taking the burden of this type of concern off our backs. We can suppose that the purpose of this, for humans, would be something like "taming" the intellect, that is, to direct it only to what is useful and to prevent it from turning its critical eye to rationally judge things in which we need to firmly believe in order to live well — such as the value of life, happiness, feelings, etc. This would make our intellect an intelligent tool to satisfy only our needs that, possessing reinforced authority due to the idea of God, would clear all doubts, subjecting our intellect to the interests of life — which, as we have seen, are aimed at perpetuation, not truth.

Everything makes it seem that religiosity — being faithful to the divine will — at first appears as a function of the interests of human life itself, as something that has a humanistic undertone — making us believe in ourselves. Thus, after being translated into the form of useful and emotionally satisfying maxims, it then represents the essence of our needs and regulates our basic notions of living, stabilizing them. In this perspective, it becomes obvious why, in the religious sphere, total trust, unrestricted credulity, faith, is considered precisely the highest of all virtues, and doubt, the path to perdition, a sin. In short, perhaps that is exactly why it is so difficult to objectively discuss the existence of God with theists, because there is an abyss that separates the two points of view — one sees God as a concept, and the other as a parental entity —, and it is hard to believe that individuals are capable of judging with impartiality what they adopted to justify their lives.

This is exactly the conclusion that Le Bon presents us regarding the problem of the perpetual internal struggles of which our mind is the stage: *The intellectual element resigns itself, in most cases, to suffering affective and mystical influences, without, however, consenting to confessing its defeat. This is precisely why we generally renounce discussing our affections and beliefs. This analysis would, in fact, be very painful; we don't always believe someone else's lie, but we easily give credit to our own.*

Now let's see what are the details that the shortcuts of intuitive understanding ignore — that is, the purposes behind the consciousness of the human machine. To act, we need value premises whose function is to serve as a reference to our will. What exactly is the use of a solid will? We need it to achieve goals. When we succeed, when we achieve our goals, what is the meaning of that? In other words, what is the use of success? It generates satisfaction, well-being, pleasure, happiness — after all, isn't that what we want?

Almost everyone agrees that happiness — or pleasure, satisfaction, etc. — is apparently an ultimate goal. So questions like "why is being happy good?" or "why is being successful good?" would have no reason to exist. On an individual level, in a way, this may be true. However, let's try to delve a little deeper into this issue.

What criterion defines what causes pleasure or suffering? Let's see: Why do injuries cause pain and not pleasure? Why is hunger bad? Why does sex generate pleasure? Why are we attracted to healthy bodies? Why is rotten food bad-smelling and repulsive, and nutritious food good-smelling and tasty? Why are we afraid of death? Why is winning good and being defeated bad? For example, if an individual had his sensations of pleasure and pain reversed, and thus felt enormous pleasure when damaging his body and terrible pain when reproducing or eating, isn't it obvious that he simply wouldn't survive long enough to reproduce — and wouldn't even try to —, and that therefore this variety of individual with reversed sensations would quickly disappear from the face of the earth? Imagining the existence of a population of this variety, at best we would have the brief spectacle of a crowd tearing itself apart in a bloodthirsty delirium.

From this perspective, a generic response that covers most cases comes to mind: pleasure and pain correspond to everything that, respectively, is favorable or contrary to the workings of life — survival in the short term and reproduction in the long term. Therefore, anything that leads to the strengthening or propagation of life generates pleasure and is therefore desired. And everything that weakens/destroys it generates pain and is, therefore, avoided. The premises of value of the human body were evolutionarily sculpted in a pragmatic approach, that is, according to their capacity to provide perpetuation.

We agree that this generalization is quite simplistic, and does not correspond very well to our current reality. This point will be discussed in detail in the next chapter. For now, let's make a short digression to discuss, with details that interest us here, how the selection of the fittest happens.

In evolutionary terms, successful individuals are the ones who reproduce their kind of genes the most. In each generation, a certain number of individuals is born, each with a subtly different genetic load. However, these individuals are ephemeral. They all disappear in just one generation. The only thing that can transcend the individual, through his children and relatives, are his genes. And which genes remain? The genes that are most efficient at reproducing, of course. As Steven Pinker reminds us: *The criterion by which genes get selected is the quality of the bodies they build, but it is the genes making it into the next generation, not the perishable bodies, that are selected to live and fight another day.*

Thus, a variety of genetic load may predispose an individual to fight fiercely for survival, but if it does not cause him to also fight for reproduction, he will be the end of the line for his genes, since they will not be passed on to any descendant, dying and disintegrating along with the reproductively unsuccessful individual. That's why it's important to keep in mind, as Dawkins noted, that *Not a single one of your ancestors died young. They all copulated at least once.*

Since we're talking about adaptation, let's think about the function of death in evolutionary terms. Strangely enough, death is an extremely efficient adaptive tool — in fact, essential to the maintenance of life in the long term (except for some beings that use other techniques to produce genetic variability and, therefore, technically, they don't die, except by accidents). All beings that have a more or less determined period of life and then, inescapably, die, actually have genes that are using a very effective technique of keeping the species in a constant variation of genetic content, which, in turn, always go through the filter of selection of the fittest.

It is certain that, if such beings did not die, this would condemn them to an inevitable extinction, because, with the passage of time, the environment is transformed in such drastic ways that there would come a time when the immortal organism would become obsolete, unable to adapt to the different environmental conditions that would eventually become inhospitable. However, since the evolutionary mechanism of trial-and-error infused life with the technique of limiting the temporal permanence of beings — periodically forcing them to recombine their genes to create new, subtly different organisms, discarding the parental carcasses —, that makes life extremely efficient in long-term adaptation to changes, greatly enhancing its capacity for perpetuation.

By the way, it is interesting to note that, from this perspective, it is also clear why most incapacitating or lethal diseases occur in individuals only after their adult reproduction period. It couldn't otherwise, because those who had serious illnesses *before* they could reproduce simply died or became disabled and, thus, left no descendants. However, diseases that appear only after the reproductive period do not undermine the individual's chances of having children, to whom their deleterious characteristics will be passed on freely. That is why we become more fragile and susceptible to diseases as we age — such diseases appear too late to function as selective factors.

On the other hand, regarding the selection of favorable attributes, an individual may, for example, have an astronomical IQ, but if he fails to behave in a reproductively viable manner, regardless of how special that characteristic is, it will cease to exist at the time of death. On the contrary, if that individual puts his high IQ at the service of survival and reproduction, then he will be excellent at developing tactics to survive and be a good breeder, far surpassing his competitors. Consequently, his intelligence will be passed to his children, then to their children, and so on.

Over generations, this selective mechanism proves to be very efficient. In the first generation, the genes of the best breeders survive. In the second, the genes of the best of the best. In the third, the genes of the best among the best of the best — a filter that leads to progressive and continuous refinement. Thus, with a little imagination, we realize that this type of selection tends to make us highly competent and specialized in just one thing: perpetuation. Of course, nothing prevents us from being competent in countless other things. However, none of those things will really be essential. The only fundamental rule in the game of life is to be able to perpetuate ourselves. The rest makes no difference.

Therefore, assuming that this selection has been going on for several million years, and that there are always more individuals being born than the Earth can sustain, and therefore intense competition for survival and reproduction, then it is quite reasonable to admit that individuals who do not have a "reproductive imperative" simply do not exist — and, if any do emerge, it will make no difference, as they will disappear within a generation.

Therefore, it can be said that, in all its manifestations, biological life, for a simple matter of long-term reproductive selection, has a "meaning in itself", which is not a purpose, but a mechanical, inertial goal: the tendency to continue existing.

Of course, in the case of humans, that meaning ceased to be totally mechanical when consciousness, the capacity for reflection and deliberation, emerged in us. Although potentially unnatural, the intellect of modern human allowed for greater behavioral malleability, making us a much more adaptable, versatile and, therefore, successful animal.

This mechanical meaning of life — perpetuation — can be represented on two levels, as follows:

Universal level

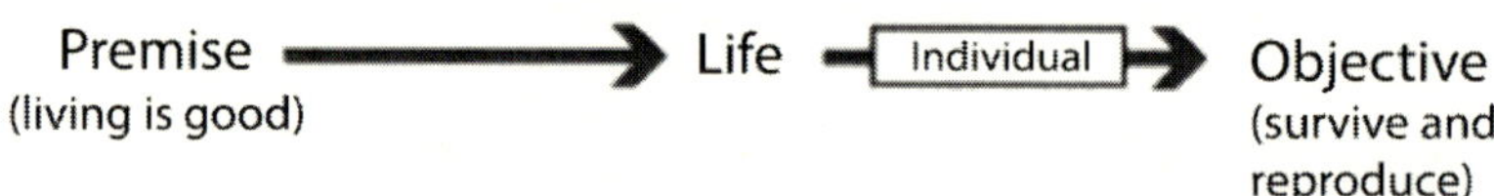

Individual level

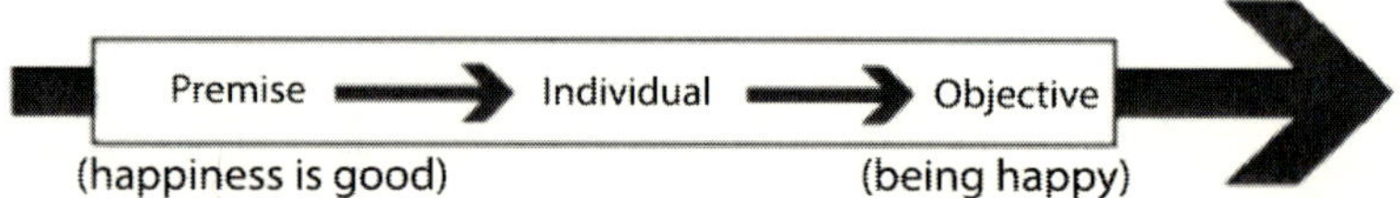

Interpreting this figure, it would be as if life — that is, DNA — "wanted" to be perpetuated through individuals, using things such as pleasure, happiness, and well-being as rewards for actions that favor its perpetuation. That scheme is metaphorical, of course. Even so, it is useful for elucidating the mechanics of life in its global behavior, as well as in its individual manifestation.

The complexity that life developed through this mechanism is astounding, and the fact that life evolved to the point of being aware of itself is something even more remarkable. We are machines that know that they exist, and this may sound trivial because we're used to the idea, but when we stop to think about it carefully, this fact turns out to be rather absurd.

Approximately 3.5 billion years ago, some informational molecules capable of self-replication emerged from purposeless chemical reactions — from physics and chance. The selection of the fittest sifted through the molecules that, in practice, are nothing more than organized energy. Little by little, those that were more efficient at self-reproduction accumulated mutations due to the imperfection of their own replication systems.

These molecules became progressively more sophisticated in their ability to reproduce themselves. Perhaps first they acquired something like the ability to synthesize a certain enzyme that would facilitate the harvesting of energy, then a protein that would provide greater mechanical resistance to the body, some primitive photosensitive structure — which now, in its ultra-sophisticated version, constitutes our eyes. In the beginning, life shouldn't be much different from something like an extremely simple bacteria, a small machine that created copies of itself.

Then, accumulating mutations over billions of years, we finally reached the stage of human complexity. DNA reached a stupendous level of sophistication, synthesizing information to create a survival machine with trillions of cells finely engineered so that such machine could easily adapt to the requirements imposed by the environment. With its various senses, it captures information at different levels of reality, and uses its cognitive capacity to articulate that information in its favor — that being the reason we have awareness. Quite impressive for a biological agglomeration, when you think about it.

Returning to the graphic scheme presented earlier, we'll see that the premise that "living is good" is just an approximate translation of the mechanical behavior of life in human terms, in order to make the idea intelligible. Of course, in practice, life doesn't "want" anything — it just behaves as if it did. But if life doesn't "want" anything, why does it spread? Because it works. That's all. There's no "reason". Like any machine, life doesn't need a reason to work.

Thus, life behaves like any material process in our reality. The study of these processes, carried out at different levels by different sciences — Physics, Chemistry, Biology, Physiology, etc. —, did not reveal any purpose, just intricate patterns of an entirely mechanical biology.

So, as far as we can tell, there's nothing magical. Life is a mechanical system that is regulated through the selection of the best reproducers. In its origin, organic life is the result of a mechanical process that is automated on its own, whose trigger can be any entity capable of organized self-replication. Therefore, it would not be bold to say that we are true "viruses" that developed in matter. Our bodies are a means that DNA found to reproduce, to propagate — that is, to infect more matter and transform it into living beings that house it temporarily. Those who evade this rule disappear; those who follow it will reproduce children who, like their parents, are likely to be good reproducers.

Drawing an analogy between our material reality and the virtual reality of a computer, we could imagine a computer in which information constantly interacts according to certain internal programs, in which such information would be equivalent to the matter of our reality and the programming would be equivalent to our physical laws. Suppose that a virus capable of self-reproduction appeared on that computer. At first, it would work as a small program that created copies of itself. Thus, it begins to infect that computer, using its own "digital laws" to provide its self-preservation. If this virus also acquired the capacity to mutate, the various types of viruses that would emerge could compete to dominate the available digital space in a way analogous to biological living beings, so that they would become increasingly sophisticated and specialized.

Thus, figuratively speaking, we can think of our material reality as if it were a computer and of our DNA as if it were a virus. The difference is that, instead of digital information, life uses information encoded in the chemical bonds of DNA chains. Corroborating this reasoning, Richard Dawkins says that:

DNA viruses and computer viruses spread for the same reason: an environment exists in which there is machinery well set up to duplicate and spread them around and to obey the instructions that the viruses embody. These two environments are, respectively, the environment of cellular physiology and the environment provided by a large community of computers and data-handling machinery.

This outstanding scholar, creator of the theory of the selfish gene, offers us a perspective that is the opposite of the notion of life to which we are used, an objective view of life, in which the key element is not the organism, but the perpetuation of what originated it, its DNA:

[Don't] look for them [the genes] floating freely in the sea. They abandoned that freedom long ago. Now they huddle in huge colonies, living safely inside gigantic clumsy robots, walled up from the outside world, communicating with it through indirect and tortuous routes, manipulating it by remote control. They're in me and in you. They created us, body and mind. And its preservation is the ultimate reason for our existence. They were transformed, those replicators. Now they're called genes and we're their survival machines.

Let us now think about the mechanisms that were developed to provide this "infection" of reality. Doesn't it seem amazing that a chemical virus has reached the stage of creating a biological machine with a self-aware onboard computer that has the intelligence tool to guarantee its own perpetuation? A virus that created a machine with pleasure and suffering programs linked to what provides survival? And that we're here seeking happiness for exactly that reason?

It's almost commonplace to say that pleasure and suffering are the primary references that guide our lives. They are the most fundamental programs of our biological existence, and they work as very efficient tools to coerce us into actions that are useful for our preservation. Of course, no one can explain why feeling pleasure is good or why feeling pain is bad. This is because they do not exist as ends in themselves, that is, they do not exist to be good or bad, or subject to a clear description — they exist only because they are efficient in coercing us into behaviors that promote the perpetuation of our DNA.

All our emotions and feelings, obviously, exist in us for merely practical reasons, and that is why acting in search of pleasure, happiness, and satisfaction is very easily confused with acting in accordance with fundamental feelings, that is, impulses generated involuntarily by the body. If the "reasons of the heart" have a connection with anything, that thing is certainly perpetuation.

The fact that practically all mothers love their children is clear evidence of genetic selection via survival of the offspring that is manifested at the behavioral level. Would anyone know how to rationally explain why a mother should love or care for her children? Certainly not. We could even use some rational arguments to try to dissuade her:

> *Your body was deformed during pregnancy. You probably experienced nausea during your pregnancy. Labor pains are terrible and, after birth, your child will just eat, present you with metabolic waste, and sing incredibly annoying cries — an enormous job, and very stressful. While he is growing up, you will have to support and educate him, at least until the end of his youth. And after all that, he will simply say: "Bye, now I want to be independent, have a good life!" You'll never be rewarded for the enormous effort that went into raising it — and*

what's all this for? For nothing, absolutely!

It is evident that we are talking at a statistical level — thus excluding cases of parents who do not exhibit caring behavior. In addition, culture is a factor that influences how we think it is correct to treat our children, that's obvious. However, if there were not a fundamental instinct that transcended cultural influence, that guided us to the perpetuation of our offspring, we would slowly see the human species walk towards the abyss and finally vanish from the face of the Earth — something which definitely does not seem to be happening.

In any case, it is clear that such an argument will have no effect. She will continue to love her offspring as before, because a mother does not have to wait for logical arguments to love her child and, without a doubt, her love is immune to any kind of rational criticism. The reason doesn't matter to the one who loves — after all, no one decides to love deliberately, saying to themselves "I will love this or that", but simply obeys an impulse that appears spontaneously and involuntarily. This means that the motives that lead us to do so are emotional, not rational. In fact, this point is very curious, since we see that the behavior of the species can be predicted relatively well in terms of reproductive investment, as Robert Wallace explains:

[Such predictions are based on the principle that the greater the reproductive "investment" we made in another individual, the more likely we are to sacrifice ourselves for that person. We see the application of this everywhere. You can wreak havoc on tapeworm eggs without risking being attacked by an angry parent. At least, I haven't recently read news of a tapeworm attack. Tapeworms have very little investment in any egg, so their sacrifice and care are minimal. A stray egg is simply replaced in the next egg-laying. (...) An antelope mother, who went through pregnancy and lactation, has a considerable investment in her only child and will therefore defend it. If marauding hyenas try to grab her baby, she will resist and fight at the risk of her own life. However, when it becomes clear that the battle is lost, the antelope may abandon its child. The reproductive economy says that it must do so in order to live to reproduce later. The genes of mothers who fight for too long tend to disappear in the population. Naturally, the same happens with genes from mothers who flee at the first sign of danger. The bottom line is that altruism can be predicted in terms of repro-

ductive investment.]

This brings us to an important finding: if we were purely rational beings, with total control over ourselves, we would be able to manipulate our own emotions — but we cannot, since we feel an involuntary and irrational love for our children, and also for ourselves, for relatives, friends, etc. Why does this happen? Outside this context, it is almost impossible to find any reasonable explanation. However, from an evolutionary perspective, it is easy to understand the reason for this: mothers who did not show the tendency to love and, therefore, to take good care of their children, simply had low reproductive success — babies are very fragile at birth — and, over time, were obliterated in number by mothers who had a stronger emotional bond with their descendants, since their children tended to survive in greater numbers due to the greater care provided. Thus, the genes of caring mothers were passed on through their children, while the genes of careless mothers disappeared from the population.

This, once again, shows that our perspective on reality, that is, our representation of reality, far from being impartial, is extremely adapted to our needs and focused on efficiency. Exactly the conclusion reached in the sixth chapter: we interpret the objective world according to our subjective.

Returning to the initial question, we conclude that the question of the meaning of life can be answered from two perspectives:

1) In the universal perspective, the meaning of life is something mechanical, and corresponds to the tendency to just continue existing — to survive and spread genes to the next generation. As we have seen, as a matter of long-term natural selection, our body is designed according to this purpose and, therefore, our entire biology, emotions, and senses gravitate predominantly around it;

2) From the individual perspective, the meaning of life is represented by personal will, which is anchored in a value premise that serves as a reference and, based on this premise, the individual pursues objectives that may or may not be consistent with the mechanics of life. Therefore, at this level, it is the direction of the individual will that determines the meaning/purpose of life.

Apart from the basic issues of survival, in order to act, to achieve objectives, we will inescapably have to resort to values that are arbitrary. At the same time, without a fundamental belief that guides us, that serves as a reference to our will, we will spend our entire lives distressed about the lack of meaning in everything. Therefore, for those who intend to face this issue head-on — that is, without succumbing to the seduction of thoughtless belief —, the only way out seems to be the affirmation of values.

The affirmation of values would be something similar to "I declare that". It must be absent of any type of underlying justification, since a first questioning would be followed by an endless series that would invariably lead us back to emptiness, to that despair that screams "nothing is worth it, nothing is real — it's all in vain!" When we affirm a value, we must be aware that it has nothing special other than the fact that we have chosen it, that it is our value — everything that it represents and means is what we arbitrarily attribute to it.

We can cite some simple examples of these values: "good is everything that makes me happy", "good is everything that is most likely to be true", "good is everything that makes my willpower unstoppable", etc. From this, it can be deduced which beliefs will best serve our ends. Belief in God? The belief in reason? Belief in science? The belief in subjective feeling, in willpower, in objective knowledge, in moral discipline?

A question that is almost always present in this type of investigation is the following: is it better to be happy or to be right? Depending on the answer, it can be deduced which is the best path. Those who want to be happy will certainly find more answers in feelings and in religion. Those who want to be correct will certainly find more answers in reason and science.

However, those who want to be happy should not try to reconcile happiness with truth — likewise, those who want to be true should not try to reconcile truth with happiness. They are not incompatible things, but irretrievably different in their essence. For this reason, saying "I believe in God because I want to be happy" is an infinitely more respectable statement than saying "I believe in God because no one has proven his non-existence" — because at least it does not use silly arguments to try to mask the irrationality of such belief.

Therefore, we will not raise objections to those who decide to follow only the path of happiness, provided that, at least, they have sufficient integrity to also renounce any claim in the context of objective and scientific knowledge. They may become masters of the art of "living well" — but that's all. They may believe that they are the center of attention of a charitable providence or that they will live forever if that makes them feel good, but trying to prove such beliefs scientifically should not be the objective; what is important is the potential to generate happiness and well-being that such beliefs have, not whether they are objectively true.

On the other hand, the fundamental problem with choosing the path of truthfulness is that we have reasonable control over our thoughts, but almost none over our feelings — and when the two come into conflict, the results are potentially painful. Because of the nature of our mind, trying to induce the preponderance of rationality is often an arduous and sometimes distressing path, since living involves every part of the brain, but reasoning does not. Striving for truth implies a battle against pre-established tendencies — it is artificial like an intelligence that seeks to redefine the meaning of feeling. We know that there is a gulf between appearances and reality, and that things are certainly not as they are presented to our consciousness.

Happiness, therefore, does not have any link with truth — only with survival and perpetuation. But how important is this for the value of happiness? Why should we suffer in the search for truth if we're all going to disappear? In short, what we need to answer are these two questions: *what is the value of truth? What is the value of happiness?* It is based on the value that we give to these things, and to others that are equally fundamental, that we will be determining the objective of our lives, that is, its direction, its goal, its point — or, more commonly said, its meaning.

THE REASONS OF OUR BODY

Such as make it their business to oversee human actions, do not find themselves in anything so much perplexed as to reconcile them and bring them into the world's eye with the same lustre and reputation; for they commonly so strangely contradict one another that it seems impossible they should proceed from one and the same person. (...) We are entirely made up of bits and pieces, woven together so diversely and shapelessly that each of them pulls its own way at every moment. And there is as much difference between us and ourselves as there is between us and other people.

— Michel Montaigne

In this chapter, we will begin a quite controversial investigative process that is predominantly speculative in its nature. It should be clear that the perspective presented here refers to humans in general, to the abstraction of the "average individual" which, in fact, does not exist — it is only a theoretical model. We will try to investigate some of the predominant tendencies in human nature. In this way, behind the particular individual, behind environmental contingencies, and behind culture, we will search — quite clumsily, as we would be the last ones to deny — for general rules that apply with some precision to every human being.

Exceptions should not be seen as refutations, but as variations — and, when it comes to life, variation is something that we definitely don't see lacking. Therefore, it would be pointless to search for isolated cases that represent an exception and, raising them like a trophy, to say: "your theory is refuted, since I found an exception!" In human affairs, exceptions will always be present, because we are not doing mathematical calculations. We will never find the generic individual that incorporates everything exactly as described by any theory, because each individual, having unique genes — except for identical twins — and unique subjectivity, will always be different from any other.

Therefore, not man, the individual, but human nature — understood here as a historical and statistical predisposition in the promotion of survival — will be the object of our study. The objective will be to investigate the nature and function of some of the psychological mechanisms that, in earlier times, the human mind developed to solve problems related to its own perpetuation as a species. We can call this an exercise on *evolutionary psychology*, which, according to Geoffrey Miller:

> *try to understand human nature by asking how our ancestors survived and reproduced. The better we understand our evolution, the better we will understand our brains, our minds, and modern behavior. Evolutionary psychology seeks to understand, for example, why we seek status, find someone sexually attractive, make friends, gossip, and other answers to questions that have traditionally been overlooked by psychology. What we're now understanding is that much of our behavior is produced by brain circuits that originally evolved so that our ancestors became sexually attractive.*

It is also necessary to point out that the human mind was once an adaptive tool in the strictly Darwinian sense. But since civilization has acquired some control over the environmental contingencies that were formerly the tyrant responsible for natural selection, it ended up becoming decontextualized and not always adaptive. For this reason, it is necessary to go back to early times to be able to understand ourselves as organisms in a very unfamiliar environment.

We should note that complex cultures emerged only after the ancient period in which the mind underwent its fundamental adaptive mutations, which allowed our sophistication and social complexity. Complex cultures and civilizations, even the most ancient ones, are a very recent phenomenon in evolutionary terms. Since they appeared after such adaptations, they do not constitute factors that obstruct this analysis — that we can call "metacultural", that is, transcendent to cultures, referring to what human beings have in their psychological core. In this sense, as Daniel Goleman observed:

> *The slow and deliberate forces of evolution that shaped our emotions have been doing their job over a million years; the last 10,000 — despite having witnessed the rapid rise of human civilization and the human population explosion from five million to five billion — had hardly anything imprinted on our biological templates.*

Keeping all of this in mind is fundamental before we embark on the task of trying to understand ourselves as decontextualized survival machines. It has already been said that, in Biology, nothing makes sense except in the light of the Theory of Evolution. Here we are, somewhat boldly, stating that, in human behavior, nothing fundamental makes sense except in the light of an Evolutionary Psychology.

Our values don't exist in an organized and transparent way, and it's not always easy to figure them out. However, it's certain that they are always present, guiding our actions. Often, amidst all this intricate web of emotional and rational values that we cultivate, we end up faced with difficult dilemmas and, in order to maintain our well-being, we are forced to walk on the razor's edge. Those who want truth and well-being at the same time are between Scylla and Caribdes. This chapter aims to ensure that we can achieve a greater balance between the two things. To do so, we need to understand the true nature of our motivations, and also the factors that most strongly influence the genesis of our values.

From the perspective in which we have been analyzing the forces that move humans in their lives, we were able to identify an undeniable constant: utility. The force that drives humans, in their struggle for objectives, is utility. At first, this statement may seem rather cynical — not to say short-sighted —, because we are used to the idea that actions based on interest are driven by an unhealthy selfishness that only says "everything for me, nothing for others". However, it is not from this perspective that we make such a statement. We're not saying that people don't care about each other, but that they always care for some reason — or, in other words, that purely selfless actions are a myth.

Our thesis is that every action is always motivated by some interest, whether conscious or unconscious, internal or external, rational or irrational, known or unknown. The objective to which our actions converge is never the objective by chance — it is the objective because there is a motive that points to it. And to have any objectives, it is always necessary that we have started from some value premise.

As we've seen, values don't exist by themselves — there's no value without someone who values. Thus, *since the value of things does not in itself exist, it is determined only by desire and in proportion to the intensity of that desire*, emphasized Le Bon. The value that supports our actions is always in ourselves, whether we are aware of it or not, whether it was we who created it, or if we internalized it through external pressure. The fact is that in living beings, an assessment is always implicit in every action. Thus, if we are committed to perpetrating an action, and that action is aimed at some objective, this happens because, at some level, direct or indirect, that objective has value for us. Obviously, when something is consistent with what we value and, therefore, desire, that something can be classified as useful. It is in this sense that the statement that all our actions are motivated by interest must be understood.

We should note that it is not only between humans that there are relations based on utilitarianism, on the exchange of favors and benefits, or on cooperation to achieve similar goals. There are countless cases of relationships based on utilitarianism between many other types of living beings, which may or may not be of the same species. For example, termites feed on cellulose from wood. However, termites are unable to digest it. To do so, it has the help of a protozoan that lives inside it, which produces the enzyme called cellulase, which digests cellulose. Thus, both benefit from the product of digestion. Without such a protozoan, the termite dies. The ant is a social insect. The society in which it lives is entirely divided into specialized castes, each with its function, to allow the ant society to survive. Such cooperation is not only useful, but indispensable, as ants are unable to survive independently of the anthill — and the same can be said of bees. There is also the mutualism between fungi and algae, which constitute the lichens. Finally, we can mention the case of the bacteria *Rhizobium*, which lives in the roots of leguminous plants. The bacteria will provide nitrogen for the plant which, in return, gives it protection and nutrients. In nature there are many cases of mutual help, and we could easily multiply the examples.

To facilitate understanding, we will divide utilitarian relations between humans into two subgroups: rational or explicit utility and emotional or implicit utility. On a rational level, we speak of objective utility, and we could mention things like exchanges of favors, pacts, jobs, commercial agreements, and contracts. In particular, we could mention partnerships between individuals or companies. By making such partnerships, they aim at things such as increasing their power, their influence, their potential success, etc. For them, the objective is not to enter such a partnership because they "like being partners", but because this is useful for both parties — because with this they will be able, for example, to beat the competition or to earn more money than they would by themselves. The fact that rational utilitarianism exists among humans is nothing new and, therefore, it is not what interests us. What we intend to analyze here is implicit utilitarianism, which is manifested on an emotional level.

The perspective we are going to present is based on the idea that emotional factors present themselves in us as the deceptive surface of an underground utilitarianism. In short, we can say that, for our consciousness, emotion seems disinterested, but for our unconscious, utility exists and is objective. As can be seen, we are only advancing the conclusions reached in the previous chapter, that is, deepening the analysis of the types of mechanisms and baits that the body learned evolutionarily to use to induce individuals to perform actions that are beneficial to the imperatives of life.

It is practically impossible to identify what exactly were the evolutionary factors responsible for the genesis of all our psychological mechanisms, that is, the reason they exist in our species. However, the fact is that everything that exists in us, exists because it was useful in some sense. Natural selection does not filter the characteristics of beings by any other criterion than that of utility to survival and reproduction. It is not possible for us to define with surgical precision the role that such mechanisms played in early times, throughout human evolution, or for what specific reason they were selected and remain with us today. It is only important to note that this is how evolutionary gears work.

It would not be anything new to say that our mind has evolved certain emotional devices, and that conditioning guides such devices, allowing us to learn the types of behaviors that are important for our survival in a given environment. Our basic emotions, carrying positivity or negativity in relation to something — depending on the experiences lived —, serve as guiding elements of our actions, and thus can be understood as having an adaptive function.

The method that we will use to discover what the function was is commonly called "reverse engineering". Through it, we're able to obtain certain insights about human nature within the evolutionary perspective. Of course, the name "reverse engineering" is a bit misleading in this case, as it seems to imply the existence of an engineer who designed things. But, as we have seen, the engineer we are referring to is blind and impersonal — it's called natural selection.

It would be interesting to begin our investigation by presenting a comment by Gustave Le Bon regarding the importance of sensitivity to pleasure and pain as necessary references for maintaining our lives:

> *We will always have (...) two great certainties, which nothing could destroy: pleasure and pain. All our activity derives from them. (...) Pleasure and pain are the language of organic and affective life, the expression of satisfied or disturbed balances in the body. They represent the means employed by nature to compel entities to certain acts, without which the maintenance of existence would become impossible. (...) The language of organs, translated by pleasure and pain, is more or less imperative, according to the needs it must satisfy. Some, for example, are hunger, which they don't wait. (...) The worker, bent under the weight of work, the sister of charity, who is not disgusted by any wound, the missionary tortured by the savages, the wise man who seeks the solution of a problem, the dark microbe that agitates at the bottom of a drop of water, all obey the same stimulants of activity: the attraction of pleasure, the*

fear of pain.

Therefore, we can say that the body has a kind of language to communicate to us if something is good or not. Based on it, the body translates as pleasure, well-being, and happiness the actions and states that are consistent with the imperatives of life, and translates as suffering, pain, dissatisfaction, and sadness everything that hinders its advancement. In some cases, this language is perfectly obvious and yet contextualized, such as when we see the example of pleasure derived from intercourse as a reward for perpetuating our genes. The intense pain caused by injuries also clearly works as a punishment or warning for damaging our machine.

However, such phenomena are linked to very primitive and very fundamental questions, which is why they are so easily decipherable. Without a doubt, it would be an oversimplification to think that the human mind is something so simple. It would be practically impossible to draw up a precise historical profile of human evolution in such a way as to be able to explain how and why certain characteristics developed, disappeared, or changed over time. All we can suppose is that the selection of these traits occurred according to the criteria of being useful, neutral, or harmful for our survival.

That's why, even today, we know very little about the inner workings of our brain. The human mind has not ceased to be much less than a black box. We are only able to deduce some things indirectly, through inferences, reflections, and controlled experiments, interpreting all of this from a pragmatic perspective in order to formulate theoretical models that seek to outline in general terms what are the essential mechanisms of our mind, whose complexity we cannot understand through physics or chemistry alone.

The fact is that, in practice, if it weren't for the impulses, for the sensations that are manifested internally in us, we would never know what our body needs. When we feel an impulse or some sign of a need, we use our capacity for abstraction and reasoning to overcome the adversities of the environment and, thereby, be able to satisfy those needs or express those impulses in the form of actions. We can always noticed that, subjectively, it is very rewarding to follow the impulses generated involuntarily by our body.

For example, it is obvious that, when there is a lack of food in our body, the brain tells us, through hunger, that we should eat. However, how could we know when we should eat if the body did not inform us of this through the feeling of hunger? We would probably only remember that we forgot to eat after feeling dizzy or fainting. This is what happens to those who forget to take their medication, and only remember to do that after the symptoms that the medicine was preventing come back. We should also note that hunger is not the lack of food itself, as we could simply use an appetite suppressant to nullify the body's signal. In reality, hunger is the language that our body uses to say what it wants us to do.

Thus, when we feel hungry, we immediately translate this into the following terms: look for food. Then the conscious part of our mind reflects, devises strategies, draws conclusions, and finally discovers some way to satisfy this involuntary urge to eat, which came from a primitive level of the brain. Assuming that we were in a forest, we could go out looking for wild fruits, we could make a spear to hunt some animal, etc. When we get the food and eat it, this cancels the unpleasant feeling of hunger.

In this way, it only seems that sensations are an end in themselves when, in reality, they are not. This is pure utilitarianism in disguise, because the fact is that we don't have the power to freely choose what will generate pleasure or pain — we just use such things as references to guide our actions. In this situation, we can also see that our intellect, in fact, is just a refinement, a detail grounded on an underlying neural superstructure. Our intelligence functions as a means that the body has evolutionarily found to satisfy itself. Daniel Goleman, explaining the evolution of our nervous system, shows us the reason for this hierarchy:

> *To better understand the strong hold of emotions over the thinking mind — and why feeling and reason go to war so readily — think about how the brain evolved. Human brains, with their little over a kilo of cells and neural humors, are three times larger than those of our evolutionary cousins, the non-human primates. Over millions of years of evolution, the brain grew from the bottom up, the higher centers developing as elaborations of lower, older parts. (...) From the most primitive root, the brain stem, emotional centers emerged. Millions of years later, in the evolution of these emotional areas, the thinking brain,*

or "neocortex", the large bulb of wavy tissues that forms the upper layers, developed. The fact that the thinking brain developed from emotions reveals a great deal about the relationship between thought and feeling; there was an emotional brain long before a rational one.

In situations of danger, we can clearly see that much of our mental activity is not mediated by our consciousness. For example, if we're walking in a zoo and we accidentally run into a hungry lion, we don't stop to meditate on the potential drawbacks of the situation. When the visual system receives the stimulus containing the image of the lion, it does not reach our consciousness so that it can give the verdict on whether we should be afraid. The information is processed by the system called "cognitive unconscious", which analyzes the data obtained and automatically triggers emergency mechanisms — fight or flight —, which prepare our body for a high-risk situation. The frequency of our heartbeats increases, the palms of the hands become moist, the muscles tense. Among the consequences of this reaction is the feeling of fear, which is the conscious apprehension of the general alertness of our body. Thus, as quickly as we realize that it is a lion that is in front of us, we are already alert and with our entire body drenched with hormones to allow us to react vigorously. If, later, we realize that the lion is on a leash or that it is actually a very well-made statue, then our brain deactivates the alert. The important thing is to note that this process, at its primary level, is involuntary, and the conscious brain only perceives the results of this processing.

The same thing happens, for example, when we hear a bomb explode. The state of alert that follows the detection of the stimulus is generated before we are aware of it, since we become tense and sometimes manifest some automatic reactions — such as shouting — even before we consciously know what just happened. This is a mechanism clearly aimed at the survival of the species, since, in a wild environment, we don't have time to consciously investigate the potential risk of each situation. The faster we react to the sign of a possible risk, the greater our chance of survival. So, in terms of survival, if it was the wind or a lion that moved the leaves behind a tree, that is certainly not worth investigating — the most "intelligent" thing to do is to move away without further consideration.

When an individual is viewing images from an extremely violent movie, those images produce real responses in the body. Our conscious mind knows that in reality it is an intricate pattern of tiny luminous dots that form a series of sequential figures, giving us the illusion of movement. However, our unconscious mind doesn't "know" that. The "cognitive unconscious" captures the characteristics of the image and processes them as if they were real, coming from the environment. For this reason, the individual feels emotionally stimulated by little bright dots. Naturally, if the stimulus were mediated by consciousness and sanctioned by it, such images would have no effect on our emotions.

Intuition also falls under the category of unconscious mental processes. Who hasn't ever felt like or dislike for someone they've never seen before, right at first sight, without knowing why? This is the result of the processes of the unconscious mind, which is analyzing various factors that remain ignored by our consciousness. From this perspective, it can be said that the famous love at first sight is also a kind of intuition.

Attraction between individuals follows these same general patterns. When we are in some situation and then we are faced with a man or a woman, our mind gathers the data from the individual, compares it and weighs it according to the patterns — innate and learned — that we have of what is a "compatible" individual. In other words, it analyzes the characteristics in terms of compatibility — health, appearance, personality, intelligence, social status, etc. — to verify their potential usefulness. Once this unconscious analysis is done, the body translates the results into sensations, which are what we consciously experience.

If, for example, a girl fits our personal parameters of a compatible female, the body produces a sense of attraction in us — it makes us want to have her as a partner. If she satisfies our emotional requirements very well, it is possible that we may even fall in love with her. Of course, all of this happens at a level that is below our consciousness, as being aware of such processing would really be of no use. All that the conscious mind perceives is just a fondness and a great desire to be with the girl.

Once the desire manifests, the exact same thing happens: just like when we were hungry, the rational mind puts itself under the control of such impulses, devising all kinds of plans to win the girl over — e.g., buying flowers, being romantic, praising her, showing kindness —, always thinking that the fundamental objective is to win her over. If he manages to seduce her, he will be rewarded by a flood of pleasure. He will be overjoyed and satisfied. If she rejects him, he will feel like a failure, maybe he will become sad, sometimes even depressed.

Of course, no one in their right mind would declare their love to a girl by saying, "you know, you seem like a compatible female to me". We say such things in cipher language, such as "I like you a lot", "I love you", "you complete me", "I am in love with you", and so on. But, in the end, we like and love for one simple and unique reason: because such people are useful to satisfy our emotional needs, which are ultimately at the service of the imperative of life.

With this, we notice that there is a lot of reason behind our emotions, feelings, and sensations. What we feel only seems irrational because we are not used to analyzing such phenomena within the biological context in which they emerged, that is, within the context of the needs of our human machine. However, when we begin to view man as a sophisticated animal and his impulses as having a fundamentally pragmatic character, many "mysteries" of human behavior become more understandable.

To illustrate, let's take as an example the most controversial and apparently most inexplicable of feelings: love. Thousands of people have tried to define it, almost always in a poetic, subjective way, with metaphors and paradoxes, but for many, love remains a mystery, something that cannot be precisely defined.

There are two widespread interpretative mistakes, and they are the main reason love seems incomprehensible. The first mistake consists in trying to define just love itself, as if the act of loving were an end in itself, a pure and disinterested act, leaving its underlying reasons to the whims of what is poetically called the "heart". The second mistake, of course, consists in thinking that the motives of the heart deserve unrestricted trust, that they are the most "true" and "pure" things in us. We forget that the explanation of feelings is not in their subjective manifestation, but in their biological function.

Certainly such misinterpretations were reinforced by that myth — not to say by that lie — that we have a "soul", which carries the "essence" of our being, whose nature would supposedly be independent of the body. In other words, all involuntary feelings, because they are immune to reason and conscious will, because they function in an autonomous way, could, in this perspective, be interpreted as a reflection of that transcendent soul.

However, let's put aside such delusions and let's get to the facts. Let's see: love is a feeling that always arises involuntarily, which generates impulses that lead to well-being if they are satisfied and to suffering if they are frustrated. Doesn't that fit perfectly the profile of an innate program? And this is even more clear and evident when we realize the universal character of love, which transcends race, religion, culture, sex, age, etc.

We could make an arbitrary distinction here between two phenomena encompassed by what is usually called love. One of the facets of love is what is called "passion", which could be understood as a strong impulse to create a stable affective bond, that is, a feeling. This impetus is usually accompanied by an erotic component. The second facet would be the already established bond itself, the goodwill that is what we usually call "love". In this sense, we should note that this affective bond does not necessarily have to be established through erotic passion. It can also be created by more subtle processes: identification, coexistence, admiration, prestige, affirmation, repetition, suggestion, etc. To the various degrees of intensity of affection we give different names, such as friendship, collegiality, companionship, affection, sympathy, love, passion, etc. But, for all intents and purposes, since all these seem to be nothing more than degrees of intensity of the same continuum of affectivity, we will simply use the terms affection/emotion to designate this mental phenomenon, without artificially fragmenting it into watertight categories.

Thus, from this perspective, an extreme emotional impetus — or passion — ceases to occupy the throne of human sensations and is relegated to the same position, say, of hunger or fear: it is simply a kind of "physiological coercion" of an emotional nature — that is, a means that the body uses to achieve what, during its evolution, proved to be beneficial. As can be seen, this phenomenon represents an expression of the "reason of the body" — that reason whose criterion of truth is survival and perpetuation. For example, emotion works by taking part in reproductive phenomena — after all, no one deliberately chooses who they will be attracted to or fall in love with —, but also by promoting security through the very strong interpersonal ties it creates, leading to greater unity and cooperation between individuals.

It should be noted that, in all the ideas mentioned, emotional manifestations are always strongly linked to utility, which underlies the entire concept of Evolutionism. Of course, nobody would say "I love my parents because they're very useful". Emotion happens spontaneously in us; it is not a voluntary act. Love — that "wishing well" or "feeling good with" — is the way the body uses to say: "this is good, this is useful, keep it". But, on the other hand, when we lose something that we love, the body punishes us with sadness, and by that it means: "this is bad; don't let it happen again; protect and keep everything you love".

Obviously, we're not saying that we're born with innate stereotypical patterns that determine how we express our emotions. We are referring only to the essential mechanism of affectivity — which is a mental device with which evolution infused us to be able to deal with life. Thus understood, an affect can be seen as a consequence of the unconscious recognition of someone's usefulness in some aspect — functioning in terms very similar to fear. In this sense, just as what causes us fear is learned through our interaction with the environment, what awakens our affection and guides our ways of expressing it is learned throughout our experience — but fear and affection themselves are not learned. They're innate mechanisms, brain circuits, in fact. What we learn is only the most convenient way to use such mechanisms at the service of our well-being in the environment in which we are inserted.

At the level of human social relations, exactly the same thing occurs. Everyone likes their friends and likes to have friends. However, does someone *choose* to enjoy having friends? If they're not natural born hermits, hardly. This predisposition to socialization appears involuntarily in us, in the form of an emotional need. That's why we need to have a group of people who trust us and whom we can trust. Without friends, we feel lonely, empty, sad, insecure, meaningless. Obviously, it's nice to have friends, but in our emotional brain that's not how the reasoning works. In its proper context, to be pleasant means to be useful — and this utility, of course, is manifested in us in an encoded way, in the form of feelings.

So, when we meet a certain person and we like her, it means that we feel good in her company, either because she is funny, intelligent, erudite, beautiful, nice, companionable, caring, or has any other characteristic that we appreciate. At this level, the usefulness of the person is measured by his or her ability to satisfy our emotional needs, our requirements. We always value our friends in proportion to how useful they are to us.

Evolutionarily, it's good to have friends because we're not self-sufficient. And they provide us with a sense of security because we know that they'll be willing to help us if we need it, and vice versa. It's not hard to imagine that, in the era before the rise of civilizations, when life was a true incessant battle, seeking friendships was extremely useful for survival. Evidently, not because friendship is "natural", but because those who were left alone would probably end up dying of hunger or being eaten by some hungry beast.

Surely that's why we feel so attached to friends who understand us, who like us as we are, who are honest, sincere, who we can trust. Not because friendship is beautiful, but because it was useful during our evolution as a species — and the well-being that comes from that is just the validation of our primitive mind. Therefore, we see that friendships are based on factors of mutual interest, as if they were "emotional contracts" signed by our unconscious mind. The only difference lies in the fact that, instead of power and money, friendships provide security, well-being, and happiness.

In this sense, an interesting peculiarity of our mind is the fact that we have a kind of "impostor detector". For example, if someone we know, whom we consider a friend, does not fulfill his part of the contract that was tacitly established by friendship, that is, if he betrays our trust, that person loses his credit, his reputation is tarnished, and we tend to exclude him from our social circle. Of course, if the person is of great importance to us, we can come to forgive the disloyalty, although this is usually not a good idea.

Often, amid this situation, the famous feeling of *guilt* arises in the traitor, which, in this case, probably comes from understanding the loss of exchanging a long-term benefit — a friendship — for an ephemeral advantage obtained through betrayal — in case the advantage wasn't great enough, of course. For this reason, La Rochefoucauld rightly observed that *Our repentances are generally not so much a concern and remorse for the harm we have done, as a fear of the harm we may have brought upon ourselves.*

The existence of such a mechanism clearly shows that our relations are based on a tacit contract that aims to satisfy reciprocal needs. It is a contract based on mutual interest and which, for this very reason, is not compatible with betrayal. As Robert Wallace explains:

> *The problem is that we are an intelligent species, with a long memory and the capacity to recognize ourselves individually. Thus, if others see you defrauding, they will recognize you as an impostor, mark you as such, ostracize you, or punish you in other ways. They might refuse to save him. Thus, if impostors are identified and are not saved when they find themselves in difficulty, the fraud will not compensate. If, in relationships, there were no expectation of reciprocity, there would be no concept of fraud, of betrayal.*

With this, we certainly realize that our actions and relationships are permeated by much more selfishness than we would like to admit. We are used to the idea that when the motives that lead us to do something are purely sentimental, passionate, they are disinterested. But it's exactly the opposite. Affectivity is the synthetic language of the primitive mind, which weighs all the needs of the organism and then translates them into impulses, which the rational mind is willing to obey, like a mercenary, in exchange for subjective rewards of pleasure, well-being, and security.

The dreaded and infamous death also serves as a great example of the kind of logic behind our feelings. First of all, we can ask something very simple: why do we only suffer from the death of those who are close to us? Normally we would answer something like "because we loved that person", "because we were close", "because we were friends", and so on. But, in the end, objectively, we suffer only because that person was useful to us, because, in some sense, we were helped by them — and whenever we are suddenly subtracted from something that satisfies our needs, the consequence of this comes in the form of sadness, restlessness, anxiety, suffering, depression, despair, etc.

Thus, the reason for the pain, anxiety, and insecurity that result from a sudden change — and also the great effort needed to get used to it — lies precisely in the fact that our body, being a very efficient machine, tries to avoid superfluous expenses as much as possible. To this end, it imposes certain uncomfortable obstacles which we could call "necessity checks" — so that we only change what is strictly necessary. That's why changes are so painful.

Therefore, in the case of great losses, it is normal to feel that everything "lost its meaning" because, when we are deprived of a crutch, this causes anxiety, since it disturbs and disorients our journey towards the objectives we were aiming for, requiring a readaptation to the unusual situation that presented itself before us. Thus, we can think of our affective ties and our habits, in a certain way, as being inertial, that is, tending to remain as they are, unless some change is essential — and the body verifies that it is truly essential through the suffering that we will have to experience to carry out such a change. This does not apply, of course, to the changes that will be beneficial to us, that will facilitate our lives — these we will accept without any difficulty.

From this perspective, to miss something only means the feeling of abstinence from something that we were used to. Thus, when we fear losing something that we love, it actually means that it would be too painful or impossible to find a replacement. If we lose a friend that we like, for example, we get sad. For most people, there's no logical explanation for this, as they are used to the idea that sadness is just a "natural consequence" of the fact that they have lost a "true friendship". Of course, this is a superficial and poetic notion that doesn't explain anything. Humans tend to idealize everything, over-romanticize feelings and relationships, and that's why such things become seemingly incomprehensible. However, if we analyze this issue from a pragmatic and objective perspective, it becomes obvious why we suffer when we lose a friend.

A solid friendship is a big, long-term investment. We spend a significant portion of our lives getting to know each other, cultivating emotional bonds and trust. We have many expectations and, over time, an "emotional contract" is slowly established, a bond of sincerity and mutual commitment with that person. In this context, the emotional cost of losing an investment of this magnitude would be enormous. It would take us a long time to structure another similar friendship. To arrive at such a degree of entanglement, years and years of contact would be necessary. That's why we suffer so much when we lose a friend or a loved one: we were attached to them, we were used to them. We lost something that, on an emotional level, was very precious. In addition, after the loss, we will need to reorganize our entire emotional life, something that is very exhausting.

Thus, the idea is that when we love others, when we do things for their benefit, in the end we are not doing them a favor, but seeking our own advantage, our own satisfaction. If we love our neighbors, we do so only because we love ourselves, and the fact that the motives for this are sentimental doesn't make such action less selfish — at best, it's spontaneous.

A feeling that is also interesting is called jealousy. It seems to play a fundamental role in maintaining the balance in relationships. For example, why do men, in general, tend to be polygamous and women tend to be monogamous? The answer seems to be found in the investment that each one has in the generation of a child containing their genetic material. A man's investment is very small — only the material of an ejaculation can yield him a child. On the other hand, women need a much greater investment to produce and maintain a child.

Thus, it is natural to suppose that women should be more careful in selecting their partners, since they have higher reproductive costs, so that when they manage to maintain a compatible male in a monogamous relationship, they automatically increase their chances of raising a healthy child, because with the partnership there will be more resources available. From this point of view, jealousy appears as a defensive technique against infidelity, which, in genetic terms, means, for men, raising a child that does not have his genetic material and, for women, a substantial loss of assistance in raising the child, since the father will be busy trying to fertilize other females. In this regard, Leland Swenson made a very interesting comment:

In humans, the differences between the two sexual genders are related to the different evolutionary strategies resulting from selective pressures. Behavioral differences related to partner choice and jealous reactions to infidelity may be correlated with the best reproductive maximization strategy for each sex. (...)

semen is cheap — eggs are expensive. Males can be several times more reproductively successful if they produce as many offspring as possible, investing nothing but time and semen. On the other hand, if times are scarce, males will be more successful if they are left with just one female and invest their resources to increase the chances of survival of the offspring. The dualistic behavior of men in relationships — of seeking short-term sexual partners with a small investment or of seeking a spouse to invest in — created for women the adaptive problem of having to discern whether the particular man sees her as a temporary sexual partner or as a potential wife. Females have a greater initial investment in generating a child, and can only conceive a certain number of offspring; therefore, it is in their interest that as many of their children as possible survive. The females are interested in increasing the male's investment and the costs of desertion. Requiring a courtship is an adaptive strategy for this purpose. Courting increases the male's initial investment in the relationship and reduces the usefulness of desertion. This is because a male who deserts a female after extensive courting has already used most of his resources in his courting and, in this way, few resources will remain to court future females.

The benefit-cost ratio seems to be playing the central role in the issue of infidelity, which is frequently where we find the most tension in relationships. The male does not want to raise children with the genetic material of another individual, so he feels jealous of his partner. But at the same time, he also wants to fertilize as many females as possible to disseminate his DNA at low costs. On the other hand, when females feel jealous and demand courtships, they are seeking to maintain their reproductive success through monogamy, due to the large investments that a child requires of her, especially during pregnancy, which will be substantially reduced if she has a loyal male by her side. We should note, however, that when males are looking for a definitive female, the one with whom they want to raise their children, in whom they intend to invest their resources, they generally become as judicious as the female in their choice, working actively to maintain their partner.

In the end, men want to inseminate as many females as possible to maximize their reproductive success, and women also want to maintain their reproductive success, and they do so by trying to maintain the male's fidelity long enough. Betrayal, of course, can also be interesting to women. Females can deceive the faithful male, maintaining relations with another who is more "vigorous", while being supported by the loyal male. Since there was no DNA test in the Stone Age, he would have no easy way of knowing that the child wasn't his.

In the current context, it may seem that such ideas do not apply as well as they did in the past — after all, contraceptives didn't grow on trees in Prehistory. But this theory seems to clarify, at least in general terms, some interesting points about the sexual behavior of human beings. Maybe that's why it's so common to hear that women "don't understand" men and that men "don't understand" women — because they were shaped by evolution with different and somewhat conflicting reproductive strategies.

Another example that seems quite reasonable to explain a mechanism that the body uses to coerce us to act in a way that is compatible with the imperatives of life is the one through which we value ourselves emotionally in a social environment. It's a very remarkable fact that honest compliments work beautifully to make us feel good, to raise our self-esteem. For example, those with a beautiful, well-sculpted body almost always like to show it off — of course, to be praised, admired, and to feel desired. Nobody does hours of exercise alone — even because, alone, we don't have much motivation — and then lock themselves in a room. When we ask the reason for this, we often hear that they exercise just because they like it — but they do so because it would be embarrassing to admit the truth. No kind of personal satisfaction occurs in isolation.

In another example, if we spend ten years writing a fascinating and revolutionary book, we don't do it to put it in a drawer and spend the rest of our lives satisfied with knowing we're intelligent. We want to publish the book, we want to be read, we want to receive some return for the effort we made. Just knowing is not enough — we must, in addition, show our "power" to others, so that we can be recognized for our qualities. It's only then that we effectively *feel* rewarded for the effort.

Why is that? Because man, obviously, is not an end in itself — we are just a bridge to the next generation. We live according to the social because it is the reference according to which we measure and define ourselves. Displaying intelligence, beauty, physical strength, and the like, are some means that the human species uses to expose its "peacock tail", its qualities. In this case, the behavior would be transmitting a message like this: "look at the power of my intellect, at my great physical strength — I am a good reproducer and a fearsome adversary, meaning I have excellent genetic material".

With this mechanism in mind, it is certainly easy to understand why we are upset when rumors arise about us, which misrepresent who we really are. Why should we be concerned, if we know it's a falsehood? Rationally, this doesn't make any sense, as we know ourselves in greater depth than anyone else will ever come close to knowing. However, this is an emotional issue, not a rational one. This is because our vanity is pinching us to warn that our public image is distorted, that our social credibility is falling, and as a result we may lose social benefits.

Our vanity would be something like a device that makes us worry about what others think about us — and it is always according to what our social environment thinks of us that we weigh our value. So when others think well of us, we think well of ourselves. When others recognize us, we feel recognized.

Therefore, emotionally, we value ourselves indirectly. What we call our self-image is a reflection of what the individuals around us think about us. Most likely, this is a mechanism whose purpose is to make us act in a socially — and, in earlier times, reproductively — compatible way.

Because of this remarkable peculiarity of our nature, we always seek to do things for which we will be recognized. Thus, in order not to feel "useless", we live in an eternal struggle to impress the people around us, to show our value, our usefulness, our virtues — and, with that, without realizing it, we are competing and adapting to the selective pressures of the environment in which we live. As Geoffrey Miller explained:

Sexual selection determined our need for status, prestige, and social respect. Status isn't as useful for survival, but it's very important for reproduction. When we compete in the workplace, we are seeking status in the same way that our ancestors tried to achieve status by being good hunters or storytellers. In other words: we are always working to impress and attract sexual partners. Our culture is not separate from our biological evolution.

As we can see, vanity can be understood as a kind of "socialization instinct". Vanity causes individuals to be concerned with their self-image — and their self-image is the awareness of what they represent in their social environment. Thus, the feeling we have about our image is always a reflection of social judgments about us. Figuratively speaking, it would be like saying that our "true self" is a source of white light that is emotionally invisible to us. We are only able to see it after it reflects on external objects — the social environment — and then returns to our eyes colored by it.

Vanity, from this perspective, presents itself as the fundamental root from which our "will to power" originates — or, to put it more honestly, our desire for domination, recognition, and social prestige. Friedrich Nietzsche, with his keen intuition, understood well the nature of vanity. He noticed that we feel uncomfortable in the presence of individuals who have the same vanities as us, since it is a "peacock's tail" that is competing with ours.

Nor did escape him the fact that it is precisely because of vanity that we are concerned with the aesthetic factors of our personality. It makes us want to embellish our character and enhance our attitudes, covering them by pompous speech and impressive external appearances as its very essence:

As the bones, flesh, entrails, and blood vessels are enclosed by a skin that renders the aspect of men endurable, so the impulses and passions of the soul are enclosed by vanity: it is the skin of the soul.

It is because of this "power factor" that the occupations in which we find most satisfaction — or happiness, fulfillment — are always tied to our capacities. For example, those who have difficulty in exact sciences, such as mathematics, will most likely not follow this field of knowledge by choice, since the frustration resulting from incompetence acts as a strong demotivator.

On the contrary, we tend to like occupations that are harmonious with our individual capacities, through which we can express our best potential. Such occupations are those to which we will most likely dedicate ourselves — not because of our love of toil, of course, but because of our eagerness for the social prestige that we will achieve through this.

Understanding vanity as a quest for power in the context of a pre-established collective valuation, it could never exist in isolation. This means that our power is nothing more than a social convention — and this is a good example of how our social environment regulates our instincts. Thus, our power is always a power in relation to something — and, since we are inherently social beings, our reference for measuring this is the other, that is, the values in our social environment.

In our primitive mind, those primary instincts of domination and power always survive within a social hierarchy, in which the criterion that defines our position is our "strength" — in a broad sense — and our potency exists as a collective recognition of that strength. This type of thing can be observed in our simian cousins in a much less disguised way than in humans. In any case, it is clear that this type of need for potency is found at a relatively small level of importance, below the most fundamental needs, such as biological ones — nutrition, respiration, digestion, etc. However, it would be of no use for a being to behave in a biologically healthy way if, after having this type of need guaranteed, it did not fight for potency, for domination in its social environment — a tendency that was originally expressed in territorial and hierarchical struggles within small bands.

From this perspective, it's not difficult to understand the raison d'être of the old adage "power corrupts" — power is a very satisfying type of pleasure, and we do everything to achieve it. It seems, then, that Ecclesiastes was really correct when he said that everything is vanity.

There is also the famous and controversial issue of altruistic actions — and their related values — always revolving around a supposed "pure disinterest". Altruistic behavior, in a generic way, can be defined as any act that, with some detriment to the perpetrator, provides benefit to the one who receives it. It should be noted that the harm caused to the altruistic individual always tends to be less than the benefit resulting from their action. We will divide altruistic actions, for convenience, into three categories: 1) genetic altruism; 2) reciprocal altruism; 3) psychological altruism.

1) *Genetic altruism* consists of a sacrifice to help someone with whom we are genetically related. For example, parents helping children and *vice versa*, siblings helping siblings, etc. We should note that the higher the degree of

genetic kinship, the higher the percentage of DNA that an individual shares with another, the greater the tendency — and let's understand it: tendency — to altruistic behavior. The degree of genetic altruism can be predicted more or less precisely through a short mathematical exercise, as Robert Wallace explains:

[Genetic] altruism can be predicted mathematically with great precision, but we will also discover that the phenomenon is more complex than previously believed, because animals sacrifice themselves for relatives as much as for descendants. (...) Who would you die for? Let's ask another way: why does natural selection say that you must risk your life in order to increase your gene species in the population? If there's a good chance that you would have two more descendants if you were still alive (thus duplicating your existing genes in the gene pool), you wouldn't be well advised to die for one or two siblings; you would need to defend three at least. Nor would you want to die for less than five half-siblings, nephews, or aunts, and you wouldn't die for all your cousins, unless they were numerous enough to form a baseball team. The idea is to give up your chances of future reproduction only when it is likely that the relatives you saved would have more of their own species of genes than you would be able to perpetuate through your descendants if you were still alive.

2) *Mutual altruism*, as the name suggests, is based on mutual help, and its most obvious example is friendship. The central idea is that we strive to do favors to people in the same degree and proportion as we imagine they would do for us, if necessary. As we have already dealt with this issue just above, it seems unnecessary to explain it again. So let's just quote an observation from Wallace in this regard:

The idea of reciprocal altruism is contained in a parable from the Good Samaritan. Suppose a drowning man is rescued by a Good Samaritan, although the two are not related to each other and are totally strangers. It seems at first that we have found an example of pure altruism. However, it turns out that the Good Samaritan has a little to gain from his "selfless" act. Suppose that the man who is drowning has a fifty percent chance of dying if not helped and that the Good Samaritan, being a good swimmer, is only one in twenty likely to die if he helps him. In our plot, we also assume that if the Good Samaritan falls into the water and drowns, the victim will also drown. But if the Samaritan lives, the victim will also live. For illustrative purposes, let us assume that there is a high probability that the Good Samaritan himself will need assistance at a later time and that the rescued man will be able to give back by saving him. In fact, if the drowning man reciprocates (with the same probability of risk for each), both will have received a net benefit from playing the role of savior. In essence, each man would have traded a fifty percent risk of dying for about a tenth of the risk.

3) *Psychological altruism* is what is typically considered to be "true selfless altruism", which consists of perpetrating philanthropic actions without any expectation of reward. Let us note that the idea that altruistic actions are "superior" probably has its roots in the well-being and in the sense of "peace of mind" provided by actions of this nature — and this could be interpreted as a kind of "sponsorship" of our instincts in favor of cooperation.

As we saw earlier, the awareness of our usefulness, of our importance for the happiness of others, weighs heavily on us, since, as mentioned, we value ourselves indirectly, through their judgments about us. However, even anonymously, the reward of well-being could still be achieved through the awareness of our beneficial influence, the "conviction of our own virtue". Thus, strictly speaking, altruism does not seem to be more than a selfish search for physiological well-being rewards — after all, we are biochemical machines —, having in the back of our minds the sense that they are virtuous actions.

So, deep down, everything is done selfishly, just for our own good. In this sense, Wallace himself defends that *no one has ever done anything for anyone else. Never. I hope that this statement will be met with howls of denial, because we have all seen cases of self-sacrifice. In fact, we ourselves often sacrifice ourselves for others and we have a notion of people who sacrificed themselves for us. So what does this patently stupid statement mean?* That subjective appearances delude us with incredible ease.

Genetic altruism and reciprocal altruism are so obviously based on interest that it is not necessary to comment on them in detail. What we have left is only to fully unmask the third type of altruism, which is considered the most "authentic".

Suppose we were helping someone with whom we are not related nor have any friendship, and there was no expectation of a return on their part. What's left? The well-being derived from the gratitude of the individual who benefited from our action, as well as the awareness of our beneficial influence. However, the person in question is ungrateful and cares little about our effort to help them. What do we have then? The awareness of our beneficial influence, which is sufficient to generate well-being in us through the "conviction of our virtue". We suffer some loss to help someone and all we receive in return is the fact that we know we have helped them. Surely that is an example of true and selfless altruism, right?

Let's investigate this phenomenon a little more deeply. Let's imagine the following situation: after helping someone, we would forget that we helped them, and the person who received the benefit would also forget that. That would be a small obstacle, but it would not prevent the person from feeling special because of it, at least *before* committing their act. Then merely forgetting the act afterwards would not demotivate the individual.

Then let's worsen the situation by replacing the consequences of the selfless act. Let us take the feeling of well-being that comes from selfless action and place perfect indifference in its place. This complicates the issue quite a bit. What happens? Altruism dies here, because, after such substitution, the selfless act would become equivalent to doing charity work to rocks — and who, in good conscience, would do that? Does anyone actually do that? Would anyone take a risk, would someone express altruism to what is indifferent to them? We've never seen that happen.

Just the example above completely dismantles the idea of disinterest in any action. But even so, let's move on. We could replace the well-being reward with an unsatisfactory reward. In this situation, instead of feeling good about helping someone, we would feel, for example, unease and guilt. In such a context, who would be selfless? Who would suffer to suffer more? It would just be a masochism in which there is no material, emotional, or social reward. Evidently, no one is like that, no one feels bad helping someone, but that's beside the point. The fact is that this situation places the selfless man in the position equivalent to that of someone trying to help a hungry man by feeding him a meal mixed with a small dose of poison — and, of course, feeling good about having done so.

Obviously, no one would sacrifice themselves for someone else if they felt bad about it — if we do so, it's because, directly or indirectly, we feel good. So, as we can see, the idea of selfless actions doesn't seem very well supported, and neither the myth of altruism.

The reward of virtue is virtue itself — that's an adage that only sees the surface of the problem. Our actions are never disinterested or sufficient in themselves, and their real motivations are almost always radically different from those we imagine. The rational justification we give for our own actions is nothing more than a false surface, a veil thrown over the machinery of the human unconscious, which we ignore.

Of course, we're not dissecting some of humanity's dearest feelings just because we have some kind of sadistic pleasure in destroying delusions. The objective is clarification, understanding. We are investigating our internal mechanisms to increase the control we have over ourselves, to learn to better manage our impulses and understand their real meaning. In this way, just like Wallace:

> *I am fully aware of the risk of condemnation faced by those who try to stick pins into sacred balloons, and I know that I poked some of those balloons in these pages. Nevertheless, it is time for us to take a closer look at ourselves, so I feel justified, if not convinced of my virtue. I talked about some of our most cherished ideals and suggested that they can be explained as essentially selfish resources. I talked about love as a means of introducing our genes into the next generation's gene pool. I'm not saying that love is bad; I'm saying that love is selfish and that selfishness is good, or at least it was. Selfishness is the pervasive quality that filters through the souls of living things. It's the driving force behind our behavior, the behavior that brought us to our present successes. But the world is changing. Things are different now and maybe it's time to change our behavior. To have any hope of adapting to a modified plan, we must come to understand our motivations as they really are and not as we would like them to be.*

So, if we honestly want to have a real understanding of our nature, we need to accept the fact that not everything in us is like we imagine. We need to understand that the rational mind is not as independent and influential, that we are not as flexible as we would like to believe. Just as the body has several specific physiological mechanisms that are essential to our survival, our mind also evolved psychological mechanisms — neural circuits — for the same purpose; it evolved certain emotional devices that act as guides for our actions. In this process, the weight of environmental influence is certainly relevant, but it was far too exaggerated. From the beginning, our mental structure has always been far from a blank slate on which culture and experience, alone, imprint their hands.

Intelligence is like a sophisticated pleasure mercenary at the service of our primary needs. Figuratively speaking, we could represent emotions and reason as a relationship between a tyrant and a servant. The tyrant, although extremely powerful, is primitive and lives in a "dark cave", which means its inability to understand and adapt to the complex and dynamic reality full of symbols in which we live. On the other hand, the servant finds itself in the position of an intelligent mercenary whose notion of values is tied to the reward of pleasure and the punishment of pain. In this situation, the tyrant imposes its objectives as goals to be achieved by the servile intellect in whatever way suits it, receiving pleasure rewards in exchange. If the servant — the intellect — disobeys, if it deviates from this path, it will receive punishments in the form of suffering, which are highly discouraging. In turn, the tyrant's objective is dependent on the fundamental biological requirements of the organism itself, which is the final authority in matters of valuation.

We could say that genes are the "legislative" factor of the body, that impulses and emotions are the "executive" factor — which can be direct or, through reason, indirect — and that reason works as a "judicial" factor — in the sense of critically analyzing the best ways to satisfy the body's needs. These three powers are hierarchical in their capacity to influence the destiny of the organism. Thus, the more important any factor is for the survival of the organism, the less freedom we'll have to control it, that is, the more inflexible and authoritarian the demand is. For example, the fact that we cannot make our heart stop beating voluntarily, but that we can stop breathing, at least for a while.

Then, hierarchically, physical laws control genes, which control the biological constitution, which controls physiology, which controls brain chemistry, which controls impulses and emotions, which control reason, which in turn understands reality and decides what action is most appropriate to satisfy the body's needs. Sometimes, in an emergency, emotion can alter this order, obliterating reason through so-called "emotional kidnappings", during which actions escape our conscious control, and reason is temporarily suppressed. Likewise, sometimes our reason can suppress the manifestation of an emotion, although its power in this sense is not really very significant.

In addition, we also need to understand that, in the end, the famous "complete happiness" is nothing more than another pipe dream that we seek. In our eternal search for fullness, for satisfaction, for well-being, for happiness, what we really do is to look for the type of occupation or situation in which the feeling of well-being occurs in parallel. Such happiness, such satisfaction, when achieved, will never be continuous, because, as Le Bon noted:

> *(...) pleasure only exists under the condition of being intermittent. Prolonged pleasure immediately ceases to be pleasure, and continuous pain soon subsides. Its reduction can even, by comparison, become a pleasure. (...) The discontinuity of pleasure and pain represents the consequence of this physiological law: "Change is the condition of sensation". (...) Pleasure is always relative and linked to circumstances. Today's pain becomes tomorrow's pleasure and vice versa. Pain, for a man who had an abundant dinner, to be condemned to eat crusts of dried bread; pleasure, for the same individual, abandoned for many days without food on a deserted island.*

We can conclude that any satisfaction will never be permanent — and we will always be in this dance, oscillating between different stimuli to reach states of well-being and satisfaction, which will always be temporary. And what does all this mean? It means that, by playing this game, we are submitting to the rules dictated by our emotions and biological needs, whose satisfaction is rewarded with pleasure.

In this regard, it seems that our freedom, our independence from the framework of happiness, of satisfaction, is quite small. Our personal tastes are a reflection of our needs — and we can't choose those tastes voluntarily. In this sense, even when we suffer in the name of something that we consider valid for purely rational reasons, this cannot be considered a disconnection from the reference of happiness, since we, for the most part, act according to long-term objectives, and not just in terms of immediate pleasure. We call this hope, that is, the expectation of a future reward or pleasure at the cost of an investment or suffering in the present.

In this way, satisfaction can be anywhere, even if it is not the perfect happiness that is idealized as an absolute wellness in relation to everything. Some find happiness in work, others in leisure, some in obeying, and others in leading. But this happiness, in the broad sense, can always be understood as the satisfaction of our natural inclinations, of our organic and emotional needs.

However, many people see the topic of feelings as something that cannot be thought of, as something mysterious that, in some way, is "above" reason. This is because feelings originate at deep levels of the brain, and the rational mind, which is the most recent layer in evolutionary terms, does not have the power to control them at will. Emotional reactions and feelings are practically immune to reason and conscious will — and this, of course, also applies to beliefs that satisfy our emotional needs. However, the simple fact that they are immune does not mean that they are above — they're just disconnected from reason.

Put in these terms, our feelings and emotions certainly lose that "mystical glow" — and that's exactly the goal. Our feelings and emotions are not "truths", but merely powerful bonds and impulses, forged unconsciously and emanating from the depths of our mind, manifesting in our behavior. Our mental constitution, like everything else, was not defined by its veracity, by its logic, by its coherence. Quite simply, its value was defined by its ability to provide survival. Just like our liver, our emotions didn't evolve to make sense, but to work.

Therefore, we must not confuse efficiency with intelligence. Efficiency is blind to becoming and, if it adapts, it is only because it was programmed to do so in advance. The human body is efficient, but not intelligent. For example, if we perform a blood transfusion with an incompatible type, the body will destroy it as a foreign element — this is not a sign of intelligence, but of simple blind efficiency. Even if the transfusion was going to be beneficial, the body is not structured to recognize such benefit. This is because evolution built us blindly, by trial and error, according to the principle of "good enough to survive". The body is like a computer: stupid, but efficient. It was only through the use of abstract and rational intelligence that we discovered ways to circumvent this mechanical rejection for our own advantage, verifying the existing blood types and which are compatible or incompatible with each other in a transfusion.

There is a good example to show that impulses and sensations should not be seen as criteria of truth. Obese individuals, by nature, tend to overeat. This certainly generates pleasure in them. However, their conscious mind knows that if they follow their impulses without any kind of control, despite the pleasure and well-being they feel, this will have several negative consequences for their health. That is why, against their natural tendency, they restrain their impulses, their desires. And even if such an effort is aimed at the well-being of the organism in the long term, the primitive mind does not "know" this, continuing to act as if we were living in the Stone Age.

Those who have ever been on a weight loss diet know very well how awful it is to go against these decontextualized tendencies inherited from the past. However, it is certain that, in the environment in which humans evolved, that is, in an environment with a violent dispute over food, this obsession with consuming as many calories as possible was not a problem, but a great advantage in terms of survival.

We could also mention the difficulty of giving up the habit of smoking or the use of other addictive drugs, the struggle to overcome a failed relationship, to change ingrained habits, to control phobias, and so on. In all these cases, the rational mind knows what's best for the body's health, but has no direct control over it. That's why we suffer so much to accomplish such changes. In that sense, it would be useless to say to ourselves: "from now on, I will no longer feel this or that need". We need to use strategies to accomplish this kind of thing. In this case, the most common thing is to try to control the body indirectly, placing it under the pressure of specific conditions, manipulating variables that aim to alter our emotional disposition in a predictable way, according to our rational objectives — for example, a comedy movie to cheer us up, a party to relax, physical activities to relieve tension, coffee to give energy, etc. Thus, despite our impulses telling us otherwise, the fact is that, sometimes, not listening to what we feel is the most intelligent thing to do.

If we can say that there is some "truth" hidden in our feelings and in our emotions, that truth is evolutionary — true as an expression of historical and statistical realities in the promotion of survival. Through these feelings, our body speaks in evolutionary language. Our primitive constitution follows these general rules, and the idea behind it is: act like this or that, as it almost always works.

However, it's not because it worked before that it will work again, because they're only true as statistics — they're not always applicable, they're not always convenient. In other words, this is exactly where the value of rational reflection on actions becomes clear. Thus, if we do not want to give up on the little intelligence that we have, we must go a step further, and use our reflection not only to satisfy our impulses and needs, but also to be able to see in the long term what the consequences of this will be.

With such words, we're just trying to say that no feeling is sacred, even though some of them seem sacred. In practice, there is no really palpable difference between the mechanisms of fear and love — the difference lies only in the fact that we see the first objectively and the second subjectively. We look at fear as something "obvious", but we never dare to look at love the same way — that's why we've never been able to understand it.

Like any mental mechanism, love has nothing true and nothing false — it's just another letter of our emotional alphabet. A kind of affective bond that is manifested as a desire for what, to our primitive mind, seems useful in some sense. Thus, in practice, there is virtually no difference between struggling to lose weight, to quit smoking, to get used to a new keyboard, or to get over a relationship — it's the conscious mind versus the inertia of the unconscious mind. A matter of conditioning, of habit.

In this case, we can think of the brain's behavior, metaphorically, as that of a muscle. If we don't put it in a high-pressure situation that gives it the signal, the stimulus to adapt, it won't do it at all, because the human body always avoids superfluous expenses. For the same reason that a muscle never grows spontaneously, our habits, beliefs, and personality traits will tend to remain the same if there is no pressure for change.

Therefore, since our emotions are blind to the current reality, it makes sense to use the eyes of reason to guide them. We need to learn to use intelligence to understand them and direct them in the direction most favorable to our objectives, which exist in our complex modern cultural context. Undoubtedly, it is difficult to face them objectively, since we tend to interpret reality and judge the value of things according to our subjective emotional disposition, and in this situation the rational mind often ends up with tied hands. However, when we become aware of this mechanism, it is easier to deal with them objectively, and we realize that we don't have to obey impulses that don't make any sense, and that there is certainly nothing "wrong" in that — despite the fact that sometimes we "feel" that it is wrong. To exemplify how much our psychological predisposition is decontextualized with the current environment, let's mention a comment by Steven Pinker:

> *But what about the Darwinian imperative to survive and reproduce? As far as everyday behavior is concerned, there is no such imperative. Some people watch a pornographic movie when they could be looking for a partner, those who give up food to buy heroin, those who postpone the pregnancy of their children to pursue a career in the company, those who eat so much that they end up going to the grave sooner. Human addiction is proof that biological adaptation, in the strict sense of the term, is a thing of the past. Our minds are adapted to the small food-collecting flocks in which our family spent 99% of its existence, and not to the disordered contingencies created by us since the agricultural and industrial revolutions. Before photography, it was adaptive to receive visual images of attractive members of the opposite sex, as these images originated solely from light reflecting off fertile bodies. Before narcotics in syringes, they were synthesized in the brain as natural painkillers. Before there were movie movies, it was adaptive to observe people's emotional struggles, because the only fights you could witness were between people that you needed to psychoanalyze every day. Before there was contraception, children were inevitable, and status and wealth could be converted into more numerous and healthier children. Before*

there were sugar bowls, salt shakers, and butter bowls on every table, and when lean cow days were never far off, it never hurt to eat all the sugar, salt, and fatty foods you could get. People can't guess what's adaptive for them or for their genes. These give them thoughts and feelings that were adaptive in the environment in which the genes were selected.

As we have seen, civilization does not create our feelings, our emotions, our affections, nor our fundamental predispositions. Our great behavioral malleability is a genetically determined pre-existing potentiality. It is something inherent to our species, not something that we "learn" through experience, or from culture. Civilization merely influences our potentialities, modulates them, directs them in this or that direction, develops, sophisticates, and exalts them, or allows them to atrophy, or conceals them. But, fundamentally, they continue to exist, implicitly or explicitly, in any and every civilization, differing only in the meaning and direction we give them.

For this reason, it makes no sense to try to force sophisticated and specific adaptive explanations to everything we do in our modern society, because our mind is not modern — our society has become modern. Our mind, the mind of *Homo sapiens*, has essentially the same basic brain structure as a human of the Stone Age. It doesn't understand what behaviors are currently adaptive, because it was formed in a very different context, in which it was the tyrant called environment who imposed what was adaptive, not our tastes, not our will, not the surrounding social situation.

For example, our society says how we should behave sexually. Another society says that we should behave differently. However, the sexual instinct is the basis of all this, and cultures only diverge in their interpretation of the instinct and in the ways in which they consider correct to express it. And even if the interpretation is done in a non-adaptive sense, this is not a problem, because our desires can be satisfied in any way — "artificially", so to speak. As Pinker explained: *The body certainly does not know how to discern one from the other, it is unable to guess what is adaptive, because, at the level of particular individuals, evolution is completely blind.* So it doesn't matter how our desires are satisfied — as long as they are. A man's sexual desire, for example, can be satisfied by a healthy woman, by a woman without a womb, or by a corpse —

they are just as effective as long as they are able to satisfy the need.

So does this mean that we should ignore all these stupid obsolete impulses and become rationalistic ice stones? Quite the contrary. Combating our impulses head-on just because they are decontextualized, in addition to causing a lot of psychological distress, is a great foolishness, and that's not the idea we're trying to convey. Explaining the function and meaning of our feelings, emotions, and impulses doesn't mean underestimating them — if they were contemptible, they wouldn't even deserve our attention. Therefore, all of this should not be understood as a declaration of war of extermination against our emotional world, since it is part of our intimate nature and, as such, will never be eradicated. Quite aptly, Nietzsche observed that:

> *Formerly, in view of the element of stupidity in passion, war was declared on passion itself, its destruction was plotted; all the old moral monsters are agreed on this: il faut tuer les passions. [passions must be killed] The most famous formula for this is to be found in the New Testament, in that Sermon on the Mount, where, incidentally, things are by no means looked at from a height. There it is said, for example, with particular reference to sexuality: "If thy eye offend thee, pluck it out". Fortunately, no Christian acts in accordance with this precept. Destroying the passions and cravings, merely as a preventive measure against their stupidity and the unpleasant consequences of this stupidity — today this itself strikes us as merely another acute form of stupidity. We no longer admire dentists who "pluck out" teeth so that they will not hurt any more.*

The idea consists only of trying to understand and manage in the best possible way the impulses and emotions that drive us, in order to avoid making the same mistakes over and over again because we do not objectively understand the meaning of what we are feeling. Therefore, we should not ignore, but understand as much as possible about our affection, our emotions, our feelings, since they represent a large part of the equation of our lives. Everything that has been said about our emotions, in reality, is only a warning that we should remove them from their divine pedestal and begin to ponder, in a logical way, the implications of the actions inspired by them. We often see individuals acting irrationally and using love to justify their incoherent actions. Nothing could be more absurd. Love justifies irrationality as much as hunger justifies obesity. May the romantics forgive us.

X

MANKIND, THE WORLD, AND THE NOTHINGNESS

In some remote corner of the universe, poured out and glittering in innumerable solar systems, there once was a star on which clever animals invented knowledge. That was the highest and most mendacious minute of "world history" — yet only a minute. After nature had drawn a few breaths the star grew cold, and the clever animals had to die. One might invent such a fable and still not have illustrated sufficiently how wretched, how shadowy and flighty, how aimless and arbitrary, the human intellect appears in nature. There have been eternities when it did not exist; and when it is done for again, nothing will have happened. For this intellect has no further mission that would lead beyond human life. It is human, rather, and only its owner and producer gives it such importance, as if the world pivoted around it. But if we could communicate with the mosquito, then we would learn that he floats through the air with the same self-importance, feeling within itself the flying center of the world.

— Friedrich Nietzsche

In the beginning, our planet was the center of the Universe. Well, we were the masterpiece of an almighty God who loved us — nothing could be more just. After a long time, the astronomers of the Middle Ages arrived, and shook the foundations of the geocentric thinking of the time, demonstrating that the Earth was not the center of anything — it is Earth that revolves around the Sun, and not the other way around. Besides that, our planet is not the only one — there are several others as well. This diminishes us a bit, but that's okay, because our planetary system is all that exists. It would have been good for our ego if all the discoveries were limited to that, but that's not what happened. Now we know that the stars that we see in the sky at night are other suns. Thus, our planetary system is no longer the only one: there are many other stars with many other planets revolving around them. In truth, it's not just a lot of suns: it's *really* a lot of them. In fact, it's billions of suns — 100 billion suns! That's such an absurd number that we can't even imagine what it means. However, we realize that it makes us something very, really very small. And all of this gets even worse when we realize that we're much smaller. All this colossal structure is contained in just *one* galaxy, and it shocks us to think that, in addition to ours, there are 100 billion other galaxies in our Universe, with approximately another 100 billion suns in each, and these, probably, being orbited by many planets. At the very least, it's a slap in the face for our arrogance. Anyone who, faced with this, says that we represent a grain of sand will be making an exaggerated compliment.

But scientists didn't just look outside the Earth. They also turned to themselves, placing man as an object of study. Thus, in parallel with the discoveries of Astronomy, those of Biology came to finish dynamiting the small rest of our sense of importance. The researchers of human physiology and anatomy have already thoroughly unraveled us. There's no magic at all — we're just animals, biological machines. They found no soul or spirit, only viscera. The heart has no feelings — it's just a muscle. Feelings, so sublime, are merely chemical reactions in our brains. Our personality, which we cultivate and value so much, which we consider indestructible, is as fragile as the disposition of our neurons — a small damage, and the person we were ceases to exist. Our individual goals are not as ours as we think, but they are undoubtedly as ephemeral as ourselves. The human species, like any other, is nothing more than a variety of biological robots controlled by DNA molecules.

We live in a world that is a subjective fiction, a mental representation lost among countless other possible perspectives. Our senses only see the surface from an angle of reality and, for them, everything else is dark and impenetrable. We cannot open the curtains of reality to look at what is behind appearances. All we can know is everything we can touch, in the dark, with the fragile and trembling hands of our intellect. All our knowledge, therefore, is nothing more than a sophisticated assumption.

We will never be completely certain about anything. Rationally seeking absolute truths is naive, it's like running desperately to reach the horizon — the longing for such truths, contrary to what we would like to believe, is not born from the search for knowledge, but from the search for peace of mind. And those who still think that, in seeking knowledge, they are fighting for a supposedly noble cause, are mistaken, because this is nothing more than self-flattery. Nobility doesn't exist. We fight because we want to, we fight for nothing and, in the end, we will become nothing.

That is the very strange reality in which we find ourselves immersed. For billions of years, we were dust. But somehow, about 3.5 billion years ago, that dust woke up. It changed over the ages, until, at a certain moment, that dust became aware of itself — the dust saw that it was a man. And that man, in turn, found himself in an unfamiliar world, without a reason to be. Then he realized how absurd was the very fact that he existed. As a passenger on a train that inexorably leads to the abyss of nothingness, man asks himself: but why here, why now? And in the face of such questions, the universe remains silent. Then we ask ourselves: what is life? Apparently, nothing more than a long succession of random events that finally gave birth to machines blindly programmed with murderous precision, and with that impassive efficiency became the objective of a pointless world. We can then think: What am I? And it's simple: we're *Homo sapiens*, a model of survival machine.

When we stop to reflect about such things carefully, perplexity takes hold of our consciousness. We feel static, not quite sure what to think. Then the feeling of disquiet comes and, if we can still preserve our lucidity in the face of all this, the more we delve into this analysis, the more that anguish grows within us. As if we were dreaming, sometimes it seems that we are going to wake up from this cold and absurd reality — something in us is reluctant to admit that this is all there is to be experienced. Our hope always tries to persuade us to reinterpret what our eyes tell us, but every morning we wake up and see that all of this is real, inescapably real.

Among such thoughts, the reality around us simply comes to a standstill. Our life hangs in the balance, and there comes upon us the overwhelming realization that none of what we are living has any meaning — human existence as the emptiest contingency. The idea that we are living just because we "happened" is far too bizarre. Humanity, in this frantic race, seeking happiness, money, success, advancement, glory, power, knowledge; the immense competitiveness, which is growing by leaps and bounds, moving the gears of our world more and more rapidly; and also ourselves, fighting, struggling in this anthill of people called Earth — all of this to get nowhere. It sounds crazy.

Why, when we think about all this, do we get this feeling of paralysis, of emptiness, of lack of reference? There's a painful reason for this: it's precisely the delusions that fuel our motivations. Any objective that we imagine is rationally unjustifiable in and of itself. It is from the passion for our delusions that we draw our strength.

When we understand such things for the first time — and it's never easy to get used to them — it is natural to feel a certain weakening, a certain disconnection, because understanding dissipates, for a while, the strength of our illusions. Reason, in a way, has the capacity to "dissolve" them, even if only temporarily — but that's not something we should regret. Even so, such dissolution of delusions is the prerogative of only a few individuals under certain privileged conditions: only when we become sufficiently complete, free, and courageous enough to dispense with our delusions. This is because, when necessary for our subsistence, illusions become unshakable, immune to any arguments: lies metamorphose into truths when we need them. Nobody questions the value of life inside a burning house; a hungry person never questions the value of food — either for the soul or for the body.

As we've seen, it's not rationality that, for the most part, tells us what to do — it just guides us about *how* to do it. Reason cannot decide anything purely, without a Dionysian passion telling it what to do. Thus, we can say that, apart from objective knowledge, the rest of our opinions and beliefs are not rational in their genesis. Our "philosophy of life", in practice, consists only of a rationalization of our human needs. Through this, we try to justify our actions, giving them a mask of rationality. However, behind all our reasoning, lies the irrational shadow of our prejudices and unconscious desires.

Thus, it is inevitable that we end up as mostly superficial beings, since our subsistence is based on self-deception. The fact is that, if our significance were proportionately dosed to the beliefs we need to nurture in order to feel motivated, we would be gods — and what better example could we find of this phenomenon than religions?

Our sense of importance must be constantly fed by reasons that ignore reason itself, pointing directly to our needs of self-preservation. From this perspective, we can say that being forgetful sometimes represents a blessing, since it would simply be impossible to live with the constant company of the paralyzing ghosts of the void.

Obviously, we do not intend to promote the generalized annihilation of all our delusions. We do not intend to extirpate them because that is not possible — nor is it desirable. Without these little lies, our life would be nothing more than a boring tragicomedy. *Without madness*, Fernando Pessoa asked, *what is a man more than a healthy beast, a postponed corpse that procreates*?

We're just trying to outline certain boundaries. We are trying, as far as possible, to maintain the distinction between subjectivity and objectivity, thus aiming at two things: understanding what we really are and, thus, learning to deal with our nature in an objective and efficient way, getting as close as possible to our ideal of life — whatever it may be. On the other hand, we also want to avoid dogmatism, mysticism, and all that emotional blindness that paralyzes the progress of human knowledge. The search for scientific knowledge must be carried out with our feet very firmly attached to the ground, always with the utmost objectivity, so as not to lose from sight — inflated by anthropocentric delusions — the reality of the human condition.

It is important to insist on this separation, because whenever mystics invest in their unreciprocated love with logic, the result is a deplorable hindrance to the progress of knowledge. It is a biased mistake to start from our personal desires, from our beliefs, and then start looking for their correspondence in reality. If we want to be unbiased, we must always have the honesty to start only from objective facts — and not from our metaphysical dreams — to infer what is real.

Throughout history until today, attempts have always been made to prove the veracity of religious beliefs — and they have always failed. Even so, they survive, retaining all their vivacity — and that's no surprise. Any type of mystical belief can dispense with verification precisely because it has an existence that is autonomous, independent of reason, independent of the facts. Thus, it must be understood that the function of all mystical, religious, and transcendental beliefs is simply to satisfy emotional needs of the human being.

God, bliss, transcendence, elevation, nirvana, spiritual peace, contact with God — these are all things as true as a love poem. Being a "child of God" is a state of mind, a feeling, it is something that is experienced, not something that is scientifically proven. Beliefs of this kind serve to provide well-being and security, to reduce anxiety through definitive answers about the world, about morals, about life, etc. However, it seems that most individuals have not yet realized that the happiness a belief can provide cannot guarantee its veracity.

As we can see, when we analyze and understand an illusion rationally, when we remove it from its magical pedestal, it loses much of its strength, which resided precisely in misunderstanding it, or in its unquestionable character. This type of honesty, when focused on existence as a whole, makes us, step by step, aware of our complete insignificance — and, after having done so, we can hardly return to what we were. Enlightenment is a path that, in addition to being painful, is without return — hence being followed by so few. By our own integrity, we have been reduced from the crown of creation to an infinitesimal point that is neither useful nor useless — which simply doesn't matter.

Undoubtedly, we can still give some meaning to lives, but our sense of importance has been irreparably shaken by the rude blows of science. And, in fact, what it hit was just the part of us that had been inflated by anthropocentric daydreams, because the fact is that we were never important. This just took us by surprise, because it was impossible for us to imagine that we're all so little. We projected our hopes into the unknown — and were victims of our own expectations. Now we have reaped the frustration and disappointment that none of what we dreamt was real.

Very well, here we are, alone, in the inhospitable desert that is hidden behind our delusions, to which we referred at the beginning of this work. The difference lies in the fact that we, atheists and freethinkers, are able to survive under such conditions. We endure such aridity without invoking consolation in parallel realities, where we will be rewarded *post-mortem* for all our unhappiness and frustration. From life, we expect nothing more than living, and few understand how much courage is contained in the lucid statement that our life is nothing more than an ephemeral glimpse — those who laugh at this have little understanding of themselves and of the world in which they live.

If we are humble, it's only because we are honest, not because we are obedient. Our smallness is not virtue — it's a fact. We simply admit what we see — our immeasurable insignificance compared to what exists. It's a situation that tastes acrid, and we know it very well. But what could we do? We can't stay kids forever. This mystical infancy must be overcome if we don't want to spend the rest of our lives immersed in an ocean of false dreams.

This understanding of reality, besides being painful, is not very intuitive. That is why it is only intellectually, through serious reflection, that we find ourselves faced with such conclusions. Only in this way do we grasp the enormous emptiness of existence — and that is precisely what makes us aware that our freedom is absolute. The fact is that, in this situation, man is exempt from any responsibility in any perspective you can imagine. There are simply no authorities — none. There are no duties — none. There's no good and there's no bad. There's no better or worse. There's no right or wrong. After all, what is a human being if not an agglomeration of atoms that knows it exists? A machine alone in the world, aware that it exists and that, one day, it will cease to exist?

If anything is certain, it's that we're all destined to die. In that regard, it doesn't matter what we do with our lives. It is completely irrelevant whether during it we were atheists or believers, kind or mean, hardworking or indolent, honest or hypocritical, selfish or altruistic. All of us will one day be stripped of our senses. Our "I" will be suppressed from existence and our body will be converted to decay — and not long after that, there won't even be memories of what we were.

If we want to imagine what death is like, we just have to try to "remember" when we weren't born yet — it's like sleeping forever, with no dreams. There will be no rewards at the end of this game, just the eternally blank face of nothingness. It may sound pessimism, but it's not. Human existence boils down to that. If the idea sounds depressing, it's because reality is indeed depressing. Man is simply there, suspended in a vacuum, thrown into existence, into this ever-changing world, without meaning, without reason or purpose. Therefore, free from any obligations, free from any specific destiny.

However, let us not be naive: this is certainly not equivalent to saying that man is the master of his destiny. Behind your supposed free will are hidden your many genetic prejudices, your countless limitations, and all external conditioning — things that are undoubtedly beyond our control. And even assuming that our will was completely free, that wouldn't make much difference, since it is not the only force that acts in determining the destiny of individuals. Therefore, to say that man is free is not equivalent to saying that man is omnipotent — "everything is allowed" does not mean "everything is possible". We must see our limitations: we are just a bunch of amino acids witnessing this ephemeral and curious pastime called life.

The important thing is to bear in mind that a considerable part of the structure of values and meanings that we carry is created by ourselves. That is, everything that has value, has it only because we recognize that value and accept it as true — and isn't doing so just equivalent to creating that value? If we didn't attach value to diamonds, what would they be if not tiny shiny pebbles that are difficult to find?

Thus, if we want to be at least intellectually free, we must never lose sight of the fact that all meanings, values, and goals are merely a reflection of human nature. We must ignore the fictitious authority of cold, fossilized, idealized, and impersonal values. We shouldn't listen to the dogmatic moralists who tell us about "good virtues in their own right" — they are nothing more than tyrants, whether they know it or not. We should never bend our knees to any kind of abstraction chimera — on the contrary, let us put them on their knees before us! Let us be the masters of our virtues, not the virtues our masters.

The only true values are our human values. They must have life, they must breathe, they must be our creation, they must appear as the fruit of our individuality, of our authenticity, of our recognition, of our inner and personal need, and in our defense — thus representing our intimate nature, our position in the face of reality.

Values of all types are established through a mechanism based on authority — in a kind of imposition. The difference is that, in enslaved and resigned men, values are established through their submission to the authority of external ideas, sacrificing their individuality in the name of supposed higher truths. On the other hand, with the enlightened man, values are established through understanding — the imposition comes from the inside out, and in that he is his own authority. Thus, our values appear as a reflection of our intelligence, our desires, and our needs — the values, here, long before suppressing our individuality, are its highest expression.

Therefore, in view of all the facts that we presented, *we deny* the existence of any kind of truth, value, or impersonal duty. As truth is transformed into abstraction as a law suspended above man, as it judges — approving or condemning — solely on the basis of itself, as a value in itself, regardless of the specific circumstances of each situation, of each individual, it becomes despotic, restrictive, oppressive, tyrannical. When truth is allowed to take on a life of its own — and this undoubtedly brings us back to the idea of God — it becomes a dogmatic, authoritarian, and intolerant monster that represents an enormous threat to human freedom.

When common foundations are imposed on the construction of all individualities, when all men are assessed with the same scale, when the fundamental value of all is leveled through the lie of the "moral world order", of the "equality of souls before God", or through respect for the authority of any fantasy of abstraction, the insult committed by this is substantially the same: the suppression of individuality, the imposition of equality between the different — a massive attack on human freedom, a stab at the heart of our authenticity. Surely in vain one would search for a crime more revolting than this.

Appendix

I shall be told, I suppose, that my philosophy is comfortless — because I speak the truth; and people prefer to be assured that everything the Lord has made is good. Go to the priests, then, and leave philosophers in peace! At any rate, do not ask us to accommodate our doctrines to the lessons you have been taught. That is what those rascals of sham philosophers will do for you. Ask them for any doctrine you please, and you will get it.

— Arthur Schopenhauer

ON FREEDOM AND FREE WILL

It may be true that we act as we choose. But can we choose? Isn't our choice determined by causes that elude us?

— J. A. Froude

No book entitled *Atheism & Freedom* could be complete without an investigation into the famous dilemma of free will versus determinism. This justified the creation of this short postscript that attempts to clarify the question a bit.

In this type of investigation, it is very common to notice that explanations always leave a gap: forget to point out that free will and freedom are not the same thing. Such a distinction, with any luck, will become clear throughout this essay.

Freedom has always been a term considered "indescribable", whose essence has occupied many great minds. After all, do we have any individual freedom to decide our actions, or is our sense of free-choice just one of the many subjective delusions that populate our minds? This old problem is still very current. Science has already helped us a lot in this regard, and it has solved several puzzles that will give us a guideline for some of our inquiries.

We know that a significant part of the foundation of our lives and actions is not subject to our will. We have no direct control over our feelings, over our tastes, over most of our organs, over the biological constitution of our bodies, over our senses, and so on. Several factors are not controlled by us and, in this regard, we must admit, it is a point of determinism.

It is worth emphasizing that we are also largely determined by our genetic load. The entire structure of our body — our potentials, our abilities, our physiology, our organs, average height, physical constitution, skin, eye and hair colors, etc. — is determined by our genes. As for the influence of genes on our behavior, it's worth listening to what Pinker tells us, in order to better understand how heavy is their influence on traits that, at first glance, seem arbitrary:

> *Another expansion of our vista comes from the startling similarities between identical twins, who share the genetic recipes that build the mind. Their minds are astonishingly alike, and not just in gross measures like IQ and personality traits like neuroticism and introversion. They are alike in talents such as spelling and mathematics, in opinions on questions such as apartheid, the death penalty, and working mothers, and in their career choices, hobbies, vices, religious commitments, and tastes in dating. Identical twins are far more alike than fraternal twins, who share only half their genetic recipes, and most strikingly, they are almost as alike when they are reared apart as when they are reared together. Identical twins separated at birth share traits like entering the water backwards and only up to their knees, sitting out elections because they feel insufficiently informed, obsessively counting everything in sight, becoming captain of the volunteer fire department, and leaving little love notes around the house for their wives. People find these discoveries arresting, even incredible. The discoveries cast doubt on the autonomous "I" that we all feel hovering above our bodies, making choices as we proceed through life and affected only by our past and present environments.*

The great behavioral similarities of identical twins raised separately demonstrates that our personality, for the most part, does not seem to be under our control — or, at best, isn't as free as it seems. In everyday life, our free will seems to exist because our genetic constitutions are unique. However, the case of identical twins shows that such appearance is really nothing more than that — an appearance. For this reason, a large part of the illusion that we choose everything freely is due to the simple fact that we are genetically distinct.

The only remaining question that gives rise to the possibility of having free will is this: do we have any real control over our thoughts and actions? Or are our actions and thoughts just unpredictably deterministic events? Let's move on.

The differences between identical twins can be due to two factors: 1) They have a certain degree of free will to choose their destiny; or 2) Their interaction with specific environmental factors makes the individual genuinely distinct from everyone else, but without any choice involved.

Suppose the following situation: two identical twins, at birth, are placed, at the same time, in two parallel worlds that are exactly the same. Two environments in which they would face precisely identical situations. These two individuals would live with the same friends, would be born in the same historical context, would be educated by identical families, living in the same house, living in the same city, breathing the same air, etc. They would live lives in which both the genetic factor and the environmental factor are fully controlled — two equal realities occurring independently, in parallel.

Doesn't it seem reasonable to assume that these two individuals would ultimately be the same person? Apart from genetic differences and environmental divergences — the influence of external factors —, what could be left of our free will? If we suppose that man does, in fact, result from a unique interaction between his genes and his environment, that would be a complete denial of human free will. In fact, this is a purely speculative hypothesis, impossible to prove, since it is not possible to isolate and control the environmental component in its influence on organisms. But the example gives us consistent indications that we are not far from reaching a conclusion.

In this line of thinking, it seems that the executioner who unleashes the death blow against our free will is physical law. On the one hand, all material reality behaves in a strictly uniform way. But, on the other hand, quantum theory shows us that reality, although governed by inexorable laws, does not have an exactly predictable nature. For example, given a state *x* of organization of matter, even if we are aware of all the data regarding the state of organization of that matter, its behavior would still be unpredictable.

This shines a faint light of hope that is then obscured by doubt: matter, in some specific aspects, behaves unpredictably, but what does it matter? After all, that does not mean that we can influence it. Being determined by something predictable or unpredictable is still determinism. Thus, if the unpredictable aspects of physical phenomena are, as one might suppose, deterministic in their nature, this only denies the fatalistic idea that we have some destiny mapped out, but it does not free us in any way.

In any case, whether reality is predictable or not, the fact is that it makes no sense to think that, just because we are thinking living beings, just because we have the capacity to deliberate about things and about our actions, just because we can act with intentionality, we are somehow "above" physical laws. Just as our muscle cells cannot "choose" to transgress physical laws and bend a tempered steel bar with the diameter of ten centimeters, what sense would it make to think that our neurons are not subject to such laws, being able to transgress them when we "choose" to do something?

If we are material beings, if our brain is material, then our mental phenomena necessarily submit to physical laws. It sounds like unmeasured pretension to think that our intellect transcends and escapes the physical laws of our material reality. *Aren't the facts of the mental world*, Ingersoll inquired, *produced as necessarily as the facts of the material world? In this way, isn't what we call the mind exactly as natural as what we call the body?* Indeed. It seems that the acceptance of materialism implies determinism — in other words, the rejection of the idea that we have free will.

Strangely enough, some say that determinists are just crooks trying to escape the consequences of their actions, since, if there is no free will, neither can there be the concept of guilt or responsibility — since these presuppose the idea that human actions are perpetrated freely. The absence of free will, according to this view, would end up annihilating morality and, therefore, also the distinction between right and wrong.

As we know, there is no objective difference between right and wrong. In this way, could we commit crimes and claim that we did not have free will and, therefore, we are not guilty? That doesn't make any sense, but of course we could — we could also say that we're capable of jumping to the Moon with a single leg.

This allegation, as we can see, attempts to exempt the individual's social guilt by ignoring the distinction between what is objective and what is subjective. In fact, we didn't have free will — but even so, the transgression would be our fault. Being guilty of a crime is not an absolute and objective concept, but a purely subjective one. This, however, does not invalidate anything, since our consciousness "lives" in this subjective world.

It was our society that invented the subjective notion of being guilty when committing certain acts. Thus, being a criminal is nothing more than transgressing the rules created to maintain our well-being in society. Therefore, the fact that we are not metaphysically free does not mean that, if we were arrested, this would be an injustice — because we are dealing with physics, not metaphysics. In this sense, it should be noted that today, if we murder someone, we will be arrested. However, in ancient times, before humans invented such rules of social conduct, we could kill anyone at our pleasure, without any problem, and we wouldn't be "guilty" of anything, as the concept of guilt didn't even exist.

This whole argument may seem strange and paradoxical, but we're just not used to the idea that we're machines. And we're not just machines: we're social machines. For this reason, we must comply with certain rules agreed by our society. If any machine does not obey those rules, which were created by legislative machines to guarantee the well-being of all machines, then it must be punished with isolation from the other machines — and being "guilty", being "criminal", is just that. It means being a machine that's ill-adapted to living in society, representing a danger to others.

Thus, the fact that an unlawful act was perpetrated intentionally does not make it "free", since the deliberation process is just our system of neurons working as deterministically as an electrical circuit. Nor should good deeds be attributed to some "free will", as our vanity would like to believe.

We're just robots interacting with robots, clumps of atoms interacting with other clumps of atoms. We are robots that create social rules to be perpetuated more efficiently, that have a neural system capable of understanding reality and of agreeing on rules of coexistence aimed at the well-being of all. Now, in this perspective, it seems evident that the fact that we have no free will is irrelevant to morality.

So why do we have this illusion of freedom? Why do we interpret our actions as voluntary, resulting from a free will? What really seems to happen is that, after the involuntary manifestation of the will, we give it a supposedly rational explanation and attribute its manifestation to our will. This interpretation creates a fictitious cause, and the metaphysical phantom of free will appears as the causal agent — when, in reality, we are the cause, our organism as a whole is the cause.

Taking a practical example, such as choosing the color of a t-shirt, this could be understood as a very complicated interaction between the manifestation of our genes, the chemistry of our brain, our emotional state, our conditioning, our accumulated knowledge and many other things, all of this being processed by our mental computer — consciously and unconsciously —, finally culminating in our desire and in our action to choose a specific t-shirt and not another. As Pinker explains:

> *The experience of choosing is not a fiction, regardless of how the brain works. It is a real neural process, with the obvious function of selecting behavior according to its foreseeable consequences. It responds to information from the senses, including the exhortations of other people. You cannot step outside it or let it go on without you because it is you.*

If we stick only to the subjective explanations of our actions, this will refer us to magical causes of "free will", isolating our actions as events closed in and of themselves, unrelated to the world in which they are inserted. In this sense, if we ask the individual why they chose that color of t-shirt, they will say something like: "I chose it because I wanted to". If we ask why he felt like it, we'll probably hear: "I felt like it because I wanted to". And, in a big loop of imaginary causes, we will arrive at a "I wanted to because I wanted to" or a "I chose because I chose". If we don't get out of this circular reasoning and place this action in a successive line of physical events that represent his life, his action, in itself, will not make sense — it will seem like his choice took place in a parallel universe. Thus, if we want to understand it, we must analyze this process in physical, not psychological terms. If we understand our will as a purely physical process, we will see that the choice of the color of the t-shirt was, at present, the only possible behavioral manifestation.

Our will, from this point of view, would be the result of an enormous calculation between countless variables that are extremely rich, diverse, intricate and obscure, giving us the impression that we have freedom of choice. We feel free because all these factors are completely incomprehensible and unpredictable to us. But, in the end, all of this would boil down to monstrous biological calculations, resulting in what our desire should be in the present situation. In concordance with this idea, Lloyd exemplifies:

> *Some stimulus comes into my brain from outside. It is sensed by my senses and the signal is sent to my brain. That signal interacts with my brain, changes the physical and chemical state of my brain, and the result is some behavior from me. My body follows what my brain instructs it to do. Where was the free will? There wasn't any. (...) That I have no free will seems a logical conclusion which must be drawn from the simple facts that my brain is made of matter and that it interacts with the world through the senses.*

Do physical laws determine electrical impulses? Chemical reactions? Biology? Sensations? Perception? Conscience? Our lives? Yes. We can physically intervene at all these levels and see results reverberating on each one predictably. The study of this determination, however, is not the responsibility of a single science, for obvious reasons. Analyzing consciousness with the eyes of Physics would be like trying to see the craters of the Moon with the naked eye. Each science studies a limited range of events to be able to construct knowledge accurate enough to be useful, and each has different tools for its object of study.

However, ignoring our technological limitations, if a scientist fully knew the structure of an individual's brain, it seems reasonable to assume that such scientist would be able to predict their exact behavior, their reaction to an argument, or to any stimulus, just as it is possible to predict the behavior of the computer that we have on our tables. After all, why should we think that there is any difference between data processing carried out by neurons or by electronic microchips? The uncertainty refers to the quantum world of subatomic particles, not to the world of electrical circuits.

Even if we can't predict behavioral reactions completely, we can do it partially. We can observe cases in which the cause-effect relationship is clearly established. To illustrate this point, it is enough to note that any psychotropic drug that alters neurotransmitters — chemical messengers in the brain — can substantially affect our behavior and our thinking.

Let's take a benzodiazepine as an example, *diazepam*, which is an anxiolytic that decreases the degree of excitability of the nervous system. It is normally used to combat states of agitation, tension, stress, etc. Its sedative action is linked to GABA, an inhibitory neurotransmitter that acts on the limbic system, whose action slows down serotonergic reactions, reducing anxiety. It performs a regulatory function on the level of excitation of the cells that are receiving input information. Diazepam basically mimics GABA by binding to gabaminergic receptors. It sounds complicated, but the result is simple: we feel calm.

The administration of diazepam changes our brain chemistry, which in turn determines our mental state, our consciousness, and our behavior. That's why people start to think and act differently when under the use of medications such as diazepam. The molecules in the tablet fall into the bloodstream, interact with our brain, alter its neurochemical configuration and, with that, we begin to see and feel reality in a different way. The material substance of the drug, affecting the nervous system of our machine, alters its behavior. Thus, it doesn't matter what are our beliefs, our lifestyle, our temperament — the way in which we manifest all that will change if there is any change in the level of neurotransmitters. It seems quite natural that this should be so.

These changes in our behavioral patterns as a function of our brain chemistry refer us to a concept called *state dependency*. For example, suppose that an individual is normally peaceful. But, under the influence of alcohol, he becomes aggressive. His aggressiveness is a state dependency, since it only occurs together with the physiological changes caused by alcohol. The important point here is to realize that emotional states and specific memories are more easily evoked when we reconstitute the physiological context in which they appeared. Neurobiology expert Iván Izquierdo explains:

> *Memories are acquired under the influence of a certain dopaminergic, noradrenergic, serotonergic, or beta-endorphin brain "tone" and a parallel hormonal "tone". These modulators and hormones generally facilitate the formation of memories by acting on specific mechanisms in the areas of the brain that make them and, in a certain way, incorporate information into them. (...) [The] evocation of memories of a certain emotional content depends on the hormonal and neurohumoral state in which it is occurring. The more this state is similar to the one in which memories of a similar nature were acquired, the better the evocation will be. (...) Memories dependent on a particular emotional*

state are, so they say, "waiting" for a certain constellation of biochemical phenomena to appear again. Appropriate stimulation can bring them out fairly quickly.

Because each situation or substance induces a specific physiological pattern, and our body links those patterns to memories, we will more easily recall memories of happiness when we are happy, memories of fear when we are frightened, memories of sexual content when we are sexually stimulated, etc. For example, when poets are looking for what they call "inspiration", they are looking for a neurochemical state in which they can access certain types of memory and thoughts that they consider appropriate for their art. In the same way, it is common for victims to return to the crime scene so that this may help them remember more details.

When we are in a depressed state, with low serotonin and noradrenaline in the brain, we do not access memories of happiness and well-being, but of negativity, suffering, ruin, anguish, disgrace, death, failure, and the like. We have no control over the type of memory and feelings that the depressive condition will evoke. Our ideations will manifest according to the pattern learned in the depressive state — we will involuntarily think about what is related. This pessimistic and persecutory view of reality can be considered a state dependency, since we only think about such things when we are depressed.

Thus, depressed, we may think that reality has collapsed over our heads, that every goal is a vain effort, that everything conspires to suffering, and that the best part of life is that it ends. However, the fact is that this interpretation of reality stems from something much less dramatic — a low level of such neurotransmitters in our brain. If we abruptly induce an increase in this level, we will feel that we are the masters of an iron will, with the world in the palm of our hands, and its tragic aspects will no longer seem so relevant or threatening.

So, as we see, we don't need to invoke free will to explain human behavior through subjectivisms. As Skinner stated, the *Autonomous man [free will] serves to explain only the things we are not yet able to explain in other ways. His existence depends upon our ignorance, and he naturally loses status as we come to know more about behavior.*

Let us note that the physical determinism of the material world only dismantles the idea of metaphysical free will, but it does not threaten our freedom, our actual possibilities. We have a freedom that resides precisely in the contingency, in the possible configurations of the world in which we live. Our freedom is contained in the possibilities of physical determinism and biological determinism — although both are ultimately the same thing.

So what does it mean to think about our freedom within physical and biological determinism? It means thinking about what we can be, but without being able to choose — the same idea that Schopenhauer expressed in this maxim: *Man can do what he wills but he cannot will what he wills.* In other words, Biology, under the command of Physics, determines us as puppets. Therefore, it makes sense to think that our freedom is not really internal, in the form of free will, but rather a freedom to "become", a kind of freedom that we cannot control or predict very precisely — something like a deterministic becoming, with myriad possibilities of being. We are machines that, based on the same physical structure, can be programmed to behave in several different ways, just like computers. That's what freedom is.

Our freedom must have, from this point of view, a necessary connotation of absence. Analogous to atheism, which means the absence of theism, freedom could be seen as not being trapped. Thus, being free would not really be a positive state, something actual, but an absence of restrictions. A freedom that only exists subjectively, in relation to something that restricts our options.

The world has never had a good definition of the word liberty, said Abraham Lincoln. Why? Because they think of it as something real and positive, that actually exists. How could we find a positive definition for something that has no content, that exists only as an absence? Their mistake seems clear.

However, we can say that, in this situation, the idea that knowledge frees us is still true. It does not free internally, of course, but by expanding our knowledge, we enrich in number and in depth the repertoire of means through which we can satisfy our desires and achieve our goals — and we should understand those desires and goals not as something that we freely choose, but as something with which the contingency "presents" us. Therefore, if knowledge expands our horizons, if it enriches our understanding of the world, then we can say that it frees us from the shackles of ignorance, that restrict our choices.

The most important thing is to realize that our desire for freedom can be understood as the desire to escape external pressures, to be detached from any type of external coercion that hinders or obstructs the satisfaction of our desires. Thus, being free to do whatever we want presents itself as the fundamental idea — and it doesn't really matter if that "want" is free.

Considering our intimate need for personal satisfaction, it is easy to understand how religion can easily be an obstacle in this sense. Religion imposes impersonal duties that must be followed as if they were our own, and this directly conflicts with our need to satisfy our unique desires, which are entirely individual. Religion, therefore, further diminishes the little freedom we have.

With its dogmatism, religion tries to transform us into an ideologically standardized flock. This mind shackle has the absurd intention of leveling our personalities, our most original self, by dictating what we should do with our lives. Strictly following impersonal rules is pretty much the formula for unhappiness. However, the frustration generated by all this ideological imprisonment is balanced by the psychological comfort that absolute references provide — and by the rewards that will come "beyond the grave". However, without these exuberant psychological lures, it is unlikely that religion would achieve any success in finding new victims.

From this perspective, it's not hard to figure why religions insist so much on the false idea that we have a free will. This free will supposedly granted by God is a kind of subterfuge invented by those who wanted a pretext to punish us if we did not follow the "sacred laws" imposed by religion — or, at least, to frighten us through the idea that God would. In the end, generating the same result: obedience. Not following God's will is a sin — do we need to say more? It would therefore be naive to think that religion emphasizes free will for fortuitous and disinterested motives. Nietzsche explains more about it:

> *Today we no longer have any sympathy for the concept of "free will": we know very well what it is — the most suspected artifice of theologians that exists; an artifice that aims to make humanity become "responsible" in the fashion of*

> *theologians, that is, to make humanity dependent on them... Here I offer the psychology of any and all attribution of responsibility. — Wherever responsibilities are sought, the instinct to want to punish and judge is usually at work there. One has deprived becoming of its innocence if being in this or that state is traced back to will, to intentions, to accountable acts: the doctrine of will has been invented essentially for the purpose of punishment, that is of finding guilty. All ancient psychology, the psychology of will, has its presupposition in the fact that its authors, the priests at the top of the ancient communities, wanted to create for themselves a right to impose punishments — or they wanted at least to create a right for God to do so... Men were thought of as "free" so that they could be judged and punished — so that they could be blamed. Consequently, every action would need to be considered as desired, the origin of every action as being located in consciousness (— with which the most fundamental manufacture of counterfeit coins was transformed, within psychologicism, into the principle of psychology itself...). Today, when we enter the opposite movement, when we immoralists seek again with all force, above all, to remove from the world the concept of guilt and the concept of punishment, purifying psychology, history, nature, institutions and their sanctions from these concepts, there is no more radical antagonism in our eyes than that in relation to theologians who continue to infect the innocence of becoming with the notions of "punishment" and "guilt", by means of the concept of the "moral world order". Christianity is an executioner's metaphysics...*

Thus, from beginning to end, our life can be described as a state of organization of matter that tends to self-replicate — and our brain, from this perspective, would be a powerful computer processing a gigantic amount of information — sensory, abstract, emotional, etc. — with the objective of guiding our body to the goal of self-perpetuation.

Even if we are particularly rational individuals, the idea that we are just a legion of chemical viruses made of matter, in a data-processing war, all struggling to be eternal, still sounds somewhat astonishing. In this situation, our whole life would be nothing more than an informational game, an administrative battle between genes that are more or less efficient at using physical laws to make the robots they control achieve the ultimate goal of perpetuation.

Not that, in this regard, we have any obligation to perpetuate our genes — we don't, in fact. But this tendency is a kind of commitment of life to itself, due to its own evolutionary history.

So, both in biological and in physical terms, it makes no sense to think that we are internally free. In fact, we weren't even born to be free or happy, but just to reproduce. And if we can't understand our own lives in depth, it's because we weren't born to understand the world scientifically. As biological machines, we were born for each other, and all we need to understand is what we must do to spread our genes to the next generation.

Perhaps our illusion of great freedom is merely a reflection of the incapacity of our psychic apparatus in the face of a disquietingly complex reality. Perhaps an illusion that reinforces our motivation or obedience. Perhaps an evolutionary accident with no use. It's hard to understand why we believe that kind of thing. However, when it comes to the question of being free in material terms, the important thing is to be able to satisfy our needs and desires — because it's efficiency, not freedom, the essential rule of life.

Thus, taking a conception of life as a physical information system, as a machine programmed to self-perpetuate, it not only can dispense with free will, but is also absurdly incompatible with that idea. To make them compatible, it would be necessary to postulate the existence of a transcendental "Ghost of the Machine" that not only escapes physical laws but also influences them — and then throw out the window all the knowledge we have about the human brain. Something that sounds like a delusion analogous to those that gave rise to all the chimeras that populate worlds beyond reality.

ABOUT THE AUTHOR

I welcome any knowledge with a hammer. I hammer down everything that is presented to me to verify its consistency. If it crumbles before my eyes, I think: there is a dream castle built by fragile creatures. If it resists, I welcome it as another room in the house where my thought resides. It doesn't matter if reality crumbles over my head in the face of my own self-destructive attacks — self-criticism, for me, will always be an essential austerity. That's what honesty is.

My name is André Díspore Cancian. I was born on February 19, 1982, in a small Brazilian city called Catanduva.

It was as a self-taught person that I did my studies on the topics that I discuss here. I began to have a deeper contact with philosophy and science starting at the age of seventeen, and among some of the influences that were most striking in my thinking and in my vision of the world are the names Nietzsche, Schopenhauer, Cioran, Freud, Pessoa, Russell, Sagan, and Dawkins. That's why I always say, with a touch of dark humor, that almost all my friends are dead, and they only left me their books — but rather the dead friends than the imaginary ones. In any case, it can be seen that my main interests revolve around science, philosophy, and psychology.

I currently manage two internet portals that address free thinking: *Ateus.net* and *Paraíso Niilista* (niilismo.net). *Ateus.net* represents my philosophical and scientific defense of atheism, with the objective of making it as impartial as possible. The *Nihilistic Paradise*, in turn, is where I write without any objective or commitment to anything; it is my individual space, built according to my personal tastes, in which I publish reflections, texts, and poems sporadically.

Admittedly, I have been an atheist since I was fourteen years old, because at that age I reached sufficient intellectual maturity to think about such issues critically. However, taking the correct definition of atheism, which is "lack of belief in the existence of God(s)", then it can be said that I have always been an atheist — before implicit, now explicit. So I never "chose" atheism. I was born an atheist and remain so today. I remain an atheist because atheism seems the most sensible position in the absence of evidence for the existence of a god.

So, as far as my view of gods and deities is concerned, I think that they don't exist, but I don't believe that, because I don't allow myself any kind of fixed certainty on any subject. Therefore, my adopted *ism* consists of the so-called "standard skeptical position", that is, skeptical atheism.

It is true that I could have limited myself to defending atheism, but I also criticize religion, since I consider it to be something pernicious, a shackle, a true obstacle to the progress of human knowledge. Making unrestricted credulity — faith — a virtue was the most indecent perversion ever perpetrated against human freedom. However, I admit that everyone has the right to believe whatever they want. Conflict arises only when individuals express the desire to have their beliefs above criticism — something which they insist on calling "respect".

Well, I certainly don't expect that kind of "respect" for my atheism, in the sense of "don't criticize, don't analyze, leave it alone". Attack it as much as you can and, preferably, refute it — after all, who wouldn't want to be the epitome of the Universe, of the divine creation? I am an atheist only because I suffer from a disease called intellectual integrity, which does not allow me to place the comfort provided by static convictions above the painful and frustrating search for truth. I certainly don't want to sound like a dreamer here — read "war on error" or "most likely", not "absolute truth".

In any case, it should be clear that I am and have always been open to evidence. I'm not an atheist simply because I decided that no god exists and that's it. I merely weighed the available evidence against and in favor of the existence of this entity and concluded that there are no reasons that justify the belief in its existence. If, for example, an individual came to me who could categorically demonstrate the existence of a god, there is no doubt about this: I would cease to be an atheist at the exact moment. I am not and will never be an irrevocably convinced atheist, because, as Nietzsche correctly stated, *convinced men are prisoners*. In this way, as a freethinker, I will always keep my mind open. The only thing I refuse to do is to give credence to any hypothesis without plausible justification for doing so.

From what I've realized to date, in practical terms, being an atheist doesn't make me any different from anyone else. Theoretically, being the center of creation or just a rational animal should make a lot of difference in how we will live our lives, but in reality it doesn't seem to make almost any. Probably because in our daily lives we are concerned with our human needs, which are present in both believers and non-believers, differing only in the explanation given for them. In this sense, individual personality seems much more predominant in determining behavior than religiosity or its absence.

Regarding morals, I am an amoralist — this does not mean that I am amoral, but only that I defend the lack of objective moral values. I have a profound aversion to the regrettable attempts to establish the superiority of one value over another in a universal and impersonal way. A static morality that starts from the top down, from the generic to the specific, can only be two things: a tyranny or a utopia.

But, in practice, my morality is a simple rational and utilitarian selfishness. I adopted the tactic that seems most efficient and practical to promote my well-being, which consists of this maxim: all the best for me and that's all. And for the others? For others I only do and wish well if, in return, they are useful to me too — directly, indirectly, or just potentially. I see this attitude as something quite natural, leaving nothing to be desired for myself or for others. They are fair and honest mutual assistance agreements. But, of course, a sincerity raised to that degree is quite unusual, so some may think that I am a "repulsive" and "sick" being because I understand this cynical behavior as something natural. In this case, I just think the person didn't understand the reasoning very well, because the fact is that practically everyone behaves like that. In any case, I have absolutely nothing against those who decide to follow different paths, because one pretension that I will never express will be that of wanting to say how someone should behave or what's the best way to live.

Personally, when it comes to my worldview, I consider myself a nihilist. I'm an atheist and a nihilist, but to say both at the same time is redundant. An atheist may just be an atheist, but every nihilist is an atheist. Atheism boils down to not having a belief in gods. Nihilism represents a radical break with everything, a rejection of everything, a disbelief in everything — not even that we exist, not even in matter, not even in the absolute. It's not a skepticism that got wrapped up in doubt. Nihilism doesn't even ask, because it doesn't accept the concept of truth, knowledge, ignorance, or that of an object to which all of this could refer. It's like a "nothing to declare" from someone who realized that there's not even a wall against which to hit their head, or even their head, properly, while thinking about it. It's a purely intellectual position, of course. A strictly practical nihilist would be a person in a coma. But no one acts the way they think and no one feels the way they think. Living and understanding are different spheres. Nihilism stems from the apprehension of the emptiness of existence, but the nihilist does not react to emptiness with anguish, pessimism, and despair. He does not take his vision as something to be overcome, nor as something true or false, but like anything else: nothing.

We can translate nihilism into something more palpable as equivalent to the idea that our existence — which may not even be something effective — is a great absurd coincidence without any meaning, that nature, with its laws, is fundamentally irrational, that there are no reality-creating gods or a transcendental essence wandering around in our bodies, that there is no kind of value in itself, much less the possibility of hierarchizing subjective values, that we are here for nothing and that, without a doubt, we are all condemned to death. That sounds extreme to some people, but I find those ideas fairly obvious. To see them, all we have to do is open our eyes with painful honesty and remove the flowers and anesthetic poetry that are mixed with our knowledge.

As far as I can see, it is true that we do not fully understand what we are, but, in my eyes, life has ceased to be something intrinsically mysterious — what remains a mystery is the reason why we are reluctant to admit it. From my point of view, everything we are experiencing is nothing more than a mechanical result of impersonal physical factors that culminated, through self-replicating informational entities — in our case, DNA —, in our existence as self-aware machines, having, by their very nature, the objective of perpetuation, which in turn has none.

Of course, we have the illusion that we are special, but that happens only because we are life itself, and we cannot escape that partial perspective when thinking and judging the value and importance of things. This situation tends to make us egocentric, causing us to naturally overvalue the human species. Are we special because we have a refined rationality? Yes, as much as a platypus is special because it is an oviparous mammal with a duck beak. Each species is born with its survival weapons, and our main weapon is intelligence. So if we think about it carefully, we'll see that not all self-deception is necessarily bad. Our erroneous beliefs may not be consistent with the facts, but it is likely that we will find some value in them if we interpret them according to their usefulness to life.

This way of seeing things, however, is not pessimism. This is merely an objective statement. I do not claim that life is a great disgrace or pure suffering, since this is subjective and depends entirely on how we look at reality. Whether life is a blessing or a burden depends on each one's eyes and peculiarities. That's why I don't think of our life as a curse, but only as an emptiness where everything is ephemeral and meaningless — but, for that very reason, free.

I could not deny, however, that my personal view of reality is somewhat dark — but that is my individual position, and I have no intention of generalizing my personal conclusions and impressions and imposing them on others. It just amazes me that life is so insignificant, so gloomy, during which we keep so few memories worthy of a spontaneous solitary smile, within four walls. It amazes me that we live at the expense of the mirage of aspirations and intangible dreams, while, in fact, in the present, throughout childhood, youth, virility and old age, we vegetate at the taste of the wind in our immense castles of small trivialities, surrounded by concerns as trivial as necessary to escape from ourselves, because it is certain that, freed from the concern of ensuring our existence, free from such everyday futilities that make our lives go unnoticed, we would become an "annoyed burden" for ourselves — and, while we are alive, we will be in such tragicomic position, of which no one is to blame. William Shakespeare expresses this vision very well with the following passage from *Macbeth*:

> *Tomorrow, and tomorrow, and tomorrow, creeps in this petty pace from day to day, to the last syllable of recorded time; and all our yesterdays have lighted fools the way to dusty death. Out, out, brief candle! Life's but a walking shadow, a poor player, that struts and frets his hour upon the stage, and then is heard no more. It is a tale told by an idiot, full of sound and fury, signifying nothing.*

On the other hand, in relation to the experience of being alive, I think that it is not worthy of much seriousness or commitment. After all, living boils down to a mere pastime that, predominantly, is boring and dull, and the best that can be achieved from life is to forget it, since, in my opinion, it becomes better and happier the less consciously we feel it. In fact, *in purely rational terms, if we consider life objectively, it is doubtful that it is preferable to nothing* — I think that Schopenhauer is covered by reason, but covered only by reason. We're not purely objective and rational beings, obviously. The fact that we hold on to life in such a desperately passionate way — despite its endless tribulations —, I think, has no logical basis — we are like clockworks that don't know why they keep ticking. This all seems to happen because of our basic instinct for self-preservation, a bloody legacy from our evolutionary past.

As far as the infamous death is concerned, I don't see any mystery. Worrying about death itself seems one of the most efficient ways to waste time with meaningless speculation, and treating it like some "unfathomable mystery" seems like a great foolishness whose purpose is to allow the cultivation of childish hopes regarding a possible *post-mortem* existence. Why is it so hard for us to accept that death is part of the functioning mechanism of life? It is not necessary to think much to conclude this, just observe: we are animals that are born, grow, reproduce, and die, like any other. We are born and have an indefinite interval of time to do, or try to do, whatever we want with our lives, and then death simply marks the end of our existence as a biological system. So I have no problem accepting it naturally. Fearing death would be the equivalent of fearing a good, eternal night of deep sleep — in fact, it would make much more sense to fear life. In any case, those who stay on this point for a few moments soon realize how the notion we have of death affects our way of living. In this regard, I think that a quote from Montaigne will serve to clarify my point of view: *To meditate on death is to meditate on freedom; those who have learned to die have unlearned to serve; no harm will affect those who in existence have understood that the deprivation of life is not an evil; knowing how to die exempts us from all subjection and coercion.*

Finally, should we believe in hypotheses that, currently, cannot claim for themselves any support from the known reality, that make of ourselves what we are not — but would like to be —, just because that is comforting? Or should we face reality and human nature honestly, as they present themselves to us? The choice is up to each one, because no one has the obligation to be atheist, skeptical, materialist, freethinker, nihilist, rational, scientific, or even coherent. But personally, I stick with the second option, because my desire was never simply to believe, but to know, even if, for me, that means admitting that I am ignorant, possessing a knowledge that is always provisional. Even so, I will always prefer the honesty of the doubt — it's what insists on questioning everything that has already been solved. This is the type of consciousness that I consider of first importance for there to be progress in any type of knowledge.

REFERENCES

ALCOCK, James. “The belief engine.” *Skeptical Inquirer*, Maio de 1995.

ASIMOV, Isaac. “The relativity of wrong.” *Skeptical Inquirer*, Outono de 1989.

AUGUSTINE, Keith. “A morte e o sentido da vida.” *Ateus.net*. 2000. http://ateus.net/artigos/miscelanea/a-morte-e-o-sentido-da-vida/ (acesso em 2000).

______. “O caso contra a imortalidade.” *Ateus.net*. 2000. http://ateus.net/artigos/critica/o-caso-contra-a-imortalidade/ (acesso em 2000).

DAMÁSIO, Antônio. *O erro de Descartes*. São Paulo: Cia. das Letras, 1996.

DAWKINS, Richard. “A improbabilidade de Deus.” *Ateus.net*. 2000. http://ateus.net/artigos/critica/a-improbabilidade-de-deus/ (acesso em 2000).

______. *O gene egoísta*. Rio de Janeiro: Itatiaia, 2001.

______. *O relojoeiro cego*. São Paulo: Cia. das Letras, 2001.

______. *O rio que saía do Éden*. Rio de Janeiro: Rocco, 1996.

______. “Os vírus da mente.” *Ateus.net*. 2000. http://ateus.net/artigos/miscelanea/os-virus-da-mente/ (acesso em 2000).

DESCARTES, René. *Discurso do método*. São Paulo: Martins Fontes, 1996.

DO VALLE, Huáscar Terra. *Tratado de teologia profana*. São Paulo: Alfa Ômega, 1998.

EDWORDS, Frederick. "O fundamento humano das leis e da ética." *Ateus.net*. 2000. http://ateus.net/artigos/miscelanea/o-fundamento-humano-das-leis-e-da-etica/ (acesso em 2000).

FAURE, Sebastien. "Doze provas da inexistência de Deus." *Ateus.net*. 2000. http://ateus.net/artigos/critica/doze-provas-da-inexistencia-de-deus/ (acesso em 2000).

FREUD, Sigmund. *O futuro de uma ilusão*. Rio de Janeiro: Imago, 1984.

______. *O mal-estar na civilização*. Rio de Janeiro: Imago, 1997.

GOLEMAN, Daniel. *Inteligência emocional*. Rio de Janeiro: Objetiva, 1996.

HUME, David. *Investigação acerca do entendimento humano*. São Paulo: Cia. Editora Nacional, 1972.

INGERSOLL, Robert G. "O que é religião?" *Ateus.net*. 2000. http://ateus.net/artigos/critica/o-que-e-religiao/ (acesso em 2000).

______. "O que substituiria a Bíblia como um guia moral?" 2000. http://ateus.net/artigos/critica/o-que-substituiria-a-biblia-como-um-guia-moral/ (acesso em 2000).

______. "Por que sou agnóstico." *Ateus.net*. 2000. http://ateus.net/artigos/critica/por-que-sou-agnostico/ (acesso em 2000).

______. "Sobre a Bíblia Sagrada." *Ateus.net*. 2000. http://ateus.net/artigos/critica/sobre-a-biblia-sagrada/ (acesso em 2000).

LE BON, Gustave. *As opiniões e as crenças*. São Paulo: Brasil Editora, 1956.

LEWIS, Joseph. "Um manifesto ateísta." *Ateus.net*. 2000. http://ateus.net/artigos/critica/um-manifesto-ateista/ (acesso em 2000).

LLOYD, Nikolas. "Por que não tenho livre-arbítrio." *Ateus.net*. 2000. http://ateus.net/artigos/miscelanea/por-que-nao-tenho-livre-arbitrio/ (acesso em 2000).

LOFTUS, Elizabeth F. "Criando memórias falsas." *Ateus.net.* 2000. http://ateus.net/artigos/miscelanea/criando-memorias-falsas/ (acesso em 2000).

MACKIE, J. L. *Ethics: inventing right and wrong.* London: Penguin, 1977.

MENCKEN, Henry L. *O livro dos insultos.* São Paulo: Cia. das Letras, 1988.

MILLER, Geoffrey. *A mente seletiva.* Rio de Janeiro: Campus, 2000.

MONTAIGNE, Michel. "Da incoerência de nossas ações." *Ateus.net.* 2000. http://ateus.net/artigos/filosofia/da-incoerencia-de-nossas-acoes/ (acesso em 2000).

NIETZSCHE, Friedrich. *Assim falou Zaratustra.* Rio de Janeiro: Civilização Brasileira, 1981.

______. *Crepúsculo dos ídolos.* Rio de Janeiro: Relume Dumará, 2000.

______. *Genealogia da moral.* São Paulo: Cia. das Letras, 1998.

______. *The antichrist.* Tradução: H.L. Mencken. Torrance: Noontide, 1980.

PINKER, Steven. *Como a mente funciona.* São Paulo: Cia. das Letras, 1998.

RANDI, James. *Flim-Flam!* New York: Prometheus Books, 1982.

RUSSELL, Bertrand. *The problems of philosophy.* New York: Oxford University Press, 1917.

______. *Why I'm not a Christian.* New York: Touchstone, 1957.

SAGAN, Carl. *O mundo assombrado pelos demônios.* São Paulo: Cia. das Letras, 1997.

SANTI, Pedro Luiz Ribeiro de. *A construção do eu na modernidade.* Ribeirão Preto: Holos, 1998.

SARGANT, William. *Battle for the mind.* Westport: Greenwood Press, 1957.

SASSON, Sezar *et al.* "A Evolução biológica." In: *Biologia; introdução à biologia*. São Paulo: Gráfica e Editora Anglo, 1991.

______. "A origem da vida." In: *Biologia; introdução à biologia*, 97-105. São Paulo: Gráfica e Editora Anglo, 1991.

SCHOPENHAUER, Arthur. *O mundo como vontade e representação*. Rio de Janeiro: Contraponto, 2001.

______. *Parerga and paralipomena*. Tradução: E. F. J. Payne. 2 vols. Oxford: Clarendon, 1974.

SMITH, George H. *The case against god*. New York: Prometheus Books, 1979.

WALLACE, Robert. *Sociobiologia: o fator genético*. São Paulo: Ibrasa, 1985.

ISBN: 978-65-00-73903-9

Made in United States
North Haven, CT
24 March 2024

50418877R00169